Science as Active Inquiry

Science as Active Inquiry

A Teacher's Guide to the Development of Effective Science Teaching

3rd Edition

Selma Wassermann and
J. W. George Ivany

ROWMAN & LITTLEFIELD
Lanham • Boulder • New York • London

Published by Rowman & Littlefield
An imprint of The Rowman & Littlefield Publishing Group, Inc.
4501 Forbes Boulevard, Suite 200, Lanham, Maryland 20706
www.rowman.com

86-90 Paul Street, London EC2A 4NE, United Kingdom

Copyright © 2022 by Selma Wassermann and J. W. George Ivany

All rights reserved. No part of this book may be reproduced in any form or by any electronic or mechanical means, including information storage and retrieval systems, without written permission from the publisher, except by a reviewer who may quote passages in a review.

British Library Cataloguing in Publication Information Available

Library of Congress Cataloging-in-Publication Data

Names: Wassermann, Selma, author. | Ivany, J. W. George, 1938- author. | Wassermann, Selma. Teaching elementary science. | Wassermann, Selma. The new teaching elementary science.
Title: Science as active inquiry : a teacher's guide to the development of effective science teaching / Selma Wassermann, J.W. George Ivany.
Other titles: New teaching elementary science
Description: Third Edition. | Lanham, Maryland : Rowman & Littlefield, [2022] | First edition: 1988. Second edition: 1996. | Includes bibliographical references and index. | Summary: "A practical guidebook to enable teachers to address their concerns about teaching science as active inquiry, in addition to providing them with the tools and techniques for developing a science program that models how real scientists work"—Provided by publisher.
Identifiers: LCCN 2022006558 (print) | LCCN 2022006559 (ebook) | ISBN 9781475864854 (Cloth) | ISBN 9781475864861 (Paperback) | ISBN 9781475864878 (ePub) Subjects: LCSH: Science—Study and teaching (Elementary) Classification: LCC LB1585 .W29 2022 (print) | LCC LB1585 (ebook) |
DDC 507.1—dc23/eng/20220225
LC record available at https://lccn.loc.gov/2022006558
LC ebook record available at https://lccn.loc.gov/2022006559

Contents

Preface	vii
Acknowledgments	ix
Introduction: This Book Is for Teachers	xi

SECTION I: PERSPECTIVES — 1

1	Perspectives on Science and Sciencing	3
2	Perspectives on Children	9
3	Perspectives on Play	15
4	Perspectives on Teaching-for-Thinking in Science	19
5	Perspectives from the Classroom: The Play-Debrief-Replay Instructional Model	27

SECTION II: ORGANIZING THE CLASSROOM FOR SCIENCE AS ACTIVE INQUIRY — 35

6	Preparing Students for Sciencing	37
7	Gathering the Materials	41
8	Making Room for Sciencing	51
9	Guidelines and Ground Rules	55
10	Debriefing: Interactions That Promote Thoughtful Inquiry	67
11	Thinking and Decision-Making in Science	81

SECTION III: FIFTY-EIGHT SCIENCING ACTIVITIES   91

12   Introduction to the Activities   93

13   Category A: Wet, Wetter, Wettest: Activities 1–11   103

14   Category B: No Fuss, No Muss, No Sticky Stuff: Activities 12–48   133

15   Category C: Who's Afraid of Spiders? Activities 49–58   237

SECTION IV: JOURNEY INTO THE UNKNOWN   267

16   Evaluating Student Growth   269

17   Journey into the Unknown   279

Appendix: Selected Readings in Science for Primary and Middle Graders   291

Bibliography   295

Index   299

About the Authors   303

Preface

It has been more than thirty years since the first version of *Teaching Elementary Science* appeared. In that single generation, science and technology have taken several giant leaps forward. Advances as yet undreamed, let alone untried, have now become a routine part of our lives. Thirty years ago, the manuscript for that first book was written on an electric typewriter. That machine, considered at that time state of the art, has been long pensioned off to sit, waiting for a buyer of junk, at "Value Village," a prehistoric relic among the detritus of rotary dial phones, black and white TV screens, Betamax videos, and old piano rolls.

There were several compelling reasons to consider a new version of the book, not the least is the year we all lived dangerously—facing a pandemic that took 600,000 lives in the United States alone, locked down in self-quarantine, until scientists at various pharmaceutical laboratories worked round the clock to come up with a vaccine that would protect us and keep us safe. It was a "lesson in science" to consider what scientists did to find their way, through experimentation, trial and error, testing, review, and recalculation, in coming up with a vaccine. How they did that was science at its most effective, most heralded, and most eventful. One can say, without hesitation, that science once again "saved us."

The changes that science has brought us have been instrumental in lengthening our lives. The time in which a brace of pigeons, necks wrung, bellies slit open, and, leaking blood, applied to infected wounds are long over. Today more than 99 percent of children born in "first world" countries survive and more than 96 percent worldwide (Pinker, 2021). In 1900, we could expect to live to be fifty—if that long. According to Pinker, the Johnstone professor of psychology at Harvard University,

To a germ, you and I are big, yummy mounds of gingerbread, there for the eating. And in the arms race between pathogens' weapons and our defenses, they can evolve faster than we can. The greatest life extenders are feats of human ingenuity that made this a fairer fight. Of the eight innovations that have saved the most lives, six are defenses against infectious disease. (Pinker, 2021)

In the list of inventions that saved hundreds of millions of lives are antibiotics, blood transfusions, chlorination, and pasteurization. Among those that saved billions of lives are the lowly toilet and sewer, artificial fertilizer, and vaccines (Pinker, 2021). It was science that uncovered the relationship between poor sanitation and diseases such as cholera, diarrhea, dysentery, and hepatitis. Scientists Edward Jenner and Louis Pasteur were among the first who developed vaccines to protect us against smallpox and rabies. Pinker argues that it is the vaccines that are the greatest invention in history, and according to him, the target of "head-smackingly stupid resistance."

That resistance was seen during the year of COVID-19, in newspapers and TV reports, of large numbers of antiscience adults who not only chose to defy orders to mask up but also insisted on their "civil right" to NOT be vaccinated. Such resistance gives one pause to wonder where and how these adults learned science? And why scientific knowledge seemed such a threat to their "individual freedoms."

So yes, there is a good reason to write a new book emphasizing inquiry methods in teaching science—a book that would provide teachers with the strategies and materials with which to educate students about the importance of science in our lives and that would "open students' minds" about the ways in which scientists take bold steps to open doors into the unknown. It is our hope and wish that what we provide for teachers will not only enable them to create more effective, more exciting, and more mind-opening science programs but also be the means through which students will become more intelligent consumers of scientific knowledge.

The first two editions (1988; 1996) of *Teaching Elementary Science* were written as a result of the authors' two-year field research with twenty Vancouver teachers, who put the ideas of "Project Science-Thinking" into operation in their classrooms. The "big ideas" behind that research were to provide the resources and the guidance to enable teachers to create science programs that would promote scientific literacy in their students. From the work of these teachers, the curriculum framework, Play-Debrief-Replay was born; that became more than a metaphor, but rather a guiding paradigm that would enable other teachers to envision and implement more effective science programs.

Acknowledgments

This new book gratefully acknowledges the work of those twenty teachers and the students in those Vancouver classrooms where the original research was carried out and, especially, to Heather McAllister, Marti Edwards, and Susan Sheremeta, whose classroom work contributed to the development of the instructional model, to the members of the research team, to all those who played a significant role in the implementation of the research, and those editors who shepherded us through the first two editions: Alan McClare at Harper & Row and Susan Liddicoat at Teachers College Press.

Thanks, too, go to Teachers College Press and, especially, to Christina Brianik for their permission to transfer the rights of the 1996 edition to the authors, to Dennis Smith for his graphic images that capture so wonderfully the essence of teaching science as active inquiry, to Maya Snow for her imaginative illustrations for the sciencing activities, and to our publisher Tom Koerner, and the editorial staff at Rowman & Littlefield for their guidance and support in birthing this book from proposal to print.

Introduction
This Book Is for Teachers

Kasim looks up at the teacher, making the rounds from science center to science center where the Grade 3 students are testing theories about which objects float and which sink and how to turn sinkers into floaters. His eyes are full of excitement. "You know what I want to be when I grow up, Ms. Baker? I want to be a scientist!"

For too many years, teaching science has taken a back seat to other academic areas that have been considered more important. Two presidential administrations have used their bully pulpits to initiate legislation that would, to their thinking, address some weaknesses in what was being taught and learned in the nation's schools. The *No Child Left Behind* Act (2001) was an attempt to ramp up student's test scores in reading and mathematics, using high-stakes testing to measure pupil outcomes. Teachers, so stressed to meet the demands of these tests, spent most of their instructional time drilling students in these subject areas, with less than zero time devoted to "untested" subjects like science, art, and music.

Another administration introduced the *Every Student Succeeds Act* (2015)—legislation intended to provide equal opportunity for disadvantaged students, holding schools accountable for how students perform on achievement tests. Again the emphasis was on high-stakes testing and teachers were put in the position of having to "teach to the test." Once more what was being measured by these tests were the academic areas more easily tested: reading, language arts, and mathematics. Once more science fell to the back seat of what was important in what students were supposed to be learning.

Given the unintended consequences of these presidential initiatives, the shortfall was that over the course of two presidential administrations, there was a lapse of more than sixteen years in the teaching of science while students, teachers, and parents wrestled with the pressure and anxiety of test preparation. In the absence of any emphasis on teaching science, is it any wonder that a large portion of the current adult population remains innocent of why and how vaccines play the key role in keeping us safe from disease. There is, alas, a huge price to pay for such scientific illiteracy.

IT'S TIME FOR SCIENCE!

There are other stories in the Naked City about the neglect of science in the elementary school curriculum. From kindergarten through the middle grades, science education has been perceived as "in deficit" with respect to its scope, its confusion of purpose, and the inadequacy of methods of instruction (Fort, 1993). There have been complaints about the dearth of science materials for any "hands-on" investigations; that the emphasis in teaching is on the collected wisdom of an assortment of science texts, the content of which has been watered down to meet various objections of the most vocal interest groups; that in some classrooms teaching science is virtually nonexistent.

Perhaps some of these claims are extreme. Yet many of them strike home. Look into these classrooms: In one, Sean a bright fifth-grade boy is describing an aspect of the evolutionary process by stating that the "feet of the fish turned into fins, which took about a hundred years." In another, Sally fills out a science worksheet answering questions such as "The sea is made of _____ water." In a third, when Neil tells his teacher that his experiment didn't lead to the "correct" results, the teacher tells him to do it again so that it will.

It is easy to blame teachers for all these faults. After all, haven't teachers been made scapegoats for virtually every societal malaise? If children are not learning, isn't it the fault of teachers everywhere? It is far easier to assign blame than it is to identify and come to terms with the profound, complex, and multidimensional factors at the root of the problems.

This book is on the side of teachers. The authors have assumed that most teachers are in the profession for one important reason: to help children grow and learn. It is also assumed that teachers work very hard at their jobs, and most of them teach to the very best of their abilities. These assumptions are taken one step further. We believe that teachers want to teach science effectively, but they are handicapped by inadequate preparation in professional coursework and insufficient background of experience with science. One cannot teach what one does not know.

As a consequence, many teachers are daunted by the subject. Science is too full of unknowns. Electric current sizzles. Bunsen burners are potential fire hazards. Spiders and other creepers are yucky. It's much safer to keep these things at arms' length, to stay within the confines and protected domains of textbook exercises and pencil-and-paper worksheets.

Since science has given us a vaccine to keep us safe from COVID-19, science is at the forefront of our thinking. Now that renewed emphasis is being placed on developing students' higher-order thinking skills, it may be possible to make clear the kinds of teaching methods that will result in pupils' learning science with an emphasis on promoting inquiry, with a full appreciation of this extraordinarily rich and exciting field of study. It may be possible to help teachers overcome some of their anxieties about science and tempt them into taking some steps, seeing them through to the development of an effective science program. Welcome to the wonderful world of science! This is the expressed goal of this new book.

HOW THE BOOK IS ORGANIZED

The book is organized into four sections. The first section, chapters 1 through 5, provides background information on the important issues that underlie an effective science program. Chapter 1 explains the difference between science and sciencing as carried out in classroom practice. Chapter 2 offers perspectives on children and their role as scientific inquirers. Chapter 3 provides a sound theoretical base for the use of investigative play in sciencing activities. Chapter 4 gives a rationale for how teaching-for-thinking and sciencing are interwoven in the curriculum framework. Chapter 5 describes the instructional model: Play-Debrief-Replay, a framework for carrying out curriculum experiences in promoting scientific inquiries with an emphasis on higher-order thinking.

The second section begins with chapter 6 that describes the ways in which teachers may prepare students for their investigative inquiries. In chapter 7, advice is offered for how teachers may gather the materials needed for students to carry out their investigative play. Chapters 8, 9, and 10 offer suggestions for room arrangement, orientation, and discussion strategies that promote further reflection on the big ideas.

In the third section, chapter 11 tackles the relationships between science and decision-making; chapter 12 introduces the activities; chapters 13, 14, and 15 include all fifty-eight activities grouping them according to their attributes: Category A: wet, wetter, wettest; Category B: no fuss, no muss, no sticky stuff; Category C: who's afraid of spiders?

In chapter 16 of the final section suggestions are offered for evaluation methods that are consonant with sciencing, and in the last chapter 17, some questions are addressed that might still create impediments for those intrepid teachers embarking on their first sciencing programs.

In total, all the chapters combine to offer teachers not only an introduction to teaching science as inquiry but include a comprehensive, fully detailed collection of hands-on activities that will give students opportunities to work as scientific explorers in the same ways in which real scientists work. The fifty-eight activities should provide extensive opportunities for sciencing at whatever level of the elementary grades, for the full school year.

Section I

PERSPECTIVES

Chapter 1

Perspectives on Science and Sciencing

SCENE A: TEACHING SCIENCE

The teacher stands behind a table on which she has set a magnet and a small collection of objects, some metal, some wood, and some plastic. The Grade 3 children are seated at their desks watching and listening as she explains.

Teacher: (*holding up the magnet*) What is this thing I'm holding?
Students: (*in chorus*) A magnet.
Teacher: Yes, it's just like the one in the picture in your book. Remember we were reading about magnets? Now, what is going to happen if I bring the magnet close to these things, like this? (*She lowers the magnet toward a metal ball and the ball "jumps" toward the approaching magnet and sticks fast.*)
Students: (*talking all at once and some shouting*) It will stick. It attracts things.
Teacher: (*managing the behavior*) Now, you know the rules. One at a time, please. Yes, Martin.
Martin: The magnet sticks to the ball because it's metal, but it won't stick on the wood and stuff.
Teacher: That's right. Martin is right. Remember how we read in the book that magnets attract some things? We call them "magnetic." Metals are often magnetic. That's why the ball is attracted. But let's see what happens with the wood. What do you think is going to happen?
Students: (*in chorus*) Nothing!
Teacher: See—you are right. Nothing happens. Wood is not magnetic. Here (*she holds out the single magnet*), some of you try these other objects.
Students: (*There is some noticeable movement within the class and some talking together, while several students walk over to the table and take turns moving*

the magnet around among the objects. After a few minutes, the teacher stops the activity.)

Teacher: I'll tell you what we are going to do. Let's make a list of all the objects and place them in two columns. We'll label the first column "Magnetic." *(She writes "Magnetic" on the whiteboard.)* We'll label the second column "Non-magnetic." *(She writes this too.)*

The activity concludes as the teacher elicits from the students the names of the objects that belong to each column.

SCENE B: LEARNING SCIENCING

A group of six children is working together around a table on which the following materials are found: a bag of ice cubes, newspapers, a ruler, balance scales, several plastic dishes and other containers, a small digital clock, a hammer, a pair of scissors, nails, and a dish of coarse salt. The teacher's goal for this activity is to provide opportunities for the students to carry out investigations to promote increased awareness of the properties of ice, under several variable conditions. The second goal is to give students opportunities to work as scientific explorers, in the same ways in which real scientists work—testing theories, gathering data, and making conclusions based on observations.

As the students work on their investigations, she observes what they are doing from a discreet distance. Sonia and Mark have placed three ice cubes on the balance scale.

Sonia: (*to Mark*) Weigh them. Tell me how much they weigh. I'll write it down.

Mark: (*Dips an ice cube into the dish of coarse salt and sets it down on another dish.*) I'm going to see how long it takes this to melt. (*He records the time.*) (*Heather and Angela have wrapped some ice cubes in a newspaper. Heather hits the wrapped ice with the hammer.*)

Walter: (*Observing Heather and Angela*) It's going to melt faster, you know. It melts faster when it's crushed.

Angela: (*to Walter*) Let's see if it does. Here, I'll put these four ice cubes into this dish and I'll put the crushed ice in this dish. Then we can see which goes faster. You may be right, Walter. I think you could be right.

Heather: Look at this. There are little drops of water already around the crushed ice, but there's hardly any water in the ice cube dish.

Walter: If you put it on the heater, you'd really get some melting.

The children continue with their self-initiated investigations for about twenty minutes when the teacher calls for a cleanup. Notes of their investigations are gathered while the table is cleared and the materials are put away. The teacher calls the group together, and they come to her with their notes. Using "teaching for thinking" questioning strategies (Wassermann, 2017), she will work with the students' observations to help them extract the "big ideas" from their investigative play experiences. She begins by asking them to tell her about the observations they have made about the ice cubes.

SCIENCE VS. SCIENCING

Science, the way it has often been taught, consists of instructing students about what is *known*—the naming and the labeling of certain bits and pieces of information. The underlying rationale is that there is a body of knowledge, well defined and utterly without equivocation, from which all the profound implications of hypothesizing, of tentatively held concepts, and of experimentation have been extinguished. There is no margin for error; answers are either right or wrong. "Experiments" to "find" what has already been found are carried out and if the student doesn't provide the "right" results, he or she is admonished to try it again until it does. The prevailing modus operandi is not to err; students are, in fact, penalized for it. It is a picture of "science" that is as simple-minded as believing that warts are caused by bad behavior.

"Sciencing," by contrast, begins with a different attitude about both the content of what is being taught and the context in which it is taught and learned. It is not by chance that the word appears in the present participle form, making it sound as if it is in motion. In fact, sciencing is being in motion; it is a generative process, a creative act, and as an act of creation, it is by nature messy. It involves the manipulation of data—trying things that don't work and "bouncing back to try again." The essence of sciencing is playing with variables. Will this work? Maybe it will. I'll set up a test and see what happens. Oh no, it's not working. I wonder what will happen if I try another way?

Sciencing involves making predictions, setting up an experimental design in which hypotheses are tested, gathering data, making observations, examining results, and evaluating their validity. In sciencing, the emphasis is on finding out. It is not about finding answers to what is already known (Ivany, 1975; DeVito, 1984).

In his seminal book, *The Youngest Science*, Lewis Thomas provides us with insight into how scientists work:

> In real life, research in science is dependent on the human capacity for making predictions that are *wrong*, and on the even more human gift for bouncing back to try again. This is the way that the work in science goes. The predictions,

especially the really important ones that turn out from time to time to be correct, are *pure guesses. Error is the mode.* To err doesn't really mean getting things wrong; it means to "be in motion." In order to get anything right, we are obliged first to get a great many things wrong. (Thomas, 1983; emphases in original)

In the landmark work on the reform and restructuring of science education generated under the auspices of the American Association for the Advancement of Science, the authors make clear that in teaching science, "the emphasis should overwhelmingly be on gaining experience with natural and social phenomena and on enjoying science." It is by "gaining lots of experience *doing* science, becoming more sophisticated in conducting investigations and explaining their findings that children can accumulate those concrete experiences that enable them to reflect on the process" (AAAS, 1993).

Sciencing calls on the ability to use higher-order thinking skills: observing, comparing, suggesting and testing hypotheses, gathering and classifying data, interpreting and evaluating results (Wassermann, 2009). Perhaps it may be said that science + higher-order thinking = sciencing.

When children learn "science," they leave school with a collection of names and labels, some of which may even be correct. But without the added dimension of using intelligent habits of mind, without being actively engaged in the process of scientific investigations, they will not be able to apply principles to new situations, interpret data intelligently, and learn what all scientists must know in order to be successful: how to fail and keep trying.

From their work with sciencing, on the other hand, the expectation is that students will become competent to chart unexplored territory; to become experienced as investigators, learning to think; to take cognitive risks; to predict and test; to evaluate wisely and thoughtfully and through the process, gain and use scientific knowledge more effectively. It is through the process of sciencing that we may hope to expect the breakthroughs that vastly enhance the quality of lives on this planet that will allow us to understand in fuller measure the extraordinary demands of living in a scientifically and technologically driven world.

It is through the process of sciencing that we better understand what diseases kill people in great numbers from what generates headlines: to distinguish actual causes from bunkum. It is through sciencing that scientists were able to expose the uselessness of the many nostrums, snake oils and sometimes poisons that people were ingesting as supposed cures (Pinker, 2021).

Now in our times of great upheaval, with global warming threatening to harm us in ways yet untold, with new viruses being spawned and spreading like wildfire, with a former president suggesting that people inject disinfectant into their bodies to combat COVID-19, with groups of people disclaiming mask wearing as an infringement on their civil rights, and rejecting vaccinations, there is more reason than ever for teachers at every grade level to create sciencing programs that advance intelligent habits of mind and that create the ethos in which children learn to prize science for the many ways in which our lives and our health are enriched, extended, and improved.

Chapter 2

Perspectives on Children

SCENES FROM THE CLASSROOM

The six-year-old students are sitting in a circle on the carpet, studying a series of photographs depicting scenes from birth to old age. The teacher says, "Tell me what you see."

Charles: I see him here, where he's a baby. Here's where he's a little boy playing and going to school. Here's where she's growing up and getting married and here's where she's a grandma.
Donald: Uh oh, Charles. You can't say that. You can't say, "Here's where *he's* a little boy" and "here's where *she's* getting married." When you're *born* a boy, you *die* a boy. Some of the other children nod in vigorous agreement, except for Fancy, who shakes her head from side to side.
Teacher: (*The teacher sees this and asks her*) Tell me, Fancy, what do you think? You seem to have another idea.
Fancy: Well, that's not right, you know. If you want to change, you can.
Teacher: (*ever so gently*) And how would you do that, Fancy?
Fancy: Well, you just go to the doctor and (*thumps her chest*) tell him to change your stuff!

There are no biological creatures more wonderful than young children. A living, breathing set of paradoxes; they are at once both in the present and in the future. They are full of sweet innocence yet crafty as old con artists; outrageously silly, yet deadly serious; short on experience and unequivocal about what they know; gently loving and demonically mischievous; fiercely independent yet afraid of monsters; unselfconscious yet needing adult approval.

They are vigorous, demanding, excessive, frustrating, and exhausting, but never boring. What's more, their capacity to be frank is disconcerting. "Say, Mrs. Melrose, how come you've got those little hairs growing out of your nose?"

If you can keep up with the pace, it is a gift to teach young children, for they will bestow on you their greatest treasures—their most intimate secrets, their hearts' desires, the depths of their feelings, as older children are less able to do, their innocence having been traded for experience. In the primary years, children's curiosity to know is unbounded. They are natural investigators and their zest for learning seems limitless.

Often this ceaseless quest to know takes the form of an endless run of questions: "How come?" "But why?" "How?" "Where?" "What will happen?"—their questions exhaust us. Yet this fervor for learning is the greatest capital of the primary teacher. To harness this energy and to convert it into productive and significant learning without diminishing its intensity or spirit—ay, that's the rub.

The middle-grade teacher has other capital. Older children have a greater capacity to understand. "Don't disturb us unless it's an emergency" is a clear directive that needs no extensive explanation. Their vocabulary base is large, and the range of their experience is greater. Many of them have already spent years on computers and tablets and their sophistication with IT often extends beyond the realm of many teachers.

While they are wise in years, for example, they know there is no Santa Claus, they still cling to idealistic hopes of what a superhero can do in righting the wrongs of the world. They have learned better to curb their impulses; they begin to see relationships between means and ends, between action and consequence. They have even learned some social graces. A six-year-old sibling, offering his teacher a Christmas gift and saying, "This handkerchief is for you but don't blow your nose in it because it cost two dollars" will get a punch in the arm from his older brother for such a serious social gaffe.

Older children are learning responsibility: to clean up their rooms, to help with the chores, to bicycle to the store to fetch another liter of milk—but they have not learned to love it. They covet their independence fiercely but resent the means by which it is attained.

The middle grader is a many-splendored gift. Personal identities and values have become more solidly formed. You must work hard to win their affection and respect. But having won their hearts they are exceedingly loyal, unremittingly generous. "My teacher said so" is the arbiter of the highest court, the final word at the dinner table.

Most middle-grade students are action-oriented and would rather be participants than observers. Participation strengthens their sense of "can do" and their sense of personal power and there are few things they won't try at least once. Logic is both their strength and the chink in their armor; they will use it to their advantage in reasoning yet must also allow it as a way of confronting their outrageous demands. These middle-grade years are the last of the precious years of childhood, before self-consciousness sets in, like hardening of the arteries, by gonads run amok.

Teachers who are lucky enough to work with children at this age level will find them frustrating and fascinating; the greatest challenge is to protect and cultivate their individuality while at the same time bringing each into full membership with his or her social group.

CHILDREN TODAY

Several dozen scholarly tomes over the past forty years have dealt in-depth with the developmental history of children. Each informs us in detail about their physical capabilities, their physical limitations, their social-emotional development, their intellectual expertise, and the range and extent of their individual differences. The texts also provide evidence of how the individual differences among children profoundly influence their abilities and their styles of learning (see, for example, Clarke-Stewart, Friedman and Koch, 1985; Bronfenbrenner, 1979; Kaplan, 1986; Segal and Yahraes, 1978; Wood, 1983).

It was in the 1980s that scholars and historians began to write about the observable changes being seen in child development, attributing these changes to certain social conditions—the role of television, the street culture, a new social ethos, and the very beginning influence of electronic media.

Books by Neil Postman, David Elkind, Marie Winn, Vance Packard, Valerie Suransky, Alex Kotlowitz, Joshua Meyrowitz, and Sylvia Ashton-Warner urged us to examine how childhood was being "eroded" away by cultural forces that were having a major impact on children's growth and development. That "sweet innocence" of childhood was now being supplanted by their exposure to adult values, behavior, and activities through the various media heretofore hidden from children's eyes.

All of the above texts were written before the enormous impact of the Information Age and the emergence of social media as an influential factor on child development. According to Karlis (2021),

> Through Twitter, YouTube, Snapchat, TikTok and other social media platforms, humans have created worlds and different realities on the internet. Nearly 15 years of social media have been integrated into our lives, and on a whole generation's childhood. We are raising the first generation of children whose entire lives have been subsumed by and through social media.

Each of these authors has written about major observable changes in the behavior of children, seen as early as the primary years. If these data tell us anything at all, it may be that teachers are facing greater challenges than ever before in their struggle to protect the natural growth and development of children in their classes. All of that was a priori to the advent of COVID-19, the lockdown of families, the closing of schools, the many deaths of loved ones, the loss of jobs, and the struggles of parents and children to remain safe and cared for in a climate of fear and high anxiety.

IMPLICATIONS FOR TEACHING

To consider a curriculum plan without first considering to what extent that plan reflects our knowledge of children today may be akin to wandering in the wilderness without a compass. Successful curriculum building is very much tied in with what we know about children and how they learn. The more we know and the more perceptively we know, the better we are able to conceptualize, organize, gather appropriate materials, and deliver the curriculum experience.

The dozen principles identified below represent what are believed to be key to effective teaching and learning (AAAS, 1993). They are offered here to establish some important guidelines that inform the instructional model presented in the next chapters. The list is not exhaustive, but the principles included are, to the authors, the very bedrock of our beliefs about the effective and healthful teaching and growing of today's primary and middle-grade students.

a. *Every child is different.* Therefore, a curriculum plan for a science program must provide for individual differences in learning capabilities and learning styles.
b. *Each child brings the sum total of his or her life experiences to each learning task.* Children whose life experiences have been rich need a curriculum that is rich in order to sustain and challenge their interests. Children whose life experiences have been more limited are even more in need of a curriculum that is rich and full in order to compensate for the deficits.
c. *Children are naturally gregarious. They thrive in a socially active environment.* Therefore, curriculum experiences must provide for extensive social interaction. Through these social interactions, language learning is enhanced, problem-solving and decision-making skills are exercised, and personal responsibility grows.
d. *Each child has a distinctly different and unique concept of self as a person and as a learner.* Therefore, a curriculum in science must ensure that each child is enabled and no child is diminished in the learning process.

e. *Most primary and middle-grade students are action-oriented and require first-hand experiences to gather data and form concepts.* Therefore, a curriculum in science must be founded in active, experiential learning if conceptual understanding is to grow.
f. *Gender differences do not influence children's ability to love science.* Therefore, a curriculum must provide equal opportunity for boys and girls to have enjoyable, successful, and productive experiences with science learning.
g. *Most primary and middle-grade students, while largely dependent on adults in many ways, want and need to function on their own power. Such autonomy is imperative in their growth toward psychological health and feelings of empowerment.* Therefore, curriculum experiences must encourage growth toward personal autonomy and independent functioning.
h. *Children have a great need to understand their world, to make sense of what is happening around them. They tend to interpret new data in terms of what they already know.* Therefore, curriculum experiences in science should provide many opportunities for children to broaden their understanding by observing, touching, smelling, listening, and testing ideas to see what works.
i. *Most children in today's world have fewer multisensory experiences. A great deal of their time is spent with electronic media: television, computer games, Nintendo, video games, and the like.* Therefore, a science curriculum should provide extensive opportunities for them to have direct, real experiences in carrying on investigations with a variety of primary materials.
j. *Most children are expressing deep concerns and fears about what is happening in the world today: wars, climate change, terrorism, violence, pathogens and disease, and the uncertainty of the future.* Therefore, a science curriculum can be used as a means of using knowledge and human resources to improve world conditions and provide children with a sense of control over their lives and their future.
k. *In the best climate for learning, children need to be respected and intellectually challenged if they are to grow up developmentally sound.* Therefore, a curriculum plan for science should preserve and protect the dignity of each student as well as stimulate their interest and enthusiasm for science by promoting understanding that intellectual functioning can be a significant attribute in solving problems.

l. *Children learn science and thinking by actively participating in doing science and thinking.* Therefore, curriculum experiences must provide many opportunities for them to engage actively in science and thinking. Learning *about* science when the teacher does most of the thinking denies the children that experience (AAAS, 1993).

CONCLUSION

It may seem redundant to suggest that any curriculum plan begins with a teacher's understanding of the nature and developmental stages of the children being taught. Yet, in too many instances, the plan comes first—with incomplete regard for where the children are emotionally, physically, socially, and intellectually.

Disregarding children's learning needs, their backgrounds or experiences, their interests, attitudes, and learning styles in creating a curriculum may be as unproductive as Sisyphus trying to reach the top of the mountain with his boulder. For a curriculum plan to be effective, to have an even slight chance of succeeding in its aims, it is built from the cognizance of where the students "sit on the medicine wheel"—each in his or her own learning position.

This chapter has presented some perspectives on where children "sit" today, and it identified several key principles of children's growth and development and learning needs. The chapters that follow are based on these fundamental principles and demonstrate how the curriculum plan for teaching "sciencing" is commensurate with those principles.

Chapter 3

Perspectives on Play

We all learn by experience but some of us have to go to summer school.
(De Vries)

The role of play in learning has received more than its share of ups and downs over the last seventy-five years. In days of yore, influenced by the work of John Dewey, play was viewed as "children's work" and recognized as an important medium in children's learning (Dewey, 1964). Play was commonplace in early childhood education and in the middle grades, "activity programs" made extensive use of hands-on experiences in the language arts, social studies, math, and science curricula.

With the Soviet launching of Sputnik in the 1960s, the demand for more rigorous education practices resulted in governmental policies that forced major changes in educational aims and methods. Play and experiential programs became suspect and teachers were encouraged to "stop wasting children's time" and to *teach* more and at earlier stages of school. Out went the sandbox and the blocks in kindergarten as frivolous, and in went workbooks and pencil-and-paper tasks, with standardized tests to assess "achievement" as a measure of not only children's levels of performance but also of teachers' competence.

Pulled once more by a newly emerging view of these seatwork activities as "mindless and crippling" (Silberman, 1973), the curriculum pendulum swung wide, and play was once again sanctioned and affirmed as imperative for the healthful growth and learning of children. Hardly had the sandbox been put in place when the "back to basics" movement once again cast play in a villainous and hedonistic role. In came "direct instruction," "formal teaching," and "increased time on task," with extended school days to "cover" more subject matter, all of which was to be tested and examined with a rigorous battery of short-answer, information-based standardized tests.

Fortunately for teachers who have been knocked back and forth by public opinion enough times to make their sandboxes spin, there is now hard empirical evidence to support the importance of play as a critical element in children's learning. Research carried out by Bruner, at Harvard (1974), revealed that children who had the opportunity to engage in free play were better prepared to solve the subsequent problems presented to them compared to the groups of children who were allowed to handle but not play with the materials as well as those who were only instructed in the principles underlying the solutions by an adult.

It was the British Infant School movement that provided evidence of the dynamic interface of children's play and the promotion of inquiry-type learning that collapsed the traditional view of work and play as separate entities in the cognitive development of children (Brown and Precious, 1970). Featherstone (1971) added his voice to support the "work-play" environment where children were free to conduct experiments and inquiries, which contributed to the promotion of their higher-order thinking skills.

In the British Infant Schools, teachers used the work-play context to engage children in the tasks of observing, comparing, suggesting hypotheses, testing theories, solving problems, making decisions, and evaluating procedures, providing many opportunities for them to develop skills in these higher-order mental functions.

Play is, of course, the main avenue of creativity and imagination, "one of the most highly valued of human qualities" (Getzels and Jackson, 1962), its role in the intellectual, social, personal, and physical development of children supported by abundant research (Johnson, Christie and Yawkey, 1987). According to Einstein, creativity is far more consequential than knowledge in furthering the significant advances of humankind. The creation of new ideas does not come from minds trained to follow doggedly what is already known. Creation comes from thinking and playing around, from which new forms emerge, like the geodesic dome, the dymaxion car, the theory of relativity, the Fallingwater House at Bear Run, and the first airplane of Orville and Wilbur Wright.

"If I don't play with it, how can I understand it?" Richard Feynman, Nobel Laureate in Physics, remarked of his work on the motion of mass particles that ultimately led to the Nobel Prize (Feynman, 1985). "The science classroom ought to be a place where creativity and invention, as qualities distinct from academic excellence, are recognized and encouraged" (AAAS, 1990).

The sad truth is that children today have fewer opportunities to engage in creative play as they once did. They are much more engaged with electronic media—television, tablets, video and computer games, and surfing the Internet, where they spend much of their "free" time. Is it possible that today's children may be more urgently in need of play activities than ever before?

CONCLUSION

The data about play in relationship to children's healthful and intellectual development have important implications for the classroom teacher. They suggest classroom practices that need our most thoughtful consideration. Several principles emerge from the literature and research that point to action:

- Research data provide evidence of the importance of play in children's cognitive development.
- Exploratory-investigative play activities enable children to grow to a fuller, richer understanding of their world.
- Exploratory-investigative play experiences promote children's problem-solving capabilities and give them practice in decision-making and in learning to explore the unknown.
- Creative play promotes the healthful psycho-social development of children.
- Creative play encourages the development of fantasy and imagination, the primary sources of innovation and invention.

Translated into classroom practices, these principles underscore the need for increased emphasis on play—on children's active involvement with a variety of media—as being at the very core of their learning in science (Bruner et al., 1974; Sutton-Smith, 1979; Pepler and Rubin, 1980; Vandenberg, 1980; Fein, 1986; Herron and Sutton-Smith, 1971).

Chapter 4

Perspectives on Teaching-for-Thinking in Science

What did you learn in school today, Arthur?
We're not learning anything. We're just developing cognitive skills.

The children sit quietly with impeccable good manners around the table. They are well groomed in their designer jeans and expensive haircuts. But their stylish appearance does not divert from the apprehension in their eyes. They are fourth-grade students, selected to participate in a demonstration of "teaching for thinking." The teacher removes a card from a large box of "thinking activities" and offers it for their study.

"How do you suppose pigeons can be trained to deliver messages?"

They are clearly stumped, and there is a long pregnant silence after which Sharon timidly queries, "I don't understand what you mean."

The teacher repeats the question, unwilling to play into their transparent ruse of soliciting clues to the "answer." The repeated question again draws silence. Finally, Des mumbles, "We didn't study birds yet."

Kevin, a little bolder, tentatively offers, "A pigeon trainer?" He forms his response as a question to protect himself from the possibility of having gotten it wrong.

These elegant, finely coiffed, stylish children are having a great deal of difficulty hypothesizing, inventing, creating, going beyond the parameters of right and wrong answers.

Within the confines of their Grade 4 curriculum, they are considered "good" students. And observably, they are quite good at performing the hundreds of school exercises that require single, correct answers. However, when it comes to a task that calls for imagination, for suggesting hypotheses, for connecting means with ends, for taking some cognitive risks, for extending their thinking into new territory, they are unable to take that cognitive risk.

How can it be possible that bright young minds become so narrowed in their functioning that creative thinking and intelligent problem-solving are tasks that daunt them? Why is it that in spite of all our affirmation about the importance of developing higher-order thinking skills, it is the least exercised skill in many classrooms?

THERE IS THINKING AND THERE IS *THINKING*

The definition of the word "thinking" encompasses a variety of mental functions. We think about how to spell *onomatopoeia*. We think about the name of the explorer who was the first European to arrive in Peru. We think about putting together a shopping list, and what items in the cupboard need to be replaced. We think about whether it's a good idea to continue to feed the gull that comes to the window tapping and begging for a handout, or to reject those demands so that the gull will find its own food. The mind is exercised in different ways in these various tasks, some of which are more cognitively demanding, and others that require less mental effort.

These more rigorous cognitive demands are often referred to as "higher-order" thinking—the ability to function capably on more sophisticated mental tasks. Like learning other skills, higher-order thinking needs to be developed through the frequent exercise of those cognitive skills. Without such emphasis on cognitive development, higher-order or any other type of skills lack the opportunity to grow and develop.

When teachers provide a lot of practice in lower-level mental operations like arithmetic calculations, spelling drills, and workbook exercises, students become experts at these lower-level cognitive tasks. Unfortunately, the ability to perform these lower-level mental functions does little or nothing to develop intelligent habits of mind. Becoming an expert at typing does not transfer to writing a literary masterpiece. Students practicing memorization of facts cannot translate this expertise to creative problem-solving. To become a successful problem solver one has to have a lot of experience with problem-solving (AAAS, 1993).

TEACHING-FOR-THINKING AND CLASSROOM PRACTICE

To promote students' intelligent habits of mind, it is necessary to give them more experience with curriculum materials that call for higher-order thought.

This is aided and abetted by the teacher's use of classroom interactions that require students to further exercise those higher-level mental functions (Wassermann, 2009; see also chapter 10). These cannot be one-off experiences, "stocking stuffers" that are used to fill an empty slot in the day's plan. For students to develop such thoughtful behaviors, these experiences must play a dominant role in classroom life. If developing more thoughtful behavior is a truly valued educational goal, these materials and instructional strategies must be woven into the fabric of the curriculum.

Instructional Materials

It is a sad truth to recognize that much if not most of the curriculum materials found in primary, middle-grade, and secondary classrooms overemphasize activities that require low-level cognitive responses (Goodlad, 1984). In other words, instructional materials that rely primarily on memorization and recall of information play a primary role in what the teacher is teaching and in what pupils are learning. It should come as no surprise, then, that children have become experts at low-level cognitive functions, since they are practicing these skills day after day, in class after class.

Upending the reigning curriculum materials monarchy is like the difference between canned soup and homemade, neither difficult nor complicated. It is a matter of knowing how. Converting lower-level tasks into activities that are more intellectually challenging is the teacher's first job and that begins with knowing the difference between the two. Where lower-level tasks call for memorizing and recalling information, the more cognitively demanding materials are concerned with promoting the process of analysis and reflection. They are open-ended and allow for many different responses that are appropriate and acceptable.

In the lower-level tasks, *certainty* about answers is *de rigueer*. The higher-order tasks dwell in the land of *uncertainty*. That critical difference is, perhaps, the reason why teachers steer clear of them. To be uncertain creates not a small amount of stress; certainty brings closure, a palpable sigh of relief. So part of the bargain is for teachers to become more comfortable with uncertainty, to leave "answers" behind, and prize the process of inquiry into the unknown.

To be more specific, in a lower-level task, pupils may be required to graph the average temperatures during August in Chicago. In a more intellectually challenging task, pupils are asked to develop hypotheses to explain what factors influence the weather systems during the summer in Chicago. In this task, the focus is on examining many possible alternative explanations. No single "correct" answer is sought.

Computing ten math examples, practicing spelling words, and selecting the correct word to complete a sentence are some examples of lower-level activities. Comparing squids and oysters, observing the swing of a pendulum, hypothesizing about how a pencil sharpener works, inventing a new video game, and designing a website about Ancient China are examples of more intellectually challenging activities. More about sciencing activities that call for higher-order thinking is found in chapters 12, 13, 14, and 15.

Teacher–Student Interactions

In Goodlad's (1984) study of schools, he described the ways in which teachers question and respond to their students. In most classrooms, he found very little emphasis on teacher–student interactions altogether. In fact, teachers did most of the talking, with teacher–student dialogue playing a minor role. When teachers and students did engage in discussions, teachers' questions called for pupils to recall specific information. What was important was that students came up with the answer the teacher wanted.

Teacher: What's the name of the animal that has a pouch?
Kevin: Kangaroo.
Teacher: Right.
Marlene: What about the koala?
Teacher: That's right, but for now we are only going to consider the kangaroo.

It is not wrong for teachers to expect students to know that kangaroos have pouches. Yet, when this type of interaction is the staple of the students' cognitive diet, opportunities for their thinking at higher cognitive levels are seriously circumscribed.

Teaching-for-thinking interactions requires the teacher's use of questions and responses that call for students to reflect on their ideas, to make a deeper analysis of their ideas, and to take cognitive risks in extending their thinking into new realms of inquiry.

An interactive dialogue that uses this approach might look like the one in the example below. In this dialogue, the teacher is calling on her Grade 4 students to examine two photos: one is a skeleton of a king-size salmon and the other is a carapace of a crab. The "big idea" behind the photo study is for students to examine the different skeletal structures, make some observations, analyze the data, and suggest some hypotheses about how they serve the purposes of motion and protection.

Teacher: Tell me what you see in these photos.
Frank: I see a skeleton and I see the top part of a crab.

Teacher: Say a little more about that Frank.
Frank: Well, this one I think is a skeleton of a big fish. And the other one might be the top part of a crab or a lobster.
Teacher: You are saying that one photo is a skeleton of a fish—a large fish. And the other is part of a shellfish. But you are not certain.
Frank: I'm pretty sure. But you can't be positive, you know. Pictures can be misleading.
Teacher: It's hard to tell for sure. I see. Thank you, Frank. Does anyone have other observations to make about the skeletons?
Ann: It looks like one is definitely a fish. And the other, I think it's like the crab's house. The thing that protects it.
Teacher: What clues in the photograph tell you that the one on the left is of a fish?
Ann: Well, for one thing, it's the shape. The shape looks like it might have come from a fish.
Teacher: So the shape of the skeleton suggests it could have come from a fish.
Ann: Uh huh. And yeh, I think my mother once made fish for dinner and there were some bones that looked like that.
Teacher: You saw similar bones when your mother cooked fish at home.
Ann: Yeh. I did.
Teacher: Thanks Ann. Are there other observations?
Joanne: Well, I think the fish bones are softer and the top part of the crab is harder.
Teacher: You are making comparisons about the texture of the skeletons.
Joanne: Yes. And one other thing. The bones of the fish are inside and the crab bone is outside.
Teacher: Fish bones are internal. And the skeletal structure of the crab is external?
Joanne: Yeah.
Teacher: Do you have some ideas to explain the purpose of an external skeleton?
Joanne: Well, for one thing, I think it is to protect the crab. Like Ann said.
Teacher: So your hypothesis suggests a crab might need protection and that is one reason for an external skeleton.
Joanne: This is a guess, okay. I think it's because the crab moves very slowly and that's why it needs an outside shell.
Teacher: Ah, thanks Joanne. You have suggested a hypothesis for why a crab might need an external skeleton, its slow movement. What about other animals that have external and internal skeletons? Any ideas?

Learning this way by interacting with students—designed to give them practice in using their intelligence to make meaning from data—does not come from wishing it were so. Like other learned skills, it takes practice, time on task, and reflection on action. The way to accomplish this is first to recognize the difference in the various interactive styles and then put them into use in classroom practice, working toward a new interactive pattern. (See chapter 10: Debriefing—for more information about teacher–student interactions.)

CONCLUSION

To conclude this chapter, it may be helpful to point to the important principles underlying teaching-for-thinking in science. These principles are at the heart of teaching science as active inquiry.

- Learning to think intelligently, like learning to read intelligently, requires substantial time on task. If we hope that our students will become more wise, more intelligent consumers of data, and more skilled at dealing with problems where answers are yet to be found, we need to provide them with many opportunities to practice these more intellectually challenging tasks.
- When teachers give students intellectually challenging tasks, they are giving them practice in higher-order mental functioning. These kinds of tasks should play a major role in curriculum activities if we hope students will become more skilled at them.
- A teacher's interactions in classroom discussions promote more thoughtful inquiry and give students more practice in being reflective. A teacher's interactive style should call for students to reflect, analyze, hypothesize, give examples, and process information.
- To teach science as an inert body of information is to deny students the opportunity to understand what science is about. Engaging them in curriculum activities that parallel what real scientists do takes them into the profoundly diverse, exciting, wondrous world of inquiry into the unknown.

Teachers who wish to embark on a course of action in which students engage in scientific investigations, with emphasis on the development of their higher-order skills, may begin by using the materials provided in this text to take the first steps to teaching science as inquiry. As in learning any new skills, the success of this way of teaching is largely dependent on teachers' willingness to commit themselves to put these new ideas into operation and become nondefensive, critical analysts of their classroom work. As in learning any new skills, growth toward mastery takes energy, commitment, self-confidence, and time.

On One Final Note

Several of the activities in chapters 13, 14, and 15 suggest that students go to the Internet (as well as to library books) to obtain background information about scientific concepts. Because the Internet is both a huge source of information and a snake pit of disinformation, one precondition to that search would be to teach students the ways and means of determining what information is reliable and what information is specious.

This postscript has been added to the chapter on "thinking" because learning to differentiate between reliable and fallacious information is also a matter of exercising good judgment and intelligent habits of thinking. Teaching students to use fact check sources, also available on the Internet, such as PolitiFact, FactCheck.org, and the Sunlight Foundation, to name a few, is one way for them to ascertain the reliability and validity of the information.

Chapter 5

Perspectives from the Classroom

The Play-Debrief-Replay Instructional Model

Marti E. teaches Grade 3 at the Fifty-ninth Avenue School in the east end of the city. It is an old school with none of the accoutrements of contemporary design—no rambling suburban clusters, no green lawns, no softening of the effect of institutionality. Just your basic red brick, three-story building, straight out of the 1930s. Marti, a veteran teacher, but new to the school, found that her classroom had become the "dumping ground" for other teachers to unload their "unwanted" kids on the newcomer. As Marti embarked on her science-thinking program, she certainly did not have the deck stacked in her favor.

Although the students were far from the intellectual elite of the school and although Marti had more than her share of students with identified "behavior" problems, she was nevertheless committed in her belief that given the "right" conditions, these children, too, could grow and learn. It wasn't easy; but do-able.

In the first few months, Marti emphasized interpersonal functioning and helped the children to learn to work productively with each other in small cooperative learning groups. Her behavioral standards were clear and consistent; her discipline never punitive and always fair. Underlying all of her work was the calm and clear communication of her caring, her warmth, her respect for the dignity of each of the children, and her explicit belief in their ability to grow and learn.

Inch by painful inch, the children learned to work responsibly, productively, and skillfully. In this climate, Marti embarked on her sciencing program. Her approach emphasized investigative play—active, hands-on manipulation of a variety of science materials, cooperative groupwork, intellectually challenging science activities, and classroom interactions emphasizing higher-order questions and responses.

Midway into the school year, classroom routines had been successfully established and the children's ability to work together responsibly, in small groups, was clearly observable. Though the children's behavior had initially been troublesome, there was little evidence of that to the observer. In fact, the children's engagement in their sciencing activities was energetic and productive, their experimentation with the materials imaginative and spirited. It was a matter of delight to the observer to see that children coming from home environments that were largely unsophisticated in terms of their educational backgrounds gave themselves so enthusiastically to their science inquiries.

To expect any less of children is to do them a disservice.

SCENES FROM GRADE 3 SCIENCING

Marti announces that work in science is scheduled for that afternoon. The children cheer. During the lunch break, she has set up five investigative play centers. Each will accommodate a group of five children, and each group of five will have a chance to work in three different centers that afternoon. At the end of the sciencing investigations, all groups will move to the carpeted area for a Debriefing session. In the days following, sciencing at these centers will resume for as many sessions as interest in the investigations is sustained.

Today's investigative play centers include the following:

1. Siphoning. This center contains two buckets, plastic tubing of varying lengths and diameters and water.
2. Magnets. This center contains bar and horseshoe magnets, iron filings, and a variety of metal and nonmetal objects.
3. Floaters and sinkers. This center contains two plastic tubs filled with water and a variety of objects including pieces of wood, modeling clay, plastic bottles and caps, sponges, chestnuts, toothbrushes, pieces of Styrofoam, and a funnel.
4. Sound. This center contains tuning forks, buckets of water, rocks, string, elastic bands, and bottles.
5. Observing. This center contains a large, hairy spider in a glass jar and some magnifiers.

Having moved to their investigative play centers, each group begins work by deciding on the procedures to be used during their inquiries. These arrangements are discussed and decisions made without adult supervision. When the procedures have been clarified, the groups' sciencing work begins. In every center, emphasis is on investigative play in cooperative learning groups that emphasize children's active engagement with the tasks.

As part of each activity, there is a requirement that the children record the observations they have made during their investigations. At the end of each activity, all children participate in the cleanup, making the center ready for the next group's entry.

The observer sees the five centers in dynamic operation, the room filled with the noise of scientific explorations under way. The teacher moves from group to group observing the children's work, but she intervenes only occasionally, sometimes to reflect what is occurring. She does not raise challenging questions at this time, for they are likely to redirect the children's thinking away from their own investigations and toward the teacher's view of how the inquiry should proceed.

It is important to note that Marti's responses to the children's investigations are neither judgmental ("Oh, isn't that good!") nor directive or leading ("Why don't you try it this way and see what happens?"). They are instead reassuring ("Well, the water has spilled, but I'm sure you will find a way to clean it up."), affirming ("Yes, I can see how you have worked that out."), and reflective ("I can see you've got the water moving out from the higher bucket into the lower bucket.").

Observing the activity in one center closely, it is possible to see the amalgam of children's science investigations and play emerging as one activity: sciencing. Five children working at the floaters and sinkers center are placing objects into the water in both tubs. Discussion ensues over the plastic lid, which at first floats, then sinks. The children remove the lid from the water and place it again several times to see if the floating-sinking pattern persists. More discussion ensues over how this particular item is to be recorded.

Each item is subject to repeated "floating-sinking" tests. The objects are then classified: all the sinkers into tub 1 and all the floaters into tub 2. Sam and Harpreet are in consultation over the recording of the items. On the recording sheet, Harpreet writes: clay, toothbrush, and eraser in the "Sinkers" column. Sam writes: Styrofoam, bottle, and sponge in the "Floaters" column. Edward, Raj, and Mei are continuing their manipulation of the materials. They start to build constructions with the objects in tub 2 to determine how many floating objects can be piled on top of each other and still remain floating. This problem is not articulated, but it appears to be implicitly understood as the working problem and inquiries continue.

Edward then begins to manipulate the modeling clay in tub 1 and shapes it into a bowl. He reinserts it into the tub and it sinks. He takes it out and continues to reshape it, testing it in the water each time until it has a shape that floats. "Hey," he exclaims to the others, "look at this. When you put the modeling clay into this shape, it floats." In science language, Edward has tested a hypothesis, gathering data from several field trials, each of which was unsuccessful. He continued and found that his hypothesis was eventually supported. The other children observe the floating clay bowl and some of them begin to test other shapes.

Sam flattens the modeling clay into a large pancake shape and watches it sink to the bottom of tub 2. What is occurring in this sinking-floating center is scientific experimentation in microcosm: observing, predicting, testing, and retesting of hypotheses, gathering data, the manipulation of experimental variables, the rechecking of data, the recording of data, and the consultation among peers. Through these hands-on explorations, conceptual frameworks grow.

Sciencing along similar lines is occurring in each of the other centers as children construct meanings, incorporating new ideas into their conceptual frameworks, making connections, and thereby making better sense of their worlds (AAAS, 1993). In none of these centers does the teacher redirect the children's thinking away from their own self-initiated inquiries.

When the investigative play in sciencing is concluded for the day, the children gather in a group on the carpet for Debriefing. It is now time for the teacher to ask the children about their investigations and to use this discussion as a vehicle for promoting deeper reflection and analysis of what was observed. Marti's questioning and responding interactions encourage students to express their thoughts in a climate of safety. The Debriefing works to solidify some of the findings of their investigations, to raise new questions, to raise doubts about potential theories, and to invite possibilities for further experimentation.

In the spirit of scientific inquiry, no single "correct" answer is sought, nor does the teacher attempt to "get the students to learn a specific concept." It is rather the process of examination of phenomena observed during play that is given emphasis, so that the children may extract meaning from their experiences. Implicitly the children are encouraged to tolerate ambiguity, to entertain tentative judgments, to examine alternate hypotheses, and to suspend judgment.

In the sciencing investigations of the following days, children may choose to repeat some of the experiments that they or others have done. Or they may choose to begin new investigations that emerge from the discussions during Debriefing. Marti has also added several library books placed strategically around the room so that the students may refer to them to find information to support their ideas, and/or extend their thinking by helping them create new investigations.

In this brief scenario lies the potential for the construction of a model for teaching science with an emphasis on higher-order thinking, integrating the dimensions of science, play, and the cognitive development of children.

What resulted from these observations is the Play-Debrief-Replay constructivist model: *Sciencing*.

THE PLAY-DEBRIEF-REPLAY INSTRUCTIONAL MODEL

The Play-Debrief-Replay instructional model is grounded in the belief that investigative play in learning science is a major contributor to children's cognitive growth and to the development of their conceptual understanding of science. Data from cognitive studies with young children at Harvard University (Bruner et al., 1974) revealed that children's conceptual understandings occurred more substantially through their playing with objects than through direct, systematic instruction.

Play, moreover, invites and encourages creativity and invention, builds self-initiative, and provides for the recurring practice of skills. It teaches children to be unafraid to try, to make mistakes, and to try again. It has been observed that children's play with science materials closely resembles the creative activities of scientists at work in their laboratories (AAAS, 1993).

In the sciencing program, children's play with science materials may reflect work in chemistry, physics, biology, geology, zoology, mathematics, or combinations of these. The teacher sets out the equipment with which the investigations are to be carried out. This is usually done with some articulated goals for conceptual development in mind. Some ground rules set the behavioral standards and expectations. A specific time is allotted for the sciencing investigations. Although materials and content may vary, certain conditions are maintained:

First, play with materials is generally carried out in small cooperative learning groups. The teacher is the best judge of how many and which children make up a successful working group.

Second, when the children are at play, behavioral standards are explicit. The teacher ensures that behavioral expectations for productive group work are met. The procedures for ensuring socially acceptable behaviors are never punitive or demeaning to the self-concept of any child.

Third, in most play centers, students' investigations are given focus by an "Activity Card" that directs their inquiries in an open-ended way. For example: "Use the materials in this center to make some observations of the reflections you see in mirrors. Try as many different investigations as you can think of. Talk with each other about what you observed. Then record your observations."

Fourth, when the children are involved in their investigations, the teacher is cautious about not directing their inquiries away from their own initiatives. Interventions that seem to facilitate pupils' investigations include reflective responses ("Yes, I can see you've tried many ways to put that together."), reassuring responses ("You seem to be having a hard time figuring it out, but I think you will find a way."), and affirming responses ("You really worked hard to figure that out.").

Interventions that have been counterproductive and led to the inhibiting of self-directed investigations included responses that challenged too early in the process ("Why do you suppose that worked?"), responses that rewarded the children's efforts either positively or negatively ("That wasn't a very smart thing to do, Hugo." or "Look at the way Hugo has classified his rocks. Now that's a really good idea!").

A more appropriate time for the teacher to help students dig more deeply into scientific concepts occurs during Debriefing, where the teacher promotes analyses of the data, stimulates conceptual awareness, promotes healthy skepticism, excites imagination, challenges ideas, and asks for data to support developing theories. This is done by making it safe for every student to volunteer his or her ideas without fear of rejection, welcoming and appreciating every student's contribution, and showing genuine interest in all discoveries.

Analyses are encouraged through the use of higher-order questions such as the following: What are the supporting data? How was that discovery made? How did you figure that out? Why do you suppose that strategy worked? How might you explain that?

In these discussions, new hypotheses emerge, discoveries are examined and explored. One important caveat in the Debriefing is that the discussions do not end with closure. In fact, closure would tend to inhibit the next stage in the instructional model. When the discussion is left "suspended," there is an increased motivation for students to continue their investigations in Replay.

Several suggestions are offered for more productive Debriefing discussions:

- All ideas volunteered by the students are accepted and acceptable. In order for the students to feel safe about offering their ideas, the teacher refrains from making judgments about their ideas, such as "right" or "wrong" or "good" or "bad."
- The teacher's interactions are intended to promote further examination—that is, to help a student "process" his or her idea. This is enabled by reflective responses and questions that require students to examine a particular phenomenon.
- To promote additional inquiry about their investigations, the teacher uses questions and responses that allow for further cognitive processing of the ideas, and that do not seek answers or lead students to "learn" specific pieces of information.
- When the teacher talks too much and tries to articulate the students' ideas for them, their opportunities to think for themselves are diminished.

Thinking is best encouraged by giving students a chance to articulate their own ideas.
- An important part of learning science is to develop a healthy respect for ambiguity. That is why the teacher avoids bringing closure to the Debriefing. When closure is brought, the need for further inquiry, for further thinking, ceases. Without closure, students' motivation to investigate and to discover on their own is maintained.

After Debriefing, the teacher ensures that students have access to books, articles, and Internet sources that give them more information about the topics under investigation. Because Debriefing does not end in closure but rather leaves questions unanswered, this is a strong motivator for students to pursue information gathering hard data to support or refute their inquiries.[1]

Replay follows Debriefing, generally over the next few days. Replay may involve repetition of the original investigations. It may be a time when investigations are replicated and confirmed or when new hypotheses are tested. New materials may be added to the play centers. The entire process is cyclical and terminated when the teacher or students implicitly or explicitly concur that certain materials no longer have interest for them. It is then time to collapse that center or centers and create new sciencing opportunities.

CONCLUSION

This chapter presented an instructional model, Play-Debrief-Replay—a way of teaching and learning in science. In this instructional model, elements of what we know about children and how they learn, about current practices in teaching and learning in science, about the role of play in children's learning, about the emphasis on thinking in the curriculum have been fused together into a coherent instructional framework that will result in the kinds of learning outcomes we all want for our students (Wassermann and Ivany, 1988).

The chapters that follow include explicit help for teachers who are interested in moving these ideas into their classroom practices. By making classroom applications specific, it is hoped that teachers can more easily bridge the gap between these ideas and the day-to-day life of the classroom thus ensuring potential success for every teacher in sciencing.

---

[1] Chapter 10 provides a detailed description of the teaching strategies used in Debriefing. The appendix contains a list of children's books for many of the topics under investigation in the fifty-eight sciencing activities

Section II

ORGANIZING THE CLASSROOM FOR SCIENCE AS ACTIVE INQUIRY

Chapter 6

Preparing Students for Sciencing

Scenes from the Classroom:
   This afternoon a group of twelve student teachers is heading out to Nelson School to observe Heather's sciencing program. Heather's middle-grade students offer an opportunity for the student teachers to see the Play-Debrief-Replay instructional model on site. The late April day has turned warm and fair, a welcome change from the rain in beautiful downtown Vancouver.
   Today, four centers are in operation and as the student teachers quietly slip in to the room, the children, deeply absorbed, pay little attention to this large influx of strangers. Anabella's group is at work making observations of worms in a "wormarium." They are discussing their observations and making decisions about what they will record.
   Seema's group is at the bubble center, making bubbles using several different implements and comparing results. A plastic sheet covers the carpet at this center, so the children don't have to be overly cautious about water dripping on the floor.
   Tara's group is working with mirrors, and the mirror center contains several small, flat hand mirrors, a piece of reflective metal, a large full-size mirror, a magnifying-shaving mirror, and another, more obviously curved mirror.
   Peter's group is at the pendulum center. Three pendulums with different bobs and different lengths of string are being observed and compared. The children are planning to make their own pendulums.
   When clean up is announced, the groups tidy each center and get it ready for the next group's use. All this clean up and changing of centers are carried out with the minimum of fuss and with the efficiency born of considerable practice and experience. It is a short afternoon and

after the second round of sciencing activities, Heather calls the groups together for Debriefing. She asks the children about their observations, and she asks about ideas to be shared.

The students respond to her requests for their observations, and she encourages them to formulate hypotheses and theories that flow from their investigations with the materials. The students participate enthusiastically, hands waving eagerly to share their observations, yet there is considerate attention to each speaker.

Heather's responses keep the inquiries open. They do not bring closure or lead students to learn specific facts. Through her questions, she helps them extract meaning from their investigative play experiences ("Hmmm, I wonder why that happened? Do you have any ideas about it?" "Would that happen again if you tried it on another day?" "I wonder how you could figure that out?") as well as helping them develop an increased understanding of scientific phenomena.

Debriefing also opens the doors for further inquiry: Replay.

The student teachers observing Debriefing later inquire: "How do you get the program working so smoothly?"

Developing, organizing, and managing a sciencing program is the key to its effective operation. And while there is no single way to do this, some guidelines, based on teachers' classroom experiences, are offered that may be helpful in moving ahead.

PAVING THE WAY

When a person trains to be a chef, one of the first things to learn is the importance of preparation. Regardless of the culinary undertaking, the recipe is first carefully studied and understood. Then, all ingredients are measured and laid out and all cooking utensils made accessible. The chef-in-training starts out by setting up the conditions that will make the process as problem-free as possible. Making croissants is chore enough without finding that the butter is insufficiently soft or suddenly realizing you have no egg for the egg wash.

A program that is new to students depends largely for its success in the teacher's preparation. This begins with the teacher's careful study and understanding of the instructional plan. Then, procedures, behavioral expectations, goals, all these need to be "out on the table" for the students to understand. In this way, much difficulty can be avoided.

It is therefore a given that teachers begin their sciencing program by becoming familiar with the instructional plan. Then, they will want to ensure that materials for creating investigative play centers are gathered and on hand and that workspace for the program is available.

This is followed by preparing the students for sciencing. It is recommended that this be done in two stages: first, by an "orientation," explaining to them the nature of sciencing, how the investigations are carried out, and the behavioral expectations; second, by providing guidance and supervision during the first few trials, including immediate interventions in the event of on-the-spot difficulties that might arise.

In the orientation stage of informing and explaining, the teacher makes clear the nature of the experience and the procedures to be followed. As students embark on their first investigations, the teacher is close at hand, guiding and supervising and coaching—and his or her presence slowly and gradually takes a back seat, as the students gain independence. This tapering-off process may take a few weeks, depending on the previous experiences of the students and teachers should allow for that amount of learning time as students grow in their ability to function productively in their cooperative learning groups.

SUGGESTIONS FOR ORIENTATION

1. Talk to the students about the program. Tell them what "sciencing" means, about the materials they will be using, about cooperative group work. Allow them sufficient opportunity to raise questions about their concerns.
2. Communicate your own enthusiasm for the program and for science.
3. Communicate your confidence in their ability to do this work.
4. Be explicit about the behavior you expect, about the need for cooperation, for sharing, for working together harmoniously.
5. Identify procedures for handling problems that may arise.
6. Be explicit about the way materials are to be cared for.
7. Provide a space for reference books and other informational materials that are easily accessed by students who want to look up information.
8. Be explicit about cleanup procedures and about how and where materials are to be stored.
9. Invite the students' ideas and suggestions for making the working procedures more effective.
10. Where students are to have choices about who works in what centers, make the procedures for making such choices explicit.
11. Where recording of observations is to be done, make procedures clear.
12. Undertake a "trial run" with four or five groups working at four or five centers. Have the children participate in an evaluation of the trial run. Ask for their suggestions and ideas for improving procedures.

13. In the first weeks of the program, elicit the students' participation in an evaluation of the experience directly after each sciencing period.
14. Supervise the students' work closely at first. Taper off the close supervision slowly, as students grow in their ability to work together cooperatively.

There will eventually come a time in the classroom, a magic moment, when the teacher will be able to step back and see at a glance that all the students are productively engaged in sciencing, that there is no need for close supervision and guidance, that the interpersonal relationships of the students are cooperative and not combative.

Then it is time to exhale, relax, and pat yourself on the back. Your sciencing program is at last functioning as you hoped it might.

Chapter 7

Gathering the Materials

There is considerable flexibility with regard to the extent and type of material that can be utilized in the building of investigative play centers for a sciencing program. While what can be used is considerable, it is certainly not essential to gather everything at once. Good sciencing programs can operate with appropriately selected materials. The intrepid teacher can add whatever is necessary for investigative play for those particular centers.

The following list contains numerous suggestions as to what might be considered potentially valuable for constructive investigations.

MATERIALS FOR A SCIENCING PROGRAM

Where Items Are Likely to Be Found

- Somewhere in the school: ask the custodian!
- High-school science or industrial arts departments
- Junk stores, second-hand stores, flea markets, garage sales
- Hardware stores
- Restaurant supply stores
- Toy stores
- Garden stores, pet stores
- Possible donations from parents
- Beachcombing, scrounging, rummaging, and using other artful strategies known by teachers

Materials

absorbent cotton
air pump
alcohol
aluminum foil
ammonia
animals (small): mice, lizards, hamsters, guinea pigs, chicks, gerbils, fish, turtles, and so on
apple juice
atomizer
baby carriage wheels
baking soda
balance scales
ball bearings
balloons
ballpoint pens
balls
barometer
basins
bathroom scale
batteries
beans
bedsheets
bells
binoculars
birdseed
block and tackle
blocks
blotting paper
bobs
bones
bottles
bowls
boxes
brace and bits
bricks
bubble pipes
bulbs (electric light)
bulgur
buttons
buzzer

calipers
camera
candles
carbon paper
cardboard tubes
chalk
cheesecloth
chisels
chopsticks
clay
clinical thermometer
clocks
clothesline
clothespins (wooden)
colander
collecting trays
comb
compass (magnetic)
compasses (measuring)
cooking thermometer
corks
cornstarch
crayons
detergent (nontoxic, liquid)
doweling
drums
dry cells
dry ice
earthworms
egg cartons
eggs
egg whisk (mechanical)
electric appliances (for taking apart): toasters
coffee pots, irons, mixers, radios, and so on
electric fans
electric motors (toy)
eraser
extension cords (new)
extension cords (old)
eyedropper
eyeshades
fabrics of all kids

feathers
felt pens
fertilizer
fired clay tiles
fish weights
flashlights
flour
flowerpots
fly wheel
flowers
foam rubber
food coloring
foods
forceps
fruits
funnels
fur
fuses (burned out)
geometric shapes
glass (for making slides)
glass beads
glasses (drinking)
glass jars
glass tubing
glue and paste
graph paper
gravel
gyroscopes
harmonica
hay or straw
height measure
holograms
honey
hourglass
ice-cream sticks
ice cubes
instant coffee powder
insulated copper wire
iodine
iron filings
jacks (automobile)
jars (gallon)

jugs (gallon)
kaleidoscope
kazoos
knives
lamp
laths
leather
leaves
legumes (dry)
lenses of all kinds
light bulbs (burned out)
logs
machines (for taking apart): calculators
pencil sharpeners, clocks, old dial telephones
magnetic wire
magnets of all shapes and sizes
magnifying lenses
mallets
maps
marbles
marking pens
measuring cups
measuring implements: yard sticks, meter sticks, tape measure
medicine dropper
metals (all kinds and weights)
metal scraps
metal wire
meteorological equipment
microscopes
milk powder (dry)
"minibeasties": spiders, ants, caterpillars,
worms, and so on
mirrors
modeling clay
model windmill
molds (forms)
motors
mousetraps
muffin tins
nails of all sizes
needles
newspaper

nuts and bolts
pails
paper: poster board, tissue, waxed, bond, and so on
paper clips
paper cups
paper punch
paper towels
peanuts (ALLERGY ALERT!)
peas
pebbles
pencil sharpener
pendulum frame
pendulums
picture collections
pillows
ping-pong balls
pins
pinwheel
pipe cleaners
pitcher
plants
plaster of Paris
plastic bags
plastic cake containers
plastic cups
plastic dishes
plastic sheeting
plastic tubing
plastic tubs, buckets, basins
playing cards
poster paints
potatoes
potting soil
printing ink
prisms
protractor
pulleys, double and single
rheostats
ribbon
rice
rocks
rock salt

room thermometer
rope
rubber bands
rubber suction cups
rulers
safety glasses
salt
sand
sandpaper
saws
scissors
scrap lumber
screen
screws of all sizes
sealing wax
seeds
seesaw balance on a fulcrum
shells
skeletons
skins (animal)
Slinky
snail shell
soap flakes
soldering iron
spinning tops
sponges
spools
spoons, graded sizes
sprayers
springs
spring scales, kitchen scales, scales with weights
squid (frozen)
stapler
staple remover
staples
steel wool
stethoscope
sticks
stones
stopwatch
straws
string

Styrofoam chips
sugar
syringes
tape
tape measures
teapot
tea strainers
telescope
test tubes
thermometers
thread, string, twine
thumbtacks
timer (egg)
tin cans
tissue paper (all colors)
toilet plunger
toilet roll centers
tongue depressors
tools: hammers, pliers, screwdrivers, drill, saws
toothpicks
toys: cars, airplanes, furniture, utensils
transparent flexible tubing of various diameters
trays
tree parts: bark, leaves, twigs, branches, driftwood
triangles
trundle wheel
tuning forks
umbrellas
unglazed clay tiles
vacuum cleaner
vegetables
vinegar
vise
washers
wind up watch
watch (digital)
watch with sweep second hand
water containers
watering can
waxed paper
wedge
weights

wheels of all sizes
whistles
wire
wire cutters
wooden balls of all sizes
wooden beads
wood of different types, for example, scraps, bamboo, balsa, pegboard, and so on
"wormarium"
X-acto knife
Xylophone
yeast (cakes)
yeast (dried)
yo-yos

There are, as well, IT materials that should be included. Some may be available in the school's IT lab. Some may be teacher-owned. Some may be purchased with funding from the PTA. Whichever of these are relevant for specific investigations may be added at the appropriate time, for example, tablets, iPads, graphic tablets, scanner, USB cable, headsets, and microphone.

In addition to the above, the teacher will also want to make available reference materials that attend to each of the areas of inquiry. There are literally dozens of books for children on science topics that are likely found in the school library. See the appendix for a list of some relevant children's science books.

CONCLUSION

At first glance, the above list may seem daunting. However, simple planning may take the onus off the need to spend an exhaustive amount of time gathering materials. Planning ahead by deciding which investigative play centers will be activated in the upcoming weeks will certainly reduce the amount of time needed to acquire the materials and to prepare them for use.

Since there is no required sequence to the way the sciencing activities are to be introduced or used, the nature of what is going to be used should delimit and focus the search. A good tip for teachers new to sciencing is to choose those activities in which materials are more easily accessible. There's no loss of honor in making things easy, especially at the start.

Chapter 8

Making Room for Sciencing

SCENES FROM THE CLASSROOM

I found an old, wrecked rowboat on the shore and hauled it into my class—a rowboat for science! The kids and I are sanding and painting it this week. They love it and I think it's pretty cool too.—Bev Craig, Grade 6, Prince Rupert, British Columbia

In classrooms where most curriculum activities occur in "learning centers," there would normally be one or two sciencing centers that would function along with math centers, language activity centers, social studies centers, and a variety of other theme-work or investigative centers that are created, evolve, and collapse in response to students' interests and curriculum guidelines.

Should teachers wish to explore such a "learning centers" approach, there are several texts that offer practical help. First, the classics: Virgil Howes, *Informal Teaching in the Open Classroom* and Johnson and Johnson, *Circles of Learning*. Then, more recent additions: Jacobs, Power, et al., *The Teacher's Sourcebook for Cooperative Learning*; Gillies, *Cooperative Learning: Integrating Theory and Practice*; and Practice and Joliffe, *Cooperative Learning in the Classroom: Putting it Into Practice*.

The approach taken in this text pursues a more specific curriculum path, that of the creation of investigative play centers to promote active inquiry and higher-order thinking in the curriculum area of science. Other curriculum areas have not been included, although the Play-Debrief-Replay instructional model applies to other subject areas as well.

Many elementary classrooms operate under several different types of curriculum plans, in which investigative play centers may be "parachuted in" with a minimum of difficulty no matter how instruction in other curriculum areas has been organized. There must be, however, enough room for sciencing.

ORGANIZING SPACE AND STORING MATERIALS

First, there needs to be storage space to house the materials to be used in the investigative play centers. Large-size plastic containers are ideal for larger pieces of equipment and are generally found in most schools in many sizes and colors. Failing that, cardboard boxes from supermarkets can be used as is, or they can be painted and decorated by the students. A supply of large plastic garbage bags will come in handy to line the cardboard boxes in case damp materials are to be stored. As well, a shelf for children's science books from the school library should be easily accessible for students to obtain background information for their inquiries.

Smaller pieces of equipment may be stored in shoeboxes, plastic five-gallon ice-cream buckets, cottage cheese containers, and other plastic food containers. A restaurant supply store may be stocked with other types of plastic storage containers in many shapes and sizes at bargain prices, as are thrift shops and other second-hand venues. Parents may welcome opportunities to unload some of their excess plastic containers and donate them to the classroom.

Wherever the storage bins are kept, they should be easily accessible so that the getting and putting away of materials is hassle-free. If classroom space is already overly committed, space may become available by unloading rarely used textbooks or other equipment into longer-term storage areas, possibly outside the classroom, making more room for sciencing materials.

The important consideration in creating sciencing workspace is to make the availability of needed materials and the creation of the centers as trouble-free as possible. If it is going to be a huge burden just to set up the room each day, it is more than likely that a teacher's enthusiasm will soon be eroded away by the logistic difficulties.

Creating adequate workspace is one of the major challenges of the program, and most teachers find ways to do this successfully. If space arrangement is not a teacher's particular forte, asking for advice from a colleague in brainstorming some practicable and attractive ideas may be helpful.

At best, there should be easy access to supplies that will be in constant use: water, paper towels, newspapers, scissors, measuring equipment, string, assorted paper, pens, pencils, chalk, jars, and related readings. Students should be aware of where to find these supplies without having to ask the teacher each time and should be made responsible for their care and storage.

There are multiple payoffs when students play an active role in caring for the workspace and the materials; teaching them how to do this thoughtfully and responsibly is one more part of preparing for productive sciencing. When students learn to exercise care and to accept responsibility, they are learning to become more mature, independent, and thoughtful, which encourages their personal ownership of the sciencing program.

CONCLUSION

Many teachers are in a constant battle with space requirements for their curriculum needs; few classrooms, especially those in older schools, are large enough to accommodate the number of students enrolled and the instructional materials needed for all of the curriculum activities. When students, desks, and materials are in place, that leaves little room to move around freely without getting someone's elbow in one's ribs.

In more up-to-date schools, built as recently as thirty years ago, primary rooms are more spacious and perhaps that is also true of the middle-grade rooms as well. In any event, accommodating the space necessary to allow for active, investigative play in science will be a teacher's challenge. As in most suggestions made to teachers, what will carry the most weight will be those ideas that are resonant with what the teacher believes is right, good, and of educational value for his or her students.

A teacher's beliefs that teaching science as active inquiry and developing students' intelligent habits of mind is of critical importance will find ways and means to create the space necessary for materials, work stations, and students to carry on sciencing.

Once the plan is figured out the rest is history.

Chapter 9

Guidelines and Ground Rules

SCENES FROM THE CLASSROOM

Cheryl Reflects on Creating Her Sciencing Program in Grade 5:
　Choosing a new program can be very exciting. It can also be very intimidating. There are lots of risks to be taken, lots of new roads to travel, and lots of unexpected events on the journey. Sometimes the path to innovation can have so many obstacles that progress is thwarted. Sometimes there are so many problems to deal with that the task of creating a new program becomes overwhelming.
　But I know that potential stumbling blocks can be overcome and sometimes avoided altogether when I remember to select the approach that feels right to me. That usually means that it feels reasonable to me, that I feel secure about what I'm doing, that it's compatible with other curriculum demands, that it is acceptable without conflict with the administration, that it is appropriate to the physical space available, and that it creates a minimum of stress and a maximum potential for success.

CHOOSING THE RIGHT APPROACH

Given the variety of the many issues that impact teachers' decisions, several suggestions are offered for those considering a sciencing program. Choosing the approach that is more closely aligned with teachers' needs and concerns may make for a more successful beginning.

Figure 9.1 *Dennis Smith.*

APPROACH 1: TREAD SOFTLY AND CARRY A BIG BALLOON

a. Choose a sciencing activity that feels "safe"—one for which you can obtain materials easily and one that incurs a minimum of mess. (See the Sciencing Activities in chapters 13, 14, and 15.) Let's say that you have chosen pendulums. Make five pendulums and create five working groups.

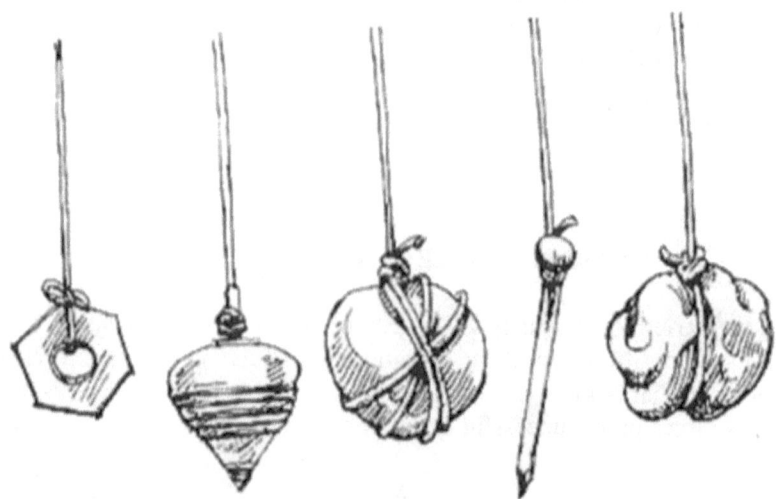

Figure 9.2 *Dennis Smith.*

Guidelines and Ground Rules 57

Figure 9.3 *Dennis Smith.*

Position the pendulums in strategic locations around the classroom so that there are, in effect, five working centers and so that the five groups may work at these centers without getting in each other's way.
b. Give clear instructions to the students about carrying out their investigations. (See the suggestions in chapters 13, 14, and 15 about writing directions on Activity Cards.) Allow about ten to twelve minutes for this introductory sciencing activity. Instruct the groups to record their observations. Include directions to the students about behavioral expectations for group work, care of materials, and cleanup.
c. Move around the room from group to group, observing what the students are doing. Be responsive but not judgmental, to what is happening. Be available to deal immediately with behavior management, if needed. Otherwise, do not direct the students' inquiries.
d. At the end of the play period, gather the students together and ask them to talk about their observations. Make it safe for all the students to share their ideas by avoiding judgmental responses. Use reflective responses to enable students to think about their statements. (See chapter 10 for specific help with questioning and responding interactions.) Limit the Debriefing to about ten to twelve minutes.
e. At the end of Debriefing, ask the students to evaluate their experiences with sciencing. What did they enjoy? What were some things that went wrong? What might be helpful to do the next time to make it work more

smoothly? Suggest that students refer to related readings on the science books shelf for obtaining additional information about the concepts under investigation.

f. The next day, follow up the sciencing activity with a Replay of pendulums. This might be done with single pendulums again, or with a double-pendulum activity, in which each group observes two pendulums, each with a different length of string and a bob of different weight. After the Replay, follow procedures *b* through *e* of this approach. Consider shifting students to other groups if there have been some interpersonal conflicts.

Figure 9.4 *Dennis Smith.*

APPROACH 2: TREAD GENTLY AND CARRY A BIG BUCKET

a. Choose two sciencing activities that feel "safe" for you—activities that you would not consider to be of high risk. (Refer to the Sciencing Activities chapters for suggestions.)

b. Gather the materials needed and set up six investigative play centers—three for each of the activities. (Use the suggestions in chapters 13–15

Figure 9.5 *Dennis Smith.*

to develop Activity Cards that focus on the investigations in each center.)
c. Allow each group to have one turn at each of the two centers during the investigative play period. Allow no less than ten to twelve minutes for each sciencing activity.
d. Instruct the students to carry out investigations using the materials in the centers. Ask them to make observations of what is happening in their investigations. As an option, ask them to record their observations.
e. Move around the room during the investigative play period and observe what the students are doing. Be responsive, but not judgmental. Be available to deal immediately with behavior management as needed. Otherwise, avoid directing the students' inquiries.
f. After each activity, instruct the students to clean up their centers and make them ready for the next group. (If the sciencing period is concluded for the day, ask the students to clean up and put all the materials away.) Allow for sufficient time for cleaning up and provide help during the cleanup as needed.
g. Debrief the sciencing activities by gathering the students together and asking them to tell what they have observed. Make it safe for all the students to share their ideas by avoiding judgmental responses. Use reflective responses to enable students to think about their statements. (See

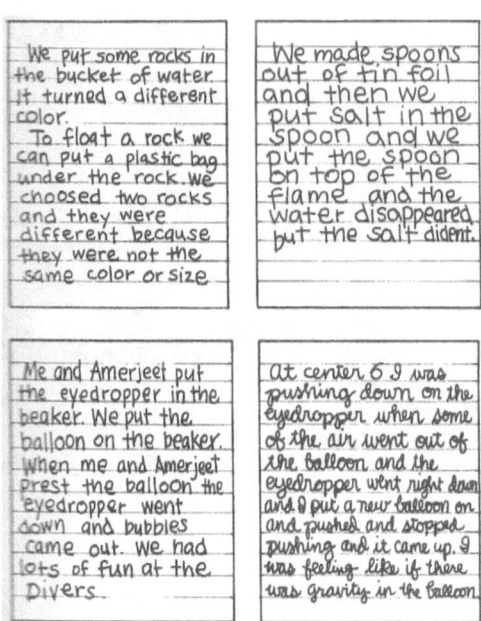

Figure 9.6 *Dennis Smith.*

chapter 10 for help with this interactive process.) Limit the Debriefing to about fifteen minutes.

h. At the end of Debriefing, ask students to participate in evaluating the sciencing experience. What did they like? What were some things that went wrong? What might be helpful to remember to do the next time? Suggest that students refer to related readings on the science books shelf for gathering additional information about the concepts under investigation.

i. Ask the students if they want to continue with their investigative play in these same centers. Get an idea of how "fresh" and appealing each center is for the students. If interest is high, maintain Replay activities using the same centers. If interest is waning, collapse the center and create a new one. If the students have been recording their observations, it might be helpful to post their notes on a science bulletin board.

APPROACH 3: TREAD FIRMLY AND CARRY A BIG SQUID

a. Choose three different sciencing activities from among those included in chapters 13, 14, and 15. Choose at least one activity that is of higher risk for you—perhaps one from the "Wet, Wetter, Wettest" group or one from the "Who's Afraid of Spiders?" group. (How about siphoning? Well, what about spiders?)

Guidelines and Ground Rules

Figure 9.7 *Dennis Smith.*

Figure 9.8 *Dennis Smith.*

b. Organize the investigative play period so that each group may participate in at least two different sciencing centers that day.
   c. Follow the procedures as in Approach 2, steps *b* through *i*.
   d. Observe the students' work in the higher-risk centers. Think about why it was a higher risk for you. If students' responses to that center were troublesome, think of some ways in which the trouble might be avoided or eliminated.

   Don't abandon the center until you have really given yourself a very good chance to get it working successfully!

Figure 9.9 *Dennis Smith.*

APPROACH 4: TREAD PURPOSEFULLY AND CARRY A GIANT PYTHON

   a. Choose five different sciencing activities and set each one up with the materials needed to carry out a successful investigative play.
   b. Include at least one activity that is of higher risk for you.
   c. Follow the procedures as in Approach 3, steps *b* through *d*.

Figure 9.10 *Dennis Smith*.

APPROACH 5: MARCH TO YOUR OWN DRUMMER

Use combinations of approaches from 1 through 4 or create your own set of procedures incorporating the principles outlined above.

GUIDELINES AND GROUND RULES

Whatever approach is used, the following guidelines may help in implementing it successfully.

- Begin with a clear idea of how you will group the students so that behavioral difficulties may be avoided and successful group functioning is encouraged. You may have to experiment with grouping arrangements before you find strategies that are more successful. Give yourself the time you need for these trial runs and don't expect total success in the first few trials.

- Make sure you have relatively easy access to the materials you need for the centers you have chosen. If you begin with elaborate plans to acquire hard-to-get materials, your efforts may soon be frustrated and your enthusiasm may soon fade.
- Try to spot the problems that arise and plan to deal with them in the early stages of the first trials. Problems may come from unwieldy group arrangements, from students' inability to work responsibly in groups, from lack of space, from the inappropriate organization—from many different sources.

Organizing a classroom for effective learning is a highly complex and creative task under the best of circumstances. Undertaking an innovative program increases the potential for things to go awry. Taking a diagnostic and problem-solving approach can be helpful, but be sure you institute corrective procedures in advance, lest you become disenchanted with the program. In some classes, it takes a good deal of time for students to grow toward responsible group behavior.

- Communicate to the students your own enthusiasm about beginning this new program. Students are very much influenced by what teachers think. If you show your own enthusiasm about sciencing, they are likely to respond enthusiastically.
- Try to avoid communicating your own anxieties or frustrations to the students. If students perceive that you are worried about their ability to undertake this work successfully, your expectations may translate into students' poor performance. High expectations of what students can do will likely yield richer and more productive results.
- Be a thoughtful, sensitive observer. Assess what is happening in a diagnostic way and use this feedback to keep building and improving the program. The most inventive and successful professionals use "reflection in action" as a means for examining existing situations, diagnosing weaknesses and strengths, and creating strategies that lead to improved practice. The teacher who is a reflective practitioner can keep the classroom dynamic and be consistently responsive to instructional improvement.

LAST WORDS

When creating a new and different version of classroom experiences, one that is unfamiliar to both teacher and students, expecting it to run smoothly in its initial stages, is setting oneself up for disappointment. Students who have become routinized to their dependence on teachers for a minute to minute direction about what to do, how to do it, and why it should be done will find it more than a little disconcerting to be asked to function as independent learners.

Working in cooperative learning groups is a learned skill; it is not learned in a day. The hard lesson is that teachers need not only give themselves time to adjust and become skilled with sciencing but equally important is to allow the students time to grow and learn responsible and productive group work.

This is done through the kind of instruction in which other skills are learned—with active involvement and assessment of that involvement as the students reflect on their behavior and actions. This is a slow process—but what aids its progress is teachers' beliefs in the students' ability to become more responsible, more cooperative, and more fully functioning group members, as well as their facilitative and supportive feedback as students reflect on the process.

Cooperative working groups do not emerge from wishful thinking. They take time to grow, let alone flourish. But the payoffs are sweet. For there will be a day, a splendid day, when the teacher will step back and observe sciencing working groups in action, every group productively engaged with the materials and with each other.

And that is sciencing at its best.

Chapter 10

Debriefing

Interactions That Promote Thoughtful Inquiry

The approach to teaching science as inquiry grew out of the work of J. Richard Suchman that originated in 1957 at the University of Illinois. The materials that Suchman developed were designed to train students in the "art of inquiry," enabling them to initiate and direct their own science investigations. Suchman was concerned that most children who enter school as natural inquirers with several years of preschool experience in manipulating objects and who form concepts based on these experiences lose that ability in school.

In school, a different kind of learning took place, in which students were expected to keep in step with their classes and were not permitted to "fool around" with materials and ideas. Students were rewarded for giving the right answers; they were required to be quiet, to listen, and to read what was assigned. They were seldom given the opportunity to make decisions or asked to make meaning from data. Suchman's research showed that as children moved up through the elementary grades, they asked fewer questions, proposed fewer hypotheses, and became less independent in their thinking (Suchman, 1966).

Teaching science as inquiry has evolved beyond Suchman's approach. Now, almost any experience that invites students to "mess around" with materials is often called "inquiry," whether students are helped to make meaning from their experiences or not. "Inquiry teaching," like many good methodologies, has evolved in both good and bad ways.

Teachers who choose an inquiry approach in science would share the belief that the process of inquiry is at least as important as the information gathered. The "teaching for thinking" approach in this text, called "Play-Debrief-Replay" evolves from inquiry teaching, with singular features. It incorporates the idea that the most effective route for gathering information in science is through the emphasis on the higher-order mental processes. In this approach, students play active roles in their own learning, are purposefully engaged, working cooperatively in small groups in productive problem-solving. Through this process, concept development grows from students' experiential hands-on investigations. In this more natural process, students are stimulated to know more and are more motivated to search through textbooks, children's books, reference materials, and the Internet to locate supporting information.

The approach is consonant with what has been advocated by the AAAS report on the need for reform in science teaching (AAAS, 1989).

Teachers who choose this or other inquiry-based approaches don't see science teaching as the presentation of "scientific truths"—a body of information to be ingested and recalled on final exams. They see science teaching as involving the skills of learning to gather information, to observe, study, and classify; to speculate, hypothesize, and generate theories; to test ideas and reject previously held assumptions in the face of new and contradictory evidence; to design investigations and experiments; and to interpret data intelligently (AAAS, 1990).

In this approach, the process of inquiry is emphasized over "correct answers." The search for answers becomes more important than the answers. Questioning results is more important than accepting them at face value, and greater tolerance for ambiguity, rather than closure, is cultivated.

Investigative play, described in chapter 3, begins this inquiry process. It is followed by Debriefing—a teacher–student interactive process in which the teacher uses reflective responses and higher-order questions to enable students to make meaning of their investigations and to examine further their conceptual understandings.

DEBRIEFING: EXTRACTING MEANING FROM PLAY

As the play stage provides for direct, hands-on experiences in manipulating scientific variables, the teacher's interactions with students during Debriefing work to help students make meaning from their play experiences. This is done through the teacher's skillful use of questioning strategies that elevate students' deeper consideration of data and further their understanding of the concepts and principles derived from their experiential play.

As the teacher questions students about their work, the questions require students to analyze their ideas as well as call for deeper reflection about certain concepts. When the teacher's interactions can do all of this, students' thinking is enhanced. One important consequence is that Debriefing, which is open-ended and lacks closure, becomes an important motivation for students to want to know more—and thus are more inclined to search through the books and other reference materials on the Science Library shelf for supporting information.

N.B. Of course, a teacher interacts with students in many ways. Interactions may direct behavior; they may admonish; they may be unrelated to the development of higher-order thinking skills. The important variable is that teachers not only understand the differences between these responses but use them as appropriate to their particular contexts.

Learning to use interactions that call for higher-order mental processing in Debriefing is a challenging task for many teachers who have been trained to use other interactive styles. These new skills are not acquired from simply reading textbook descriptions or from wishing they were so. They require the ability to discriminate between questions and responses that call for thoughtful reflection and those that reduce such opportunities. They require the ability to let go of the need to lead students to specific answers. They require the ability to avoid making evaluative judgments of what students are saying.

And here comes the curveball: they require a commitment to use and develop these skills through classroom practice, reflection on practice, and a nondefensive attitude in the ongoing analytic examination of their interactive style. The requirement to continue to use these and refine these skills is essential.

Becoming skilled in the use of these interactive skills begins with an understanding of the various ways in which teachers' responses and questions promote or inhibit student thinking.

Interactions That Inhibit Thinking

These inhibiting interactions occur in a number of ways. One is when the response has inadvertently brought closure to the student's thinking. The effect is that the student is no longer encouraged or required to think more about the issue. The burden of further inquiry has been lifted. Closure occurs when:

- The teacher agrees or disagrees with the student.
    You are right, Frank. Carbohydrates are foods that are made up of some form of sugar or starch.
    No, Rosa. You can't get that kind of reaction from the procedure you used.
- The teacher doesn't give the student a chance to think.
- The teacher tells the student what he/she thinks.
- The teacher does the thinking by telling or showing the student what to do.
    Try it this way, Marvin. You'll see you'll get much better results.
- The teacher talks too much.

- The teacher cuts the student off and does not let the student continue with his/her statement.

Closure also occurs when the teacher's response has undermined the student's confidence in his or her ideas. The effect of such responses is that students become afraid to offer new ideas or express an opinion for fear they might be shamed. For example:

Where on earth did you get the idea that ice crystals form from salt?
Solar energy is not on topic. Stick to the main idea.
We're not interested in what you found, Charlie.
That's a stupid question, Bernard. I'm surprised at you.
Obviously you weren't listening, Audrey, otherwise you wouldn't be saying that.
Now, Mei, let's remember that certain animals do NOT make good house pets.

Some Types of Interactions Delimit Students' Opportunities to Think

Certain interactions require students to retrieve information. While this is a form of thinking, it is considered to occur at lower levels of cognitive functioning (Bloom, 1956). Retrieving information requires no initiative and no originality. In recalling information, the student has no need to process it. Such interactions generally call for students to come up with *the* correct answers. In doing that, students' thinking is limited by the parameters set by the expected answer.

Such limiting interactions have certain observable effects on students' thinking. They become habituated to "right answer" explanations, and they may have considerable difficulty tolerating the ambiguity necessary for higher-order cognitive processing. Suspension of judgment, uncertainty, and exploring unknowns may make them uneasy. They grow to believe that only "answers" count.

Following are some examples of such interactions:
- Looks for a single correct answer.

What are the names of the three main systems of the human body?
- Looks for a single correct procedure.

Boys and girls, look at the way Minnie is siphoning the water.
- Leads student to the correct answer; gives clues to the answer.

Remember when we talked about skeletons yesterday? We said that the bone structure was . . . what?

- Uses voice inflection to "clue" students to the right answer.
Feel the rocks. Do they all feel the same?
- Leads students to a particular line of thinking.
Can a fish live on land? I know you really don't mean that, Harry.

Some Types of Interactions Call for Students to Think More Intelligently about Their Ideas. When These Types of Interactions Are Used, Students Are Being Asked to Function at Higher Cognitive Levels

Some teacher responses call for students to reflect on their ideas. These ask students to reexamine their ideas, reconsider them through mental processing, and assume responsibility for them. These "reflective responses" are the very bedrock of teaching-for-thinking interactions and are used extensively during Debriefing.

The use of reflective responses yields fruitful results. They will, first, communicate to the students that the teacher is listening, that their ideas are being respected and valued. They indicate to students that it is safe for them to say what they think without fear of being judged negatively. Such a forum creates a safe and generative climate for promoting thinking.

It is no small benefit that through this process students learn to think about what they are saying and take responsibility for their ideas.

Some examples of such interactions:

- Teacher reflects or paraphrases student's idea.
  S: I put the animals that live on land and those that live in the ocean in different categories.
  T: Animals that live on land were placed in one category and those that live in the water were put in another category.
  S: A grasshopper has wings but it doesn't fly.
  T: You found that grasshoppers are not flying insects.
  S: The whales. I think we have to do something to protect the whales.
  T: You are concerned about the whales, Timmy. You believe we are not doing enough to protect them.
- Teacher interprets what the student is saying.
  S: They are doing experiments with dolphins, and they are finding that dolphins can understand language. They can understand what we are saying.
  T: That idea seems to go against our old belief that animals are "dumb." You are suggesting that there is evidence that dolphins have intelligence.

A second category of teaching-for-thinking responses requires that students analyze their ideas. These responses call for deeper examination and increased cognitive risk and, therefore, create more tension. Responses that require analysis should be sensitively interwoven with reflective responses and should be voiced in unthreatening ways.

In Debriefing, the highest number of responses would fall into the reflective category. Fewer responses would fall into the "asking for analysis" category.

Here are some examples:

- Asking for examples

You said that we eat protozoa Bobby. Can you give me an example of what you mean?

You are saying that we should encourage more people to get the COVID-19 vaccine. Can you give some examples, Annie, of how we might go about doing that?

- Asking where the idea came from

It seems to me that you are saying that dinosaurs are not reptiles. I'm wondering how you came to that idea?

You think that automobile companies should abandon their manufacture of gas-guzzling cars and shift to electric vehicles. Did you read something that gave you that idea?

- Asking for a summary

I have heard you describe how the respiratory system works. Can you summarize your ideas in about two sentences?

You've been describing the effects of our overuse of plastic, Ben. Would you be able to summarize your thoughts in a few sentences?

- Asking about inconsistencies

You've been talking about the dangers of using pesticides, Leon. You have also said it's the best way to control vermin. Is there an inconsistency between those two ideas?

- Asking that an assumption be identified

You think that the reason the eggs didn't hatch was that there wasn't enough light in the incubator. Have you made some assumptions about that, Allan?

You think we should eliminate the use of plastic altogether. I wonder if there are some assumptions that need to be examined, Tula?

- Asking about alternatives

You've suggested that we might spray plants with pesticides to get rid of the bugs, but that this procedure might be harmful to humans. What might be some alternatives that you would suggest?

- Asking that comparisons be made

How does wind power compare with solar power? What are your ideas about it?

In what ways does wood compare with concrete as a building material? Can you suggest some important similarities and differences?

- Asking that data be classified

You've put together a list of foods that most of us eat for breakfast. How might such foods be classified?
What does such a classification tell us about our eating habits at breakfast?
- Asking for supporting data

You've talked about the dangers to the environment caused by our overuse of fossil fuels. What data support your ideas?

The third category of teaching-for-thinking interactions involves challenging questions. These interactions are the most aggressive and potentially the most demanding. They require students to extend their thinking into new and unexplored territory and go "out on a limb" in reaching for original ideas. In these interactions, students are at the greatest cognitive risk, and that is why they are used infrequently, with thoughtful consideration, and stated in as nonintimidating way as possible.

While some teachers may be enamored by the thought of challenging students' thinking, it should be noted that their overuse can be counterproductive since they have the effect of shifting the discussion onto new issues. Too many challenging questions in succession create a disjointed and unfocused examination of the big ideas.

Questions that challenge students' thinking and move the discussion into the examination of new issues and ideas include the following:

- Asking for the generation of hypotheses

What hypotheses can you suggest to explain why the spider can walk across the ceiling without falling?
What, in your view, explains why people smoke in the face of data about the hazards of smoking?
What do you suppose explains some people's resistance to getting the COVID-19 vaccine?
- Asking the student to interpret data

On the basis of your observations of the shape of the squid, what can you tell about the way it might move through the water?
The graph shows that the people in some of the southern states have the highest incidence of COVID infections. What do you see as the implications of those data?
- Asking the student to make judgments and to provide criteria for them

You said that the current program for environmental protection is weak. Can you describe what you see as some major weaknesses, Margo?
What is your opinion of people who refuse to get the COVID-19 vaccine? What do you see as their most cogent argument against it?
- Asking the student to apply principles to new situations

If heavy objects sink, how do you explain the fact that large boats do not sink?

The Spanish flu that occurred in 1918–1919 caused a worldwide pandemic that resulted in the deaths of 50 million people. What do you believe we learned from that pandemic that applies to COVID-19?

- Asking the student to formulate a way to test a theory, prediction, or hypothesis

You said that taking Vitamin C in large doses is a good way to cure a cold, Aldo. How would you go about testing that idea?

- Asking the student to make predictions

What do you suppose will be the effect of computer games and tablets on the ways in which young children play?

What do you see as the effects of the continued and unabated use of fossil fuels on the environment? What are your ideas about it?

- Raising a new idea or asking a question that opens up a new line of inquiry

You were talking about how the farmland in the Delta has given way to suburban housing, Marco. In what way might that have an impact on the future food market?

What are the implications of all this development for the community?

LEARNING TEACHING-FOR-THINKING INTERACTIONS: TOOLS FOR THE TEACHER

A helpful tool in learning to listen to one's teacher–student interactions begins with audio recording—a simple recording device found in many mobile phones can do the job easily. Record the Debriefing session, and play back, using the Coding Sheet found below—ticking off the kinds of responses you hear yourself making. The Coding Sheet should show a pattern of your responses. The Analysis Sheet should give you insight into what you need to concentrate on at the next Debriefing.

CODING SHEET

A. Responses That Inhibit Thinking (brings closure)

Agrees/disagrees_____

Doesn't give student a chance to think_____

Tells student what teacher thinks_____

Talks too much_____

Explains too much_____
Cuts student off_____
Heckle, is sarcastic, puts student down_____

B. Responses That Delimit Thinking

Looks for single, correct answer/method_____
Leads to right answer_____
Tells student what to do_____
Gives information_____

C. Teaching-for-Thinking Responses

a. Responses that promote reflection

Repeats statement_____
Paraphrases_____
Asks for student's idea_____
Asks for more information_____
Accepts student's idea nonjudgmentally_____

b. Responses that promote analysis

Asks for an example_____
Asks about assumptions_____
Asks for a summary_____
Asks where the idea came from_____
Asks about alternatives_____
Asks that comparisons be made_____
Asks for data to be classified_____
Asks what data support the idea_____

c. Responses that challenge

Asks for hypotheses_____
Asks that data be interpreted_____
Asks for criteria to be identified_____
Asks that principles be applied to new situations_____
Asks how a theory might be tested_____

D. Unrelated Responses

Classroom/behavior management_____

Speech mannerisms_____

Other unrelated responses_____

Analysis of a Debriefing Session

1. Describe the Debriefing session.
2. To what extent were you able to attend to students' statements and reflect ideas accurately?
3. How would you describe how your responses promoted students' understanding?
4. What were some of the best features of the Debriefing session?
5. What new insights did you acquire?
6. What did you perceive to be some weaknesses of your interactions?
7. What aspects of your teaching-for-thinking interactions need attention in the next session?

Some questions to ask yourself:

- Am I using reflective responses as my primary interactive mode?
- Am I challenging too often?
- How are the students responding to the Debriefing interactions?
- What should I concentrate on for the next session?

Another tool that may be useful is to study the two transcripts below. Making careful observations of the teacher–student interactions should provide some additional insight into how the dialogue evolves and how the teachers use reflective responses and questions that promote further examination as well as probe for deeper meaning.

TRANSCRIPT #1

The Grade 3 students were asked to examine the litter on the playground after the lunch break. The two big ideas of this investigation were, first, to alert students to the nature and amount of waste from the school population, and, second, to raise awareness of how individual behavior and choice impact health and safety.

Teacher: You were out on the playground during lunch, making observations about litter and trash left by students. Some of you took notes and others made some illustrations. When you came back to the classroom some of you said that the litter and trash were "disgusting" and suggested that the principal should take some action. Tell me about some of the things you saw.

Heather: There was litter everywhere. The kids just threw their garbage all around, even though there were trash cans for it.

Teacher: There was a lot of litter. Many kids didn't use the trash bins. (Reflects)

Heather: Yeah. It made the playground look like a junkyard.

Teacher: You were offended by how the students neglected to use the trash bins. (Interprets)

Heather: Yeah.

Teacher: Tell me about some of the observations you made about what kinds of trash and litter you saw. (Asks for observations)

Claudia: I saw some paper bags and some plastic spoons and forks. I also saw some food.

Teacher: Some of the litter was paper and some was plastic. But there was also some left-over food. (Reflects)

Claudia: Yeah. And there were some crows that had come to pick at the food.

Teacher: So the garbage attracted some birds who were eating the food. (Reflects)

Claudia: Yeah. I don't know why the kids just didn't put the trash in the bins.

Teacher: You're surprised, perhaps a little angry, that the garbage was left on the playground and that the kids didn't care about how they left the playground to look. (Interprets)

Claudia: Yeh. Even though the birds used it for lunch. (Laughs)

Teacher: If the birds made use of the left-over food that wasn't enough of a reason to throw it on the playground. (Interprets)

Claudia: I don't think it's safe to do that. And I don't think it's healthy.

Teacher: There's a problem with leaving food lying around—it may be unhealthful and unsafe. (Reflects)

Claudia: Yeah.

Teacher: I want to raise another issue. Why do you suppose students leave their trash on the playground? (Challenges; asks for hypotheses)

David: They're too lazy to put it in the trash. Or maybe they just can't find the bin so they throw it on the playground.

Teacher: You think it's a question of laziness. (Reflects)

David: Yeah.

Claudia: Or maybe they're playing with their friends and can't be bothered to go over to the bin.

Teacher: You seem to be supporting what David said. That it's a matter of laziness or being too busy. They don't want to stop playing and take their litter to the bin.

Claudia: Yeah.

Heather: Maybe it's because of what they think is more important to them. It may be more important to keep playing than to stop and take the litter to the trash bin.

Teacher: You see it as a question of priorities, Heather. What's more important—to play with your friends or to take care of your litter? (Reflects)

Heather: That's not what I'd do. But that's what some kids do.

Teacher: You'd not do that. But it's what some other kids do. (Reflects)

Heather: Most of the time.

Teacher: How did you make those decisions about what you would do, Heather? Can you tell me about it? (Asks where the beliefs come from?)

Heather: Because when I went to Disneyland somebody drops something on the ground and somebody picks it up, and I was thinking why should somebody do that for you when you should do it yourself?

Teacher: When you were in Disneyland and you saw someone picking up litter that people had left on the ground, it made you stop and think, "Why do people behave that way?" (Reflects and interprets)

Heather: And some of the commercials on TV. Like the one when the Indian sees somebody throw their garbage out the car window.

Teacher: I don't know about that one, Heather. Can you tell us about it? (Asks for more information)

Heather: Well, there's this Indian and he's walking by the road and then this lady drives by in her car, and she throws a bunch of garbage down and it lands right by his feet.

Teacher: Ah, I see.

Heather: And what I was thinking was, what he was thinking about? Because when the Indians had that land, there was no litter and they kept it pretty clean. And I was thinking about what happened.

Teacher: So perhaps you are saying that when the white people took over the land they became more indifferent to looking after the land? We have not been very good caretakers of planet earth? (Interprets)

Heather: Yeh I think so.

Teacher: Thanks so much for sharing your ideas, boys and girls. I want to ask a few more questions before we are done. I'm wondering how you see this kind of littering and garbage left around as having an effect on our health? (Appreciates students' contributions; challenges; opens up a new line of inquiry)

TRANSCRIPT #2: INVESTIGATIONS OF LOCUSTS IN GRADE 6 (CONTINUING LIVE INSECT STUDIES)

Big ideas: Locusts are certain species of grasshoppers. They have big hind legs that help them hop or jump. They have two long, pointy antennae on the top of their heads. They have wings that enable them to fly long distances.

Teacher: You were making some observations of your locusts this morning. Can you tell about some of the observations you made? (Asks for students' observations)

Leanne: Well, it was weird. Their eyes are way over on the side.

Teacher: You observed that the eyes were in an odd place—way over on the sides. (Reflects)

Leanne: Yeah.

Teacher: Do you have any ideas that might explain that? (Asks for hypotheses)

Leanne: So that they can see in front and in back of them. If anything is getting close to them fast or something.

Teacher: You think the eyes help them to see both in front and back. (Reflects) I'm wondering what might be some advantages of that, Leanne? (Asks for hypotheses)

Leanne: I think it would be for protection.

Teacher: So having the eyes there and being able to see in both directions would be a way of protection for this insect. (Reflects)

Teacher: I see. Thanks, Leanne. Are there other observations that you made?

Graeme: I saw those two things sticking out of his head.

Teacher: Do you have any ideas about them? (Asks for student's ideas)

Graeme: Antlers, I think.

Lila: Feelers. Antennas.

Teacher: Graeme, you called them antlers, and Lila calls them feelers or antennae. (Reflects)

Graeme: Antennas.

Teacher: You think they are antennae. (Reflects)

Graeme: Yeah.

Teacher: Any idea about what they might be for? (Asks for hypotheses)

Lila: They're to feel around.

Teacher: Have you seen them used in this way? (Limits thinking; asks for answer)

Graeme: I was watching them feel around with those things. Like when you are in the dark, feeling around with your hands in front of you.

Teacher: You think the antennae are used to alert the locust about what lies in its path. (Reflects by paraphrasing)

Graeme: Yeah. Like if there's something good to eat or something.

Teacher: Sends it the message. (Interprets)

Graeme: Yeah.

Teacher: There's something I was wondering about. Why might a locust need antennae to feel with, if it has eyes that see in both directions? (Challenges; asks that data be interpreted)

Kay: Well, the eyes are on the side, so they can only see this way. They can only see that way. The antennae are to feel and they can just feel in front of them, because, um, I've never seen their eyes move around to the front of them.

Teacher: The eyes seem to have a limited range, is that what you're saying? (Paraphrases)

Kay: When Gavin put his finger by his locust, he puts his antennae down. He doesn't turn around to see what's there.

Teacher: So that observation is what you are using to support your theory. (Reflects)

Kay: Yeah.

Teacher: I see. Thanks very much. Are there any other observations you want to share?

(Session continues in this fashion as students continue to examine the appearance and the behavior from their locust studies for another ten minutes.)

CONCLUSION

Learning to debrief the sciencing activities using teaching-for-thinking interactions does not occur from reading a text or from a one-off experience. To move to mastery levels of using reflective, analytic, and challenging interactions, to use these skillfully and effectively in generating the conditions that lead to the improvement of thinking skills and scientific understanding requires thoughtful attention and reflection on action. It requires a commitment to practice and a nondefensive analysis of one's own interactive style. It requires the ability to build growth gains into new performance levels.

It is not unlike learning mastery of a musical instrument. One has to learn to listen critically to his or her own music, taking cognizance of the wrong notes, of the wrong emphasis on forte and piano, on the wrong phrasing, on the wrong fingering, being nondefensive of those errors, and remembering, at the next practice session, to use that new information and those new skills in performance.

No musician expects to show skill development and know-how, let alone perfection, after only a few practice sessions. Mastery is something one works on, becoming more "tuned in" to one's performance style, over years. For some, it is lifelong professional development.

At best, such commitment to mastery of this important interactive style becomes a facet of who we are and how we talk to others. For those who have tread that pathway, those learned skills have been well worth the effort.

Chapter 11

Thinking and Decision-Making in Science

That master of irony, Jonathan Swift, would have made a meal of it—the juxtaposition of events in which what appears to be the case differs radically from what is actually the case. On the one hand, research scientists have worked round the clock to deliver a vaccine to protect a vulnerable population from a virus which, to date, has killed more than four million people worldwide. On the other hand, large groups of anti-vaxxers have gathered across the country to protest that it is their "civil right" to reject vaccinations. The reasons they cite defy credibility, such as mistrust of science, of pharmaceutical companies, and of the government.

And to further muddle our comprehension of why this perversion of fact exists, many of these same truth deniers gladly take unproven medications such as horse de-worming pills simply on the advice of talk show radio and TV sponsors.

It is difficult to fathom how it is possible for so many to be so badly informed, so mistrustful of science, and so willing to ignore data that fly in the face of their own belief systems. This would be a minor anomaly if it were true of just a few uneducated, illiterate, and perhaps paranoid individuals. But when the numbers suggest that more than 22 percent of Americans identify themselves as anti-vaxxers, and, proudly so, it gives the rest of us pause to wonder and worry. As most of the scientific literate know, these anti-vaxxers are not only vulnerable themselves, but they are also a danger to the rest of us.

The goal of becoming scientifically literate—of becoming informed about the value positions embedded in scientific decisions—is the responsibility of every citizen of a democratic society. It has been, in fact, the primary mission of a group of scientists and educators whose work on Project 2061 pointed to the urgent need for "scientific literacy as a central goal of education" (AAAS, 1989).

Life in an advanced technological society is driven by scientific decision-making, many of them based on values issues such as "what's right" and "what's good," and "what's important." Should the world population be controlled? Should we encourage the building of space shuttles for recreation? Should we plan to inhabit Mars? Should a new form of life, created in a laboratory by combining genetic material from two different species of bacteria, be released into the environment? Should the wolf population be systematically extinguished to protect the economy of ranching? Is DNA testing always reliable? Should all Grade 1 students be given tablets along with books and crayons as part of their education materials?

Should scientists be free to conduct experiments on live animals? Where should chemical plants dump their toxic waste? Should we outlaw plastic bags? Are hormone-injected cattle and poultry good for us to eat? Should we allow for a nuclear power plant to be built in the next town? Should we vote for candidates who are climate change deniers?

How can we wean ourselves and others away from the overuse of fossil fuels? What steps can each individual take on behalf of protecting our environment? What do we say to our neighbors who are anti-vaxxers?

If we accept the burdens of studying such value-laden issues as these, of becoming informed and exercising our own judgments about them, we must provide a place in our science curriculum for opportunities for students to address them as part of their science education. If we choose to unburden ourselves of such responsibility, we give power and control over our lives to "others" who will make those decisions for us, and we will have to learn to live with the consequences.

By actively confronting these and other issues in science education, students have a better chance to come to a greater understanding of their own beliefs and feelings with regard to them. They will become more disposed to using data to make informed decisions about their own values and beliefs. In that way, it is hoped that they will be able to play more active roles in making our world a more healthful place in which to live.

If we are to enjoy a future where life will be worth living, there is a great need for science education to include opportunities for students to consider how good data inform our decisions, whether they be in science or in other realms. To ignore data, to choose based on whim or caprice, or disinformation, or the words of false prophets, is not only a sign of ignorance but has grave implications for the health of our society, our culture, and our world.

Those paragraphs are by way of introduction to another thread that is being suggested as an important aspect of students' science education—the thread of promoting "scientific literacy." This includes more than promoting inquiry in the process of learning science. It includes emphasis on developing the ability to use real data to inform decisions of consequence.

IMPLICATIONS FOR THE TEACHER

Making informed choices is probably what distinguishes mature adults from the immature. We associate immaturity with indecisiveness, with the inability to make up one's mind, with impulsiveness, with the need to turn to others for help in choosing.

As some adults are dysfunctional in their ability to choose, others seem to make choices based on whim or caprice. "Foolish choices" is how we describe them, and even though foolish choices may end up presenting certain difficulties for the chooser, repeated patterns of foolish choices do not seem to prevent the same patterns from recurring. Learning that one's choice has been foolish and has ended in a disaster does not necessarily equip us to choose wisely in the next round.

Learning to choose wisely is almost certainly a learned skill, born of the ability to use data that make our choices informed. Such competence comes from using those "higher-order" thinking skills that include the ability to analyze, observe, compare, gather and interpret data, evaluate critically, and suspend judgment (Fraenkel, 1980). Wise decisions are also very much dependent on the ability to free oneself from one's prejudices and from a tendency to behave impulsively, "without thinking." What helps us through a maze of uncertainty about how to decide is our ability to consider the various aspects of situations thoughtfully and analytically and to have some view of the consequences that certain courses of action will bring.

Making wise decisions is not easy. In a world in which we are constantly bombarded by options, information, and disinformation, we make hundreds, perhaps thousands, of choices each day. Some of them are inconsequential; some are of greater import. Some of them have even greater consequences for us or for others.

Though choosing plays a very major part in our lives, learning to choose wisely does not seem to appear on any list of skills that schools consider worthwhile as part of their stated educational objectives. Perhaps it has been assumed that learning to choose is a by-product of other learning. This is a specious assumption. Perhaps it is assumed that students will have opportunities to choose in most classrooms, anyway, so there is no need for additional attention. That, too, is an unwarranted assumption that does not stand up in the presence of facts (Jackson, 1990; Goodlad, 1983).

The data from the Jackson and Goodlad studies show that in most classrooms it is the teacher who makes the important decisions and the students who are expected to obey and follow. In some cases, involving students in making decisions means trying to manipulate them into accepting a decision already made.

The implication of all of this is the suggestion that teachers give students more opportunities to make thoughtful choices and that this should occur with regularity in the science curriculum. As discussed in this book, the play stage offers students many opportunities to make choices about how they go about carrying out their investigations, about the nature of their inquiries, and about the way they work with each other. These play activities provide much practice in learning to choose as it relates to problem-solving in science and in interpersonal relationships.

Play also provides opportunities, particularly for middle graders, to work with materials that call for discussion on scientific issues with value-laden dimensions. This kind of play moves from the hands-on manipulation of materials into the realm of "minds-on" play, where groups discuss and play with ideas that stem from related readings provided by the teacher. Not only does this kind of play allow students to examine value-related issues, but it also opens up opportunities for thoughtful discussion, for the gathering of relevant data, for the development of informed opinion, and for the identification of beliefs with regard to issues under investigation.

Through such a process, students have a better chance of becoming more intelligent decision-makers (Raths, Simon and Harmin, 1980).

In these "minds-on" play activities, students are presented with some primary data, such as a photograph, an illustration, an article, a story, a news event, or a case study. These "plays" take the form of an examination of the data followed by discussions based on a series of values-related questions.

EXAMPLES OF DECISION-MAKING ACTIVITIES FOR "MINDS-ON" PLAY

Some examples of how these ideas are translated into classroom practice are included here. Many more activities are found in chapters 13, 14, and 15.

Example 1—Minds-On Activity

For their investigative play, the students are presented with a photograph of animals in an experimental laboratory for medical research.

The Activity Card includes the following study questions:

Should scientists be permitted to do scientific experiments on live animals? What are your views on this?
   What animals should be used? What animals should be exempt?
   What are some advantages of such experiments? What are some disadvantages?
   What guidelines would you propose for scientists who do these experiments?
   Where can you find information that will contribute to your thinking?

Example 2—Minds-On Activity

For the investigative play, the students are presented with a photograph or illustration of pesticides being sprayed from a plane over farm crops.

The Activity Card includes the following study questions:

Should pesticides be banned? What do you think?
What are some advantages of pesticides for farmers? What are some advantages for you and your family?
What are some disadvantages for the farmer? For you and your family?
What might be some consequences for farmers and for consumers if pesticides were banned? Would it be worth it?
Where can you find information that will further inform your thinking?

Example 3—Minds-On Activity

The students are presented with a photograph of a beach and water birds after an oil spill and the children's book, *Oil Spill*, by Melvin Berger.

The Activity Card includes the following study questions:

What happens when an oil tanker breaks up in the sea? What are your thoughts about it?
What are some consequences for the beach, the residents, the water birds, the fish, and the ocean?
We need to move the oil from where it is taken from the ground to where it is refined. Don't we need tankers to do this? What alternatives might be considered?
What would be some consequences of the actions you are considering?
Where can you find information that will further inform your thinking?

Example 4—Minds-On Activity

The students are presented with a news article about California requiring all school teachers and staff to have proof of COVID-19 vaccination or be tested weekly.

The Activity Card includes the following study questions:

Is it a good thing for a state to make such a demand on teachers? What are your ideas about it?
Should other states do the same? What data support your thinking?
Should people be free to exercise their "civil rights" and not get vaccinated, even if they are teachers? Where do you stand on that issue?

What should be done about teachers who refuse to be vaccinated? What are your thoughts?

Where can you find information that will further inform your thinking?

Example 5—Minds-On Activity

The students are presented with a news article about a president's climate change initiatives.

The Activity Card includes the following study questions:

This president has made addressing "climate change" one of his important initiatives. What is your position about this?

What, in your view, is "climate change?" What factors contribute to it?

What evidence can you cite to support your position that climate over planet earth is changing for the worst?

What role can each of us take to protect the environment? What do you think about it?

Where will you find information that will further inform your thinking?

DEBRIEFING: INTERACTIONS THAT ANALYZE AND INFORM DECISION-MAKING

One essential tool in teachers' repertoire of promoting the intelligent examination of scientific issues with value dimensions is their use of reflective responses and higher-order questions to promote thoughtful inquiry during the Debriefing of the minds-on play. While these interactions have been identified and discussed in chapter 10 (Debriefing: Interactions That Promote Thoughtful Inquiry), some additional comments have been included here that relate specifically to how best to bring to front and center where students stand with respect to their thinking, their beliefs, their values about specific science issues.

First, all types of responses identified as "teaching-for-thinking" interactions are applicable to the examination of values issues. The shift in the interactive process is on fleshing out students' belief statements and ideas and using these interactive skills to hold those beliefs up to critical scrutiny. This is done in nonthreatening ways, so that a student feels invited to respond, rather than being under interrogation.

Second, the backbone of the teacher–student interactions in examining students' beliefs is the reflective response. These responses attend directly to the student's belief statement so that their ideas are held up for their reflection and subsequent consideration.

For example,

Teacher: Tell me a little about your views on what contributes to climate change.
Hugo: Well, I think we have made the weather more extreme. There's more heat and more fires and more hurricanes.
Teacher: You see some weather conditions, like heat, fires, and hurricanes, a result of what is happening to our planet. Tell me more about what you see as some contributing factors to those conditions, Hugo.

As the teacher follows through with this interactive process, students are called upon to examine their beliefs from a variety of perspectives. Where did they get that belief? What data support it? What assumptions are being made? What actions might we consider as effective in dealing with the situation?

Such interactions sensitively carried out help inform the student's belief and pave the way for continued examination. In this process, the teacher maintains a neutral stance, so that the student is free to think his or her own thoughts and to make up his or her own mind. That does not mean that teachers *never* offer their own views; they just don't do that at this time.

Using teaching-for-thinking responses to help students examine their beliefs about values-related issues in science will enable them to reflect on what they really believe, what data support those beliefs, what is important in their lives, what they care about, and what they stand for. Strong values do not necessarily emerge from such interactions; what does happen is that students become more accustomed to and more habituated to the process of reflective reasoning, using data to support beliefs, and less inclined to make impulsive and dogmatic judgments.

When beliefs are informed by reliable data, when we have subjected them to critical analysis, we are more likely to behave in more responsible and consistent ways. Informed beliefs help us make more intelligent decisions.

What follows below are some guidelines for using teaching-for-thinking interactions.

- When students are encouraged to reflect on beliefs, teachers do not impose their own beliefs on them. Students are free to express their own points of view, and their opinions are accepted.
- When students reflect on their beliefs, teachers do not manipulate them or lead them to accept certain beliefs. Students are allowed to make up their own minds.
- When students reflect on their beliefs, teachers communicate very great regard for them and for their ideas. Implicit in what teachers are saying is:

"I respect you so much that I am able to allow you to make this decision on your own."

- When students reflect on their beliefs, they are allowed to determine for themselves what it is they really stand for. When this occurs, students may be voicing a point of view that is discrepant with the teachers.
- When students are asked to reflect on their beliefs, the teacher holds up a verbal mirror so that they may see and hear their beliefs more clearly. This may be the first time that students "hear back" what it is they are saying. It may seem a small thing but the result is that students are more inclined to think before they speak.
- In some cases, students may voice a point of view that is truly repugnant to the teacher. If the teacher cannot maintain a neutral and accepting position, he or she may be tempted to step outside of the reflective mode and express their own opinion. In such a circumstance, the teacher may have to claim that they cannot agree, cannot accept that idea. This is done in a way that communicates a disagreement between two positions and never as a put down of the student's idea.
- Although it is important for teachers to show themselves as persons who have strong values of their own and to disclose their own ideas and beliefs to students, this practice is not considered effective in helping students to reflect (Raths, Simon and Harmin, 1980).
- The effect of the reflective response may initially create cognitive dissonance in the student's mind. In attempting to resolve this dissonance, the student comes to a clearer understanding of the belief through a process of "mental sorting."
- When teachers use reflective responses with students, the initial effect may be to raise the level of students' anxiety. It may take several weeks before students feel safe about expressing different points of view and understand that many ideas are acceptable.
- Reflective responses are never used to threaten, coerce, badger, intimidate, or harm a student in any way.
- Reflective responses are only one of several types of interactions that teachers use in their discussions with students. It would be an error to assume that once teachers had learned to use reflective responses skillfully, they would use these responses to the exclusion of all others. There are times when teachers are called on to be directive, to make judgments, and to express an opinion of their own. All these responses continue to be used in the teacher's repertoire. Reflective responses are an additional resource when the goal is to promote students' intelligent examination of ideas, issues, and beliefs.

CONCLUSION: A TEACHER'S CHOICE

A hands-on experiential teaching-for-thinking program in science calls for the active involvement of students. Instead of prizing and rewarding conforming student behaviors, teaching-for-thinking requires students to function independently and responsibly on their own. Instead of learning dependency on the teacher as the source of knowledge, direction, and control, students are required to become problem solvers and to work through learning problems autonomously and collaboratively. An integral part of this process is encouraging and enabling students to think their own ideas and to make determinations of their beliefs, especially with respect to scientific literacy.

Teachers cannot have both a teaching-for-thinking program in science and conformity. They cannot have learning to choose for oneself and avoid controversy. They cannot make decisions for students and exercise all the controls over their learning and expect them to learn to do these things for themselves. They cannot have an experiential science program emphasizing thinking without the mess that is an adjunct of any productive and creative act.

In making the choice about how to teach science, the teacher is at a critical crossroads. To choose a teaching-for-thinking approach may mean relinquishing long-held, deeply entrenched beliefs about teaching. It may mean taking some risks. It is more likely to create classroom conditions that are markedly different from what is seen in the classrooms down the hall.

It may mean a journey that is full of bumps and curves, for most new paths do not follow a smooth roadway. Few of us learn to walk without falling. Yet the rewards for such a choice are great: classrooms in which students are purposefully and productively engaged in scientific inquiry, where knowledge is being generated, where students are learning to make informed choices.

Teaching-for-thinking may be a choice worth considering, but it is a choice that teachers can only decide for themselves. Should you make that choice, it is our hope that the rest of this book will serve you well.

Section III

FIFTY-EIGHT SCIENCING ACTIVITIES

Chapter 12

Introduction to the Activities

Even the most cursory glance at the activities in the next three chapters will reveal that they have not been grade-ranked. That is, none of the activities have been designated as appropriate for a particular grade level. Although such an omission may be at variance with customary practice, a good case may be made for it.

First, the assigning of scientific content to a particular grade level (e.g., if it's air pressure, it must be Grade 3) is an invented idea with little empirical evidence to support its use. Carried into the rigid grade-level application, such practice may be more counterproductive to student learning than it is enabling. As far as it is known, the study of air pressure at Grade 3 level has nowhere been writ in stone as sacrosanct. In no way will students' scientific learning be impaired if air pressure is studied at Grade 3 or 4 or 5 or 6—or even at the high-school level or all of the above.

Assumptions have been made that if air pressure is not successfully taught and learned in Grade 3, the successful teaching and learning of properties of matter, scheduled for Grade 4, will seriously suffer—something akin to the domino theory. Such "educational principles" do not stand up under critical or empirical scrutiny; they are traditions that continue to endure long after their educational value has been discredited.

In fact, the AAAS report, *Benchmarks*, presents science as "a compendium of specific science literacy goals that can be organized however one chooses" (AAAS, 1993). Rather than a series of topics that follow a rigid sequence, *Benchmarks* advocates the increasingly sophisticated examination of certain "big ideas" related to the same topics, as students advance through the grades.

Second, it is a given that any scientific investigation may be undertaken effectively and productively at virtually any grade level. Although different age groups are likely to approach an investigation differently, depending on the level of sophistication, the background of experience with science, experiences as thoughtful, trained observers, and other variables, each age group nevertheless has a great deal still to learn about the particular scientific phenomena integral to each investigation. In other words, air pressure can and should be studied throughout science, since, obviously, the more students study these concepts, the more they are likely to find out and know.

If teachers can learn to examine critically the traditions that bind us and open their minds to a more thoughtful approach to the relationship between content and grade level, perhaps they may also disabuse their students of the repugnant attitudes formed by such practices that inevitably lead to the closing of further inquiry. (*"Oh, air pressure? We had that in Grade 3. In Grade 4 we study properties of matter."*)

The truth is that even primary students can be profitably engaged in a scientific inquiry on air pressure; so may more mature middle graders. The differences lie in the sophistication of the investigations, and it is a revelation to see how different age groups can and do undertake different productive investigations with the same materials.

Having made what is, hopefully, a credible case for the consideration of sciencing activities above and beyond grade-level concerns, one additional caveat is now offered. There are likely to be some sciencing activities that, for a variety of reasons (teacher's preference, grade-level objectives, students' prior experiences, ability levels, etc.), are more or less suitable for some groups of students. It is possible that the challenges of some material or inquiries do not lend themselves easily to some primary graders.

Once again, it is the teacher who makes the thoughtful and considered choice, based on criteria that are related to the goals of promoting students' learning in science.

Instead of grade-ranking, the activities have been categorized according to teachers' expressed concerns:

Category A: "Wet, Wetter, Wettest" contains activities involving investigative play with water. This is likely to mean spillage—on tables and perhaps on the floor as well. This is made explicit just in case such activities create a problem for the teacher.
Category B: "No Fuss, No Muss, No Sticky Stuff" contains activities that are generally dry and "safe" and will not leave a mess on the tables, on the floor, or around the room. If teachers have concerns about such by-products of science investigations, they will likely want to choose, initially, sciencing activities from Category B.
Category C: "Who's Afraid of Spiders?" contains activities that some teachers may consider to be at higher risk. They may involve greater mess, the

use of more dangerous materials (such as heat sources), more difficulty in obtaining materials, or personal distaste on the part of teacher or students.

The physical sciences are heavily represented in Category A. Biological and physical sciences are included in Categories B and C. An index of the activities in each group is found on the introductory pages for each category.

PRESENTATION OF THE ACTIVITIES

Each activity has been presented in the same format to allow for its clear application to classroom practice. The format provides detailed information about how the activity is translated from the pages of this book into classroom applications. Each activity contains the following information:

1. **Activity Card.** The Activity Card contains directions that focus on students' investigative play. It is suggested that activity cards be printed out and placed in the investigative play center. Of course, the language may be modified as necessary.

    Most activity cards also include suggestions that allow students to go beyond what is on the card to extend their investigations. These more open-ended suggestions call for greater self-initiating behaviors and may not be useful for some students at first. However, as students gain skill in this process, they will eventually be able to conceive and conceptualize more sophisticated investigations and extend their work into more original realms. These more original investigations should, of course, be greatly encouraged.
2. **Materials.** Includes the materials needed to conduct the investigations.
3. **Thinking Operations Emphasized.** Identifies those mental processes that call for more sophisticated cognitive functioning that are incorporated in each inquiry.
4. **Big Ideas.** Identifies the big ideas (scientific concepts) that underlie each activity.
5. **Notes to the Teacher.** Includes information to facilitate the implementation of each activity.
6. **Debriefing.** Includes examples of questions that call for students to reflect more thoughtfully and intelligently on their inquiries. These questions are to be used selectively—that is, in a way that attends thoughtfully to the students' statements. It is not intended that all the questions listed for each activity be used in one single Debriefing session. They are not a "course of questions to be covered" but rather give examples of higher-order questions that may be used.

7. **Extending**. When students have had sufficient time to carry out initial investigative play, the teacher may wish to invite them to extend their inquiries into more substantive investigations.

    Suggestions are offered as to how this might be done. This includes using reference materials and children's science books to gather information to support their theories and hypotheses.

    Questions calling for students' examination of values issues related to these particular inquiries are included here.
8. **Creating**. As students' interests in each activity draw to their natural close, some culminating experiences may be appropriate. Activities that integrate science with other areas of the curriculum that emphasize more creative work and problem-solving are included here.

CHOOSING ACTIVITIES

Faced with fifty-eight sciencing activities, the caveats in the introductory section of this chapter, the absence of grade-level guidelines, the need to acquire materials, the newness of such an approach for some teachers, and the possible feelings of anxiety that all of this has begun to generate, how should teachers choose sciencing activities for their students?

The following ideas may be helpful. Underlying them is the belief that teachers are the best judges of what constitutes appropriate activities for their students. To that end, it is not suggested that Activity 12 is better or worse than Activity 46; or that teachers must include at least six activities from Category A, ten from Category B, and eight from Category C! In making their choices, some questions are offered as a priori considerations:

- Will I be able to obtain the materials easily enough? How much work or stress will be involved in gathering the materials?
- Does the content of the activity relate to the science content prescribed for my grade? If not, will I be able to justify its choice in an educationally sound argument to any potential naysayer?
- Will my students be able to function successfully on this task without excessive teacher direction? Does the activity call for very high levels of independent functioning on the part of the students? Will my students be able (with some help from me) to meet the challenge of the activity? Does this activity ask much more than my students are able to give at this stage of their development? Am I sure that I am not underestimating their ability?
- Does the thought of trying this activity intimidate me? Is this a high-risk activity for me? What is there about it that causes me concern?

- Does this activity involve the use of live animals? Am I clear about the ethical considerations that surround the study of live animals in the classroom?

It is probably a good idea for a teacher to choose, at first, activities that feel more comfortable and safer, whose materials don't require massive amounts of effort to acquire, that are not likely to invite disaster because teacher expectations and student behavior are still far apart, and that tie-in with school or school district science goals. To begin a science program with a "small is beautiful" approach, taking one's time to move to more uncertain territory is probably a wiser course of action. The time for taking greater risks may occur once the teacher has a few successful trials under the belt.

If an activity requires bringing live animals into the classroom, it is a good idea to introduce the activity to the whole class by setting down some ethical rules for live-animal study. Such consideration should be exercised whatever the animal, since all living things deserve our respectful regard.

Ethical considerations for live-animal study should include, *at least*, the following:

- The animal must have a suitable habitat. This includes both amount and quality of space provided. The habitat should be thoroughly researched and prepared before the animal is brought in. Climate and temperature must also be considered.
- Ongoing care and feeding of the animal are imperative. It is a great responsibility to ensure that animals are well cared for in their confinement.
- Cleaning the animal's environment is an additional responsibility; one, however distasteful, that cannot be overlooked.
- *Never* should any animal in the students' care be subject to cruel or unusual treatment that would result in that animal's pain, deprivation, or injury.
- Despite the great care we exercise in looking after and caring for our small guests, some of them might die. Should this unhappy event occur, it may be valuable (after appropriate attention to students' feelings about such a loss) to approach the demise as scientists, examining the evidence and suggesting hypotheses to explain how the death might have occurred. Such an inquiry may be helpful in preventing similar losses in the future.

Collecting animals from their natural habitat also imposes responsibilities. These are discussed in Activity 53. Such responsibilities must also be clearly identified and accepted before such collections are allowed to proceed.

Despite the greater responsibilities imposed on teacher and students by gathering and caring for living creatures in the classroom, the benefits so far outweigh the costs as to make such activities very much worth the effort.

The activities included in the following chapters should provide teachers with a more than ample supply of sciencing opportunities for the entire school year, in a program that includes science several days a week. They may also serve as models for teachers to develop their own supply of activities that reflect the interests and curriculum concerns of a particular class.

Whichever activities have been chosen and used, the experiences of the authors tell us that such a sciencing program will not only increase students' conceptual understandings of basic science concepts but will also elevate levels of thinking and problem-solving capabilities, promote socially responsible behavior, and fill students with the spirit and joy of working as scientific explorers.

SCENES FROM THE CLASSROOM

Mary Thornhill is cautiously stepping into the initiation of sciencing in her Grade 3/4 class. Her experience with teaching science is limited, and yes, she is intimidated by this more open process of teaching. She has studied the three categories of activities and decides she will make her initial selections from Category B. Knowing her students well, she concludes that investigative play with water is best left until later when students can exercise greater responsibility over their own behavior. As a matter of personal choice, she will avoid live-animal study for now, working all the while to overcome her personal anxieties.

This is the first time that Mary's students will engage in cooperative learning groups, and she uses some of the orientation strategies described in chapter 6 to introduce the students to the program. She explains the procedures clearly and makes her expectations about behavior explicit. She provides ample opportunity for them to raise questions about the work and alerts them to expect to begin work on the following day.

The activity she has selected is "Studying Flowers" (Activity 25). Following the "Notes to the Teacher," she prepares an assault on the local supermarket and manages to acquire several tired bunches of posies at reduced cost. She has also prepared five copies of the activity card since she will be setting up five working groups.

That evening, Mary studies her class list and arranges the students into groups. Joey may not be in the same group with Ben, at least at first, because putting them together is likely to spell trouble. Farah needs to work with a group that is more accepting of her special needs. She juggles the names until she is satisfied that the students in each group have the best chance of working as a cooperative unit.

She schedules the sciencing activity for just after lunch so that she has the time to arrange the tables into centers.

As the students return from lunch, she gives each one a group number and directs them to go to their respective centers. When they have done this, she reiterates the kind of activity it is and the procedures to be followed. She then distributes four different flowers at each center, plus some scissors, several sheets of paper, and an activity card. She tells the children that several magnifying lenses and a small knife are available for communal use if needed.

When the children begin to work on the activity, Mary moves about the room observing their work. Which students seem to need more direction? Which ones seem to get right down to the work? Which children seem to take leadership roles? Which ones are "fringe members" of the group?

Mary's interactions are directed toward their behavior rather than to the flower investigations, and she recognizes that this is the first step the children are taking in working toward a more responsible functioning collective. She also knows that at best, such responsible cooperative behavior may take several weeks to emerge, sometimes longer, and that she must work to facilitate this during her movements about the room.

After the students have had about ten minutes on the task, she gives a signal that the activity will conclude in five more minutes. When the time is up, she reminds them about cleanup. Waste is collected and whatever notes and diagrams the children have made are brought with them to the Debriefing. The children help to return the tables to their original positions and then take their own seats for Debriefing.

Mary has made notes of the kinds of questions she might ask during the Debriefing. Since this is her first Debriefing, she will concentrate on attending to each student's idea by using reflective responses.

MARY'S DEBRIEFING SCENARIO

Teacher: What observations have you made about flowers?
(Asking that observations be shared)

Kyle: They all had long green stems. Some of them had leaves on the stems.
Teacher: You observed that the flowers had stems and some had leaves.
(Reflects student's idea)

Kyle: Yeah.
Teacher: What other observations did you make?
(Asks for more observations to be shared)

Johanna: The flowers were of different colors.
Teacher: You noticed differences in the colors of the flowers.
(Reflects student's observation)

Johanna: Yes. And some of them had nice smells. Some smelled phooey.
Teacher: There was a difference in the way they smelled.
(Reflects student's idea)

Johanna: Yeah.
Teacher: Did you make some other observations?
(Asks for additional observations)

Sarah: The leaves had different shapes.
Teacher: You noticed how different the leaves were.
(Reflects student's idea)

Can you describe some of the differences you saw?
(Asks students to compare)

Sarah: (*Describes the varieties of leaves*)
Teacher: Thank you, Sarah.
(Appreciates student's contribution)

Ben: The petals had different shapes too. Some flowers were big and some were little.
Teacher: You saw differences in size and also differences in the shapes of the petals.
(Reflects student's idea)

Ben: Yeah.
Teacher: I was wondering if there was a way to group these flowers. Would you see any way of arranging them in groups?
(Asks for classifying)

Guy: Well, I'd put the ones that smell nice in one group.
Teacher: Perhaps you'd have a name for that group?
(Asks for identification of an attribute-alike category)

Guy: I don't know. Nice-smellers? (*Laughs*)

Mary proceeds in this fashion using a few higher-order questions and many reflective responses to debrief the initial play session with flowers. She does not attempt the more difficult challenging questions at this time. They will be used later, after Replay.

There is, of course, the initial discomfort that Mary feels about such an open-ended inquiry. No "right" answers are being sought here. Students are not being asked to name the flowers and label their parts. All of this is discrepant with Mary's old style of teaching, and she may even have some lingering doubts and hesitations about the ultimate value of this emphasis on inquiry rather than on specific information. Her awareness of these feelings helps her to manage them, and she keeps thinking about strategies she might use to liberate herself from her old ways. She is on a growing and learning path that is sometimes uphill.

In drawing her first sciencing lesson to a close, Mary asks the students to evaluate their experiences with the flower studies so she can get some ideas about how they responded to this way of learning. "What did you like about it?" "How did it go for you?" "Were there things about it that you'd like to see improved?" "What were some things you learned?"

She uses their responses to inform her plans for the following day. Tomorrow there will be Replay of the Flower studies. Her working groups may require some adjustment. On the next day of Replay, she will bring in different flowers to observe and compare as well as refer them to some of the children's books about flowers on the science bookshelf.

By then, the children may be ready to handle some of the more challenging questions in Debriefing sessions. Perhaps by the fifth day, they will be ready for one or more of the Creating tasks, and Mary is thinking about the possibility of having the children make artificial flowers with colored tissue paper and pipe cleaners. Having gotten this first field trial under her belt, Mary may be ready to tackle Activity 41: Magnets, in the next play.

CONCLUSION

With the above information as an advance organizer, it's time to move ahead to the Activities chapters, take the plunge, and begin sciencing.

Chapter 13

Category A

Wet, Wetter, Wettest: Activities 1–11

Activities that involve investigative play with water

Activity 1:   Water Fountains
Activity 2:   Rain
Activity 3:   Sinking and Floating
Activity 4:   Sound and Pitch
Activity 5:   Siphoning
Activity 6:   Absorbency
Activity 7:   Solutions
Activity 8:   Bubbles
Activity 9:   Ice
Activity 10:   Suction
Activity 11:   Life in water

ACTIVITY 1: WATER FOUNTAINS

In this center, the students work with the materials provided and make some observations about water flow. They are asked to record their observations.

Activity Card

- Use the materials in this center to make some observations about how water flows through the openings of the containers.
- Try as many investigations as you can think of.

- Discuss your ideas with each other.
- Then make a record of what you observed.

You may have some other ideas about how these materials can be used. Try your ideas and see what you can find out.

Materials

Clear plastic bottles with removable lids, with holes of various sizes punched in the sides, some in a vertical line, some in a horizontal line; yogurt containers, some with vertically punched holes and some with horizontally punched holes, also with removable lids; water; large basin to collect water; safety glasses.

Thinking Operations Emphasized

Observing and recording; comparing; suggesting hypotheses; examining assumptions; making decisions; interpreting data; applying principles to new situations.

Big Ideas

The rate at which water flows through an outlet depends on the size of the outlet, height of the water above the outlet, air pressure on the surface of the water.

Notes to the Teacher

- Reminders about cleanup procedures may be advisable before starting this activity.
- A soldering gun is an efficient tool for making holes in plastic.
- Caution: Heating plastic may produce small amounts of toxic fumes, so do this in a well-ventilated place.

Debriefing

Questions of the following types are used to promote reflection during Debriefing sessions. They should be used selectively and as appropriate.

- What observations did you make about the way the water flowed out of the holes?

- What differences, if any, did you observe in the water flow?
- How can you explain what happened? What hypotheses can you suggest to explain it?
- If you tried that with another bottle (container), what do you think might happen?

Extending

After the students have had enough time to carry out investigative play with the "water fountains," their inquiries might be extended in one or more of the following ways:

1. By adding new materials to the center, such as containers with different shapes, also with removable lids; containers with holes irregularly dispersed; different kinds of liquids, such as a mixture of oil and water.
2. By introducing new activity cards calling for ways of measuring water flow.
3. By asking more challenging questions in later Debriefing sessions, for example:
   - How do you account for the difference in the water flow when the lid is on and when it is off? How do you explain it?
   - If you wanted to change the water flow, how might you do it? Why do you think that would work?
   - What observations did you make about the relationship of the water flow to the size (shape, position) of the holes? How do you account for that?
4. By introducing questions that call for the examination of values issues relating to the topic. For example:
   - Should we be careful about wasting water? What do you think? What are your ideas about it?
   - Where do you suppose our water comes from? What are your thoughts about it?
   - What happens when the water supply is low? What contributes to the decrease in water levels? What are your ideas about it?
   - How is our water kept pure and drinkable? What are your ideas about it?
   - Some areas in the United States have been having a long drought. The crops are dying, and people are having to make do with using less water. What do you suppose causes drought?
5. By referring students to books, newspaper articles, reference materials, and Internet sources to provide background information to their inquiries.

106   Chapter 13

Figure 13.1   *Maya Snow.*

Creating

When the students appear to be approaching the limits of their interest in the "water fountain" studies, they might be asked to do one or more of the following:

1. Work with a friend. Make a "water fountain" using some of the materials found in class. Make sure that it has a "stop and go" action.
2. Work with pencil and paper to design a "water fountain" for a rabbit or other pet. Make sure that it has a "stop and go" action and that the pet will be able to learn how to use it.
3. Create a design for a Japanese-style water fountain that is soothing to the eye and the mind as the water flows. Make sure the fountain recycles the water being used. (Maya's fountain, figure 13.1).

ACTIVITY 2: RAIN

In this activity, the students spend some time outdoors on a rainy day and make observations about rain. They are asked to record their observations.

Activity Card

- Work with a partner. Make sure you have your raincoats, hats, and boots on before going outside.
- Go out into the schoolyard and make some observations about the rain. Use your eyes, your ears, and your sense of smell in making your observations.
- Use the materials in the Rain Center to help you with your observations.
- Discuss your observations with each other.
- Then come back to the classroom and record your observations.

You may have some other ideas about studying rain. Try out some of your ideas and see what you can discover.

Materials

Rulers, yardsticks, paper towels, plastic containers, umbrellas, plastic sheeting, plastic bags, marking pens, sticks.

Thinking Operations Emphasized

Observing, gathering and recording data, making decisions, suggesting hypotheses, examining assumptions.

Big Ideas

Humidity and temperature are two conditions that help determine whether the rain will fall. Rainwater may contain certain pollutants.

Notes to the Teacher

- Prior to undertaking this activity, it's a good idea to ensure that students have the appropriate dress and can be protected from getting excessively wet during their rain studies.
- Some climates and times of year are more conducive to rain studies than others. If a rainy day is a rarity in your area, you may wish to have an introductory session on rain before students go outside.
- Students should be advised NOT to taste the rainwater.
- In areas where rain is more frequent, these activities may be spread out over a longer period of time.

Debriefing

Questions of the following types may be used during Debriefing to promote reflection about rain studies. They should be used selectively as appropriate in putting the big ideas under examination.

- What observations can be made on a rainy day? What observations came from seeing? from listening? from smelling?
- How is rain different from snow?
- How could you tell if it was raining hard? How did you determine that?
- How can you measure how much rain is falling? What makes you think that is true?
- How can you tell if it is going to rain? What are your ideas?
- What do you suppose rain is good for?
- Why do you suppose you were cautioned not to taste the rainwater? What ideas do you have about that?
- How might you be able to tell if rainwater is good to drink?

Extending

After the initial investigative play period, the students' inquiries may be extended in one or more of the following ways:

1. By introducing new materials to the rain studies, such as thermometers, different kinds of fabrics (e.g., feathers, fur, plastic, and paper), magnifying lenses, and microscopes.
2. By adding new activity cards; by inventing ways to measure rainfall.
3. By raising more challenging questions in later Debriefing sessions, for example:
   - What makes rain? How do you know that it is true?
   - What's in a raindrop? What observations did you make that allowed you to know that?
   - What makes rain warm? What makes it cold? What hypotheses can you suggest that would explain the differences in the temperature of rain?
   - Sometimes when it rains, there is thunder and lightning. Sometimes there's no thunder or lightning. How do you account for that?
   - What do you suppose happens to the land when there is a long dry period without rain?
   - Some people think they can do something to make it rain. What do you think about that?
   - Sometimes, after it rains, you can see a rainbow. Where does that come from? What are your ideas?

4. By referring students to books, newspaper articles, reference materials, and Internet sources to provide background information to their inquiries.

Creating

Some of the following may serve as culminating activities for the rain studies:

1. Have the students work in groups of four or five. Ask them to try to invent a way to measure how much rain will fall in a given period (maybe one hour) on a given day. When the students have collected their data, ask that the data from each group be compared.
2. Have the students work in small groups. Ask them to compare the quantity of rain that falls in different parts of the schoolyard during one rainfall. Ask them to list all the reasons they can think of to account for the differences.
3. Ask for a "rain crew" to carry out observations and studies on each rainy day for a month. Suggest that students record their observations and report to the class once a week.
4. Ask for volunteers to find out what they can about rain forests, for example, Where are they found? What makes a "rain forest" different from a forest? What are they good for?
5. Ask students to write poetry or short stories about rain. You might wish to suggest some titles, for example:

Don't Rain on My Parade; Raindrops Falling on My Head; Thunderstorms; Singing in the Rain; Plop, Plop, Splash, Splash; I'm Always Chasing Rainbows.

6. Ask students to work with a partner. Ask them to invent a rain-making machine and to draw some diagrams of their invention.

ACTIVITY 3: SINKING AND FLOATING

In this activity, the students work with water and the objects provided and make observations about things that float and things that sink. They are also asked to record their observations.

Activity Card

- Use the materials in the center to make some observations about things that sink and things that float.

- Try as many investigations as you can think of. Talk with each other about your ideas.
- Then make some notes about what you observed.

Are there other ways to use the materials in this center? Try some new investigations and see what happens.

Materials

Water, either at a water table or in basins; assorted objects for study, such as a sponge, chalk, ping-pong balls, modeling clay, tin foil, containers with removable lids, bits of wood, plastic figures of dolls, clothespins, stones, Styrofoam chips, plastic dishes and cups, nails, paper cups, paper towels, toy boats, toy cars, plastic balls, tennis balls, plastic eggs.

Thinking Operations Emphasized

Observing and recording; gathering and classifying data; comparing; suggesting hypotheses; designing investigations; applying principles in new situations; imagining and inventing.

Big Ideas

Water has buoyancy that allows certain objects to float on the surface. Objects float or sink depending on the amount of water they displace.

Notes to the Teacher

- Before students begin work in this center, it might be helpful to remind them about procedures to be used in case of a water spill. Sponges, paper towels, and newspapers should be on hand.
- You may want to introduce just a few objects for the first play sessions and add more as later investigations get underway.
- Students may also enjoy bringing objects from home for this center, and they may be encouraged to do so.

Debriefing

Here are some questions that might be raised during Debriefing sessions to promote inquiry about sinking and floating properties:

- Tell about some of the observations you made while working in this center. What observations did you make about objects that floated? What observations did you make about objects that sank?
- In what ways were the objects that floated alike? How were they different?
- How might you compare those sinking and floating objects?
- If heavy objects sink, how come big ships can stay on top of the water? How do you explain it?
- What would you need to do in order for you to float in a lake or pool?

Extending

After adequate opportunity for initial investigations, the students' inquiries may be extended in one or more of the following ways:

1. By adding new materials to the sinking and floating center.
2. By adding salt to the water.
3. By introducing other activity cards that give specific focus to the inquiries, for example:
   - Conduct some investigations to turn some of your "sinkers" into "floaters."
   - Conduct some investigations to turn some of your "floaters" into "sinkers."
   - Keep a record of the results of your investigations about sinking and floating objects.
   - Classify the objects you worked with in this center. Establish some groups and show how each object belongs to that group.
   - Conduct some investigations to find out what difference salt water makes for floating and sinking objects. Suggest some hypotheses that might explain it.
   - Check out information about floating and sinking things in a library book or the Internet.

Creating

When the investigative play seems to have run its course, students' inquiries may be extended into more creative problem-solving tasks. For example:

1. Work with a friend. Construct a boat that will float while carrying the weight of at least three "sinkers."
2. Work with a friend. Design a floating bathtub. Draw an illustration of your design. Explain how you believe your bathtub will float.

3. Work with a friend. Design an apparatus that will keep an elephant afloat in the ocean. Draw a picture of your design and explain why you think it will work.
4. Design some investigations to show any differences for objects that float or sink if they are in lakes or in oceans.

ACTIVITY 4: SOUND AND PITCH

In this activity, the students work with the materials to create sounds and to explore the ways in which sounds are made and pitch is raised and lowered.

Activity Card

- Use the materials in the center to see what kinds of sounds you can make.
- Try as many investigations with the materials as you can think of.
- Discuss your observations with each other.
- Then write about what you observed.

Do you have some different ideas for some new investigations? Try them and see what happens.

Materials

Between eight and twelve glasses or glass jars, a metal spoon, a chopstick, a pitcher of water; paper cups; plastic cups, coffee mugs.

Thinking Operations Emphasized

Observing and recording; comparing; classifying; suggesting hypotheses; examining assumptions; summarizing; creating and inventing.

Notes to the Teacher

It's a good idea to remind students what to do if a glass jar breaks and to have a small broom, dustpan, newspapers, sponges, and paper towels on hand.

Debriefing

Here are some questions that might be raised during Debriefing. They should be used selectively and as appropriate to the discussion.

- What observations did you make about how sounds are made?
- What did you do to find that out?
- How do you explain how that happened? What are your ideas about it?
- What did you do to change the pitch of the sounds? How do you explain how that happened?
- What did you do to change the "loudness" or "softness" of the sounds? How do you explain how that happened?
- What differences did you observe about the sounds coming from the different containers? How do you explain those differences?

Extending

After the students have had adequate opportunity to carry out initial investigations, the inquiries can be extended in one or more of the following ways:

1. By introducing a wider variety of materials to the center, such as different jars and glasses; tin cans; different liquids, such as mineral oil or water mixed with sand; a xylophone; a pitch pipe; a tuning fork.
2. By introducing other activity cards, for example, asking that ways be found to measure sound.
3. By asking more challenging questions in later Debriefing sessions, for example:
   - What did you observe about the amount of water in the jar and the sound produced? How do you explain that? What are your ideas about it?
   - What did you do to change the sounds? How did that work?
   - In what ways may sounds be changed? Can you explain how that works?
   - How are the sounds that come from the jars or glasses similar to and different from the sounds on the xylophone? on the pitch pipe?
   - What differences did you observe in the sounds made by the different liquids? How do you explain them?
4. By referring students to library books and the Internet to gather background information about sounds.
5. By raising questions that ask students to examine some values issues related to the topic, such as:
   - Are there some sounds that are more pleasant to hear? What are your opinions?
   - Are there some sounds that are hurtful to the ears? Do you have some ideas about that?
   - Suppose someone is making a noise or sound that you find objectionable. What should you do about it? What are your ideas?
   - What do you suppose might occur if you did take some action to oppose noise? What might be some consequences of your actions? What are your thoughts?

Creating

When students have come to the end of their enthusiasm for the investigative play with "water music," they might enjoy participating in one or more of the following creative activities:

1. Working with a friend to make up a simple tune that they can play on their musical jars and performing it for the class. Perhaps they can use a simple recording device to record the music so that someone else might be able to learn to play it.
2. Joining a small group (quartet? sextet?) to sing some choral music that may be recorded.
3. Singing in "rounds"—like Frere Jacques, and Row Row Row Your Boat, Kookaburra, and others may be performed.
4. Comparing musical instruments, like the guitar and the piano. How are they different? What kinds of sounds are produced in each? How can the quality of the sounds be described?
5. Working with a friend, the pair may choose a musical instrument, either one found in the school or at home, and try to tune their musical jars so that at least eight of the keys match the instrument in pitch.
6. A survey may be made to find out: Which students can reach a higher pitch in singing? Who can sing the highest note? the lowest? How can those differences in voice quality be explained?
7. Introducing some classical music might also be considered, such as Handel's Water Music and Beethoven's Fifth Symphony. Discussions may focus on specific elements such as how different sounds are produced, the instruments used, and how those musical pieces affect emotions.
8. Introducing some "rhythmic" music—such as tango, hip hop, marching music—and discussing how the rhythms of these different pieces of music lead to certain kinds of movement.

ACTIVITY 5: SIPHONING

In this center, the students work with water and with clear plastic tubing to investigate how siphons work. They are asked to record their observations.

Activity Card

- Use the materials in the center to carry out some investigations of how water can be made to flow from one bucket into another.
- Try as many investigations as you can think of.

- Observe carefully what occurs and talk about your ideas with each other.
- Then make some notes to describe what you found.

You may have thought of some other ways to use these materials. Try out your new ideas and see what you can discover.

Materials

Buckets or pails of water; transparent (glass or plastic) containers of different sizes; clear plastic tubing; funnels.

Thinking Operations Emphasized

Observing and recording; gathering and organizing data; summarizing; designing investigations; suggesting hypotheses; examining assumptions; inventing and creating.

Big Ideas

Air pressure and its absence (vacuum) can be used to move liquid between containers.

Notes to the Teacher

- This activity is definitely very wet! It's a good idea to prepare for this in advance by placing plastic sheeting on the floor around the center and by giving students clear and explicit instructions for cleanup after the activity is over. Clear plastic tubing, if not available in your school, can be purchased inexpensively at a pet shop that sells tropical fish supplies.

Debriefing

Here are some questions that might be raised during Debriefing to promote reflection about siphoning:

- What investigations did you carry out in this center? What observations did you make about how the siphons worked?
- What did you do to make the siphon work?
- How do you explain that? What hypotheses can you suggest?
- How does air pressure work in the process of siphoning? What are your ideas about that?
- Why do you suppose it's important to know about how water might be moved upward? What ideas do you have about that?

Extending

When the students have had ample time to play with their initial investigations, their inquiries might be extended in one or more of the following ways:

1. By adding new materials to the center, such as water bottles with stoppers, with places to attach the tubing; spray bottles; squirt guns; bottles with holes drilled in the tops and bottoms.
2. By introducing new activity cards that call for attention to the concept of how a vacuum enables the water to flow.
3. By asking more challenging questions in later Debriefing sessions, for example:
   - What did you observe about how water flows from one level to another?
   - In what other ways can you make water move upward? What are your ideas on that?
   - What other examples can you give of water moving upward? Where else do you see this happen? What ideas do you have about how that works?
   - How does the vacuum in one of the jars help the water to flow? What are your ideas about that?
4. By referring students to background reading and to information about siphoning in library books or on the Internet.

Creating and Inventing

When the students have come to the natural conclusion of their interest in the siphoning center, their inquiries may be shifted to more creative tasks, such as the following:

1. Work with a friend. Draw a picture showing how you would design a system that would carry water from a low level to a house that was built on a very high hill.
2. Work with a friend. Talk together and invent at least ten ways that siphoning may be used in everyday situations the following.

ACTIVITY 6: ABSORBENCY

In this activity, the students work with eyedroppers and water to make observations about what happens when water is dropped on different types of surfaces.

Activity Card

- Use the materials in this center to carry out some investigations to see what happens when water is dropped on different surfaces.
- Try as many investigations as you can think of.
- Talk with each other about your observations.
- Then write about what you observed.

There may be other investigations you can do with these materials. Think of some and try them out and see what happens.

Materials

Pieces of brick, stone, fired and unglazed clay, glass, assorted types of fabrics with different fibers and textures, different kinds of paper (newsprint, construction paper, tissue paper, waxed paper, bond), different kinds of wood (balsa, plywood, pine), synthetics (several kinds of plastic), feathers, crayons, eyedroppers, water, magnifying lenses.

Thinking Operations Emphasized

Observing and recording; suggesting hypotheses; comparing; classifying; designing investigations; making decisions.

Big Ideas

Different materials have characteristic patterns and rates of absorption.

Notes to the Teacher

- These investigations, too, are likely to mean spillage of water on tables and the floor. Like siphoning, it's a good idea to be prepared and perhaps use plastic sheeting around the center. Paper towels and rags for cleanup should be on hand.

Debriefing

Some questions that might be raised during Debriefing to promote student reflection on the big ideas are included below. They should be used as appropriate and relevant to promoting student thinking in responding to their ideas.

- What observations did you make about what happened when water was dropped on these different materials?
- What similarities did you find in the way the water affected the materials? What differences did you find?
- In what ways might these materials be classified? What groups could you make? In which group would each of the materials belong?
- Why do you suppose it's important to know about those materials that are more or less absorbent? What are your thoughts about that?

Extending

After the students have had ample time for their investigations, their inquiries might be extended in some of the following ways:

1. By adding new materials to the center, such as a squirt bottle, pieces of metal, or different types of liquids, such as mineral oil, alcohol, or soda pop.
2. By introducing new activity cards, for example, investigating ways to measure rates of absorption.
3. By asking more challenging questions in later Debriefing, such as the following:
    - What observations did you make about the materials that did not absorb the water? How do you account for this? What ideas do you have?
    - What observations did you make about the materials that took longer to absorb the water? How do you account for this?
    - What observations did you make about the materials that absorbed the water quickly? How do you account for this?
    - What differences and similarities did you find in absorption when you used other liquids? How do you explain that? What are your ideas?
4. By raising questions that ask students to examine some values issues related to the topic, such as the following:
    - Someone has invented a substance that will make your T-shirt waterproof. You buy it in a can and spray it on your shirt and it will keep your shirt dry in the rain. But the plastic spray may cause some people to break out in a rash. Should this product be allowed, or taken off the market? What are your ideas?
    - Should plastic products that are helpful in some ways but harmful in other ways be allowed on the market? What are your ideas about this? Can you give some examples of such products from your own experience?

- What actions should students take with respect to finding out about the potential harmful effects of certain products? What are your ideas about that?
5. By referring students to background readings in the library or on the Internet.

Creating

When the students' interest in replaying with the materials seems to be waning, their studies on absorbency may be further extended in the following ways:

1. Work with a friend. Make a drawing of some of the observations you made in this center.
2. Draw some pictures showing your designs for a more "perfect rainwear outfit"—raincoat, cap, and boots that will keep you perfectly dry in a rainstorm.
3. Work with a friend. Think about as many materials as you can that do not easily absorb water. Make a list of these materials and classify them.
4. Work with a friend. Think about as many materials as you can that absorb water very easily. Make a list of them and classify them.

ACTIVITY 7: SOLUTIONS

In this center, the students work with dry ingredients and water to carry out investigative play with solutions. They are asked to record their observations.

Activity Card

- Use the materials in this center to make some investigations of how dry and wet ingredients combine.
- What observations did you make?
- Talk about what you found with each other.
- Then record your findings.

You may have some other ideas for using the materials in this center. Try out your own ideas and see what happens.

Materials

Assorted dry ingredients such as flour, salt, cornstarch, sugar, sand, rice, bulgur wheat, dry legumes, baking soda, dry milk powder, instant coffee; clear containers; water; spoons; clock or timer. (N.B. The dry ingredients should be labeled.)

Thinking Operations Emphasized

Comparing, observing, and recording; suggesting hypotheses; examining assumptions; classifying; designing investigations.

Big Ideas

Some materials dissolve easily in water; materials that do not dissolve easily in water may be soluble in other liquids.

Notes to the Teacher

- Before the students begin to work in this center, they might be reminded of ways to avoid an awesome mess. For example, it might be helpful if they were to wipe up after each exploration instead of leaving the entire cleanup for the end. Lots of warm water, cloths, and plastic covering for the floor are useful. This activity can be very messy, so it might be a good idea to wait until the students have achieved a relatively high degree of personal responsibility for their work before introducing it. Space might also be provided to allow for the overnight keeping of certain solutions—those that are put aside for twenty-four-hour observations.

Debriefing

The following are some questions that may be raised during initial Debriefing sessions:

- What were some of the investigations you conducted in this center?
- What observations did you make?
- What explanations do you have for how that worked?

Extending

After the students have had ample opportunity to conduct initial investigations, their inquiries might be extended in one or more of the following ways:

1. By adding new materials to the center, such as different types of liquids (oil, vinegar, alcohol, and soda pop) or by adding liquid mixtures (oil and water, alcohol solutions).
2. By introducing new activity cards.

3. By introducing more challenging questions in later Debriefing sessions, for example:
   - What are some of the similarities and some of the differences you have seen in the ways dry and wet ingredients combine? What explanations do you have for how this happens?
   - What classification systems can you set up based on your discoveries in this center?
   - What materials are more soluble? How do you explain this? What materials are less soluble? How do you explain this?
   - Some ingredients are not soluble in water but they dissolve in other liquids. What hypotheses can you suggest to explain it?
   - Why do you suppose it's important to know about the kinds of materials that are more or less soluble in liquid? What are your ideas about that?
4. By suggesting the gathering of background information from library books and/or the Internet.

Creating

When the students have exhausted their interest in working with soluble and nonsoluble materials, they might enjoy doing some more creative work such as:

1. Work with a friend. Make a ball by combining wet and dry ingredients and record what you observed.
2. Write a story about a "Secret Formula" that has certain magical properties.
3. Work with a friend and see if you can figure out how to turn a soluble ingredient into an insoluble one and make some graphic designs of how this can be done.
4. Write a "sci-fi" story about the Day When Nothing Was Soluble.

ACTIVITY 8: BUBBLES

In this center, the students work with soapy water to make some observations about bubbles.

Activity Card

- Use the materials in this center to find out what you can about bubbles.
- What observations did you make?

- Talk to each other about what you found.
- Then write about your observations.

You may wish to use the materials in this center to create some other investigations. Try out your ideas and see what happens.

Materials

A solution made of a few drops of glycerin in a gallon of water, with a capful of liquid detergent, in a plastic bucket or container; straws; flexible wire and wire cutters; a few funnels of different sizes; safety glasses.

Thinking Operations Emphasized

Observing and recording; comparing; suggesting hypotheses; designing investigations; imagining.

Big Ideas

Bubbles are thin layers of water kept intact by surface tension.

Notes to the Teacher

- Before students begin work in this center, it may be important to remind them about what needs to be done in case of spills. Sponges, paper towels, and cloths should be available for cleanup. Students might also be reminded that soapy water will smart if it gets in their eyes (safety glasses might also be provided as a caution) and that soapy water is likely to be slippery if too much of it falls on the floor. Plastic sheeting as a floor cover may be a good idea for this center. Commercially obtained bottles of bubbles may also be used in this center.

Debriefing

Some questions that might be raised during initial Debriefing include the following:

- What observations did you make about bubbles?
- What did you observe about their size? Shape? Color?
- What observations did you make about the "life" of a bubble? Which bubbles lasted longer? How do you explain this?
- What makes a bubble pop more quickly? How do you know that is true?

Extending

When the initial play has lost its productivity, the students' inquiries may be extended in one or more of the following ways:

1. By adding new materials to the bubble center, such as bubble pipes, sponges, waxed paper with holes of various sizes, paper cones, wireframes of different shapes.
2. By introducing new activity cards investigating how bubbles can be measured.
3. By introducing more challenging questions in later Debriefing sessions, for example:
   - Why do you suppose bubbles are almost always round? What hypotheses can you suggest to explain it?
   - How do you suppose you could make a square bubble?
   - Why do you suppose bubbles have colors? Where does the coloring come from? What hypotheses can you suggest to explain it?
   - Why do you suppose bubbles pop so quickly? How might you extend the life of a bubble? Conduct some investigations to see how this might be done.
   - What makes the biggest bubble? How do you explain it?
4. By referring students to library books or the Internet to gather background information about bubbles and surface tension.

Creating

To bring these studies to a culmination, the students may carry out one or more of the following creative activities:

1. Work with a friend. Design a house made of bubbles. Draw a picture of it.
2. Write a poem or make up a song about bubbles.
3. Make up a story about "The Bubble That Never Popped."

ACTIVITY 9: ICE

In this activity, the students observe the properties of ice. They are asked to record their observations.

Activity Card

- Use the materials in the center to find out what you can about ice.
- What observations did you make?

- Talk with each other about what you observed.
- Then record your findings.

You may have some other ideas about using the materials in this center. Try out some of your ideas and see what happens.

Materials

A bag of ice cubes; newspapers or a plastic tabletop cover; ruler or tape measure; balance scales; thermometer; plastic dishes or containers; clock or other timers; hammer; scissors; nails; paper towels; salt.

Thinking Operations Emphasized

Observing and recording; comparing; suggesting hypotheses; examining assumptions; designing investigations; applying principles; imagining and creating; making decisions.

Big Ideas

Water usually freezes at 32°F. When it melts, the amount of water stays the same. How fast the ice melts depends on its shape, amount, and surrounding temperature.

Notes to the Teacher

- Bags of ice cubes can often be bought at a gas station or supermarket. One bag should be adequate for one day's activity.

Debriefing

During Debriefing sessions, some of the following questions may be used to encourage deeper reflection on the big ideas:

- What observations did you make about the ice cubes?
- How are ice cubes formed? How do you know that? What assumptions might you be making?
- If you wanted to change the shape of an ice cube, how might you do that? What assumptions might you be making? How do you know that would work?
- How come ice cubes stick together? How do you explain it?
- How come ice cubes melt at different rates? How do you explain it? What assumptions might you be making?

Extending

When the students have had ample opportunity for initial investigative play, the activity might be extended in one or more of the following ways:

1. By adding some new activity cards to the center to give a different focus to the inquiries, for example:
   - Conduct some investigations to find differences between ice and water.
   - Conduct some investigations to find the temperatures of different ice cubes and the melted water.
   - Conduct some investigations to find out how you might slow down the melting of ice. Figure out how to measure and record the different rates of melting.
   - Conduct some investigations to find out how you might speed up the melting of ice. Figure out a way of measuring the rate of melting. Record your findings.
2. By raising more challenging questions during later Debriefing sessions. For example:
   - In what ways can the melting of ice be speeded up? What examples can you give to show that is true?
   - What other types of liquids might be frozen? How do you know that is true?
   - How come ice is slippery? How can you explain it?
   - How come your finger feels hot when you keep it on the ice for a long time? How do you explain it?
   - How can you measure the temperature of ice? How can you explain the different temperature readings?
   - How come Eskimos can keep warm in an igloo? How do you explain it?
3. By examining some value issues related to the topic. For example:

Snowblowers are very effective machines for moving ice and snow. But they use a lot of energy and make a big racket. Some people in North City say that snowblowers are essential machines. Others say that they should be outlawed because they consume too much energy and make noise pollution. Some critics say, "What's wrong with snow shovels?"

- What are your opinions? How should these issues be decided? Whose side are you on?
- Does your opinion depend on where you live?

4. By suggesting some background readings from library books and the Internet.

Creating

At the end of their inquiries about the properties of ice, the students may engage in other creative activities. For example:

1. Making ice carvings.
2. Figuring out ways to carry large blocks of ice from the house to the school with a minimum of melting.
3. Drawing or painting pictures of ice houses.
4. Writing stories about how it might feel to live in an ice house, or imagine what it would be like to live as Eskimos did, in an igloo.

ACTIVITY 10: SUCTION

In these investigations, the students play with the materials to investigate the concept of suction—what it is and how it works. They are also asked to record their observations.

Activity Card

- Use the materials in the center to find out what you can about suction.
- What observations did you make? Try some of your ideas and see what happens.
- Talk about your discoveries with each other.
- Then write about what you found.

You may have some other ideas about how to use the materials in this center. Try out your ideas and see what happens.

Materials

A basin of water; plastic tubing; straws; eyedroppers; toilet plunger; rubber suction cups; syringes.

Thinking Operations Emphasized

Observing; suggesting hypotheses; comparing; examining assumptions; designing investigations; imagining and creating.

Big Ideas

When some of the air inside space is removed, inside air pressure becomes less than outside air pressure. This may result in such effects as contraction and suction.

Notes to the Teacher

- The plastic tubing should be cut into several different lengths so that observations can be made within these variables. Discarded medical syringes may be obtained through the school nurse—but caution should be exercised to insure they are safe and free of any infectious disease. Rubber suction cups might be found in a toy or hardware store.
- Students using straws should not share straws with each other, and they should be cautioned about this prior to beginning their investigations.

Debriefing

The following types of questions can be raised to inquire further about suction. They should be used selectively.

- What observations did you make about how water was raised through the straws? Tubing? Eyedroppers? Syringes?
- How did it happen? How do you explain it?
- How do you know that is true? Are some assumptions being made here?
- How is the process of suction different with the syringe and the straw? How do you explain the differences?

Extending

When interest in the initial investigations seems to be waning, students' inquiries may be extended in one or more of the following ways:

1. By adding new activity cards to give the investigations a different focus.
2. By raising more challenging questions during later Debriefing, for example:
   - What kinds of machines or tools rely on suction to make them work? How do you know that is true? Are some assumptions being made here?
   - Under what conditions does suction fail? How can this be explained?
   - Think of some good ways to increase suction power. Use the materials in the center to try out your ideas.
3. By suggesting students do some background reading from library books or the Internet about suction.

Creating

To culminate the inquiries on suction, the students might work with a friend to:

1. Design a machine that uses water and suction to do its job.
2. Think up and list as many machines or tools as you can that depend on suction to work. How can these machines and tools be classified?
3. Think of a good way to increase suction power. Use the materials in the center to try out your ideas.

ACTIVITY 11: LIFE IN WATER

In this activity, the students carry out investigative play with the materials provided to examine the concept of life in water—what may live in water and how. They are also asked to record their observations.

Activity Card

- Use the materials in the center to find out what you can about what lives in water.
- What observations did you make?
- Try some investigations and see what happens. Talk about your ideas with each other.
- Then write about what you observed.

You may have other ideas about how to use these materials. Try them and see what you can discover.

Materials

Several cut flowers; glass vase; water; goldfish; goldfish bowl; several types of seeds (lima beans, acorns, rice, barley, sunflower seeds, dry peas, lentils, mung beans, alfalfa seeds, peanuts, lemon, lime, grapefruit, apple and orange seeds; melon, squash and avocado seeds); flat dishes; blotting paper; paper cups; six to eight jars of several sizes; onion, potato, radish, celery stalk, asparagus stalk, green onions, food coloring.

Thinking Observations Emphasized

Observing and recording; comparing; suggesting hypotheses; gathering and interpreting data; identifying assumptions; designing investigations; making decisions; imagining and creating.

Big Ideas

Water is extremely important for all living things. Plants and animals depend on water to live and grow.

Notes to the Teacher

- This investigative play is helped along by a few advance preparations. For example, begin several days in advance to immerse some of the seeds in water, in a glass jar. Place onion and potato in water, in glass jars. Place celery stalk in water to which a drop of food coloring has been added. These "starters" should be included in the materials for the center, as well as additional seeds and vegetables that begin in dry condition. At least one marine animal (e.g., goldfish, brine shrimp, snail) should be included in the materials for the center; these are easily obtained at the local pet shop.
- BEFORE INCLUDING PEANUTS INTO THE CENTER, MAKE SURE NO STUDENTS HAVE PEANUT ALLERGIES!
- If live animals are to be included, make sure that students understand the rules about live-animal studies described in earlier chapters.

Debriefing

The following types of questions might be helpful in promoting students' reflection about their inquiries:

- What observations did you make about what lives in water?
- How do you know that to be true? What assumptions have you made?
- What did you find out about what cannot live in water? How do you know that is true?

Extending

When the investigations with these materials seem to be losing appeal, the students' inquiries may be extended in one or more of the following ways:

1. By introducing new materials to the center such as other marine animals (guppies, shrimp, mollies), amphibians (turtles, frogs), nonmarine animals (caterpillar, ants, lizard, hamster, gerbil, other insects), salt water, sea plants (seaweed, kelp), other root vegetables (turnips, carrots, parsnip), other vegetables (tomato, squash, cuttings from green plants).
2. By adding new activity cards to give the investigations a different focus.

3. By raising more challenging questions during later Debriefings, for example:
   - What kinds of investigations were carried out with salt water? What are some differences between salt water and fresh water? What are some differences between what may live in salt water and fresh water?
   - What did you find out about animals that live in water? How do "water animals" different from "land animals"? How do you know that is true?
   - What did you find out about plants that live in water? How do "water plants" differ from "land plants"? How do you know that is true?
   - How might the animals (or plants) be classified? What groups might be set up?
   - How is it possible for a fish to live in water? What are your ideas? How is it that a cow (dog, chicken, person, etc.) cannot live in water? What are your ideas?
   - What did you find out about plants' need for water? How do you know that is true?
   - By suggesting students do some background reading from library books or the Internet
4. By viewing the film, *My Octopus Teacher* (streamed on Netflix).
5. By raising questions that call for the examination of some values issues related to the topic, for example:
   a. Occasionally an oil tanker that is transporting crude oil from where it is taken from the ground to the place where it is to be refined has a terrible accident. The tanker breaks up and the oil spills into the ocean.
      - What are some consequences of these spills on plant and animal life in the ocean? What are your thoughts?
      - What are some consequences of these spills on our own lives? What are your ideas?
      - How do you suppose the oil should be cleaned up? Who should pay for this?
      - What actions ought to be considered to prevent future spills? What are your ideas?
      - Is this a question that students should be concerned with? What do you think?
   b. Several areas in the United States are suffering from severe water shortages due to long-term drought.
      - What are your ideas about how we should be concerned about conserving water?
      - Is this something important for us to think about?
      - What examples can you give about how water is being wasted? How does this happen? What might be done to educate people who are wasteful to be more careful?

c. Should sea animals, like whales and dolphins, be captured and taken to aquariums for people to study and observe them? What are some advantages of living in an aquarium for these sea animals? What are some disadvantages? What are your ideas about it?

Creating

The inquiries may be culminated in one or more of the following creative activities:

1. Taking a trip to the aquarium for observations of fresh and salt water marine animals, leading to the construction of papier-mâché aquarium animals or a large mural that can be hung in the classroom.
2. Designing a test to find out if whales and dolphins are as smart as some people claim. How would you go about doing that?
3. Painting or drawing pictures of marine animals and collecting them in a class book.
4. Writing stories: for example, *My Life in the Sea*, by Henry the Whale; *Sea Dangers*, by Sally the Seal; *The Mermaid Who Changed into a TV Model*; *The Octopus's Garden*.

Chapter 14

Category B

No Fuss, No Muss, No Sticky Stuff: Activities 12–48

Activities that will not leave too much mess on the tables, on the floor, or around the room:

Activity 12:	Reflecting Surfaces
Activity 13:	Thermometers
Activity 14:	Electricity
Activity 15:	Air and Aerodynamics
Activity 16:	Balances
Activity 17:	Pendulums
Activity 18:	Magnifiers
Activity 19:	Light and Shadow
Activity 20:	Measuring
Activity 21:	Growing Plants from Seeds
Activity 22:	Seeds from Fruit; Fruit from Seeds
Activity 23:	Tiny Plants (1): Molds
Activity 24:	Tiny Plants (2): Yeast
Activity 25:	Flowers
Activity 26:	Foods: How Foods Change
Activity 27:	Skins
Activity 28:	Bones and Shells
Activity 29:	Skeletons
Activity 30:	Birds
Activity 31:	The World Wide Web
Activity 32:	Parachutes
Activity 33:	Tools and Machines
Activity 34:	Wind Sounds
Activity 35:	Wind Energy

Activity 36:	Sounds with Strings
Activity 37:	Static Electricity
Activity 38:	Kites
Activity 39:	Bouncing Balls
Activity 40:	Friction and Inertia
Activity 41:	Magnets
Activity 42:	Wheels and Axles
Activity 43:	Levers
Activity 44:	Germs
Activity 45:	Time
Activity 46:	Ourselves (1): Hands and Feet
Activity 47:	Ourselves (2): Pulse and Heartbeat
Activity 48:	Ourselves (3): Humans and the Environment

ACTIVITY 12: REFLECTING SURFACES

In this center, the students work with mirrors to make observations about reflecting surfaces. They are asked to record their observations.

Activity Card

- Use the materials in this center to make some observations of the reflections you see in the mirrors.
- Try as many different investigations as you can think of.
- Talk with each other about what you observed.
- Then write about your observations.

You may have some other ideas for using the materials in this center. Try them out and see what observations you can make.

Materials

Several squares of mirrors, with tapes on edges; shaving mirrors or other magnifying mirrors; dentist's mirrors; full-length mirrors; distorting (curved) mirrors; symmetrical and asymmetrical pictures; illustrations from magazines; large and small print letters; pencils, paper clips, balls of different sizes, books, other objects of different shapes.

Thinking Operations Emphasized

Observing and recording; comparing; suggesting hypotheses; examining assumptions; designing investigations; summarizing; imagining and creating.

Big Ideas

Reflection requires light. Reflected objects are reversed, as in a mirror.

Notes to the Teacher

- Glass and mirror business establishments will cut an old mirror into squares at a reasonable price, if you explain that this is for school use. Masking tape protects the edges, avoids cuts, and can also be used to hinge two or three pieces of mirrors together.
- Mirrors do break occasionally. Clear tape or adhesive backing may hold the broken pieces together.
- It is probably a good idea to remind students of procedures to follow in dealing with broken glass. Have a broom, dustpan, and newspapers available in case of breakage.

Debriefing

Below are some questions to promote reflection on the big ideas.

- What observations did you make about mirrors?
- What did you do to find that out?
- How did that work? Do you have some ideas that might explain it?
- How come objects seen in the mirror are reversed? How do you explain it?
- How do some mirrors distort your images? How do you explain it?
- What observations did you make about how light and dark affect the mirror images?
- What are mirrors good for? In what ways are they useful? What are your ideas about it?

Extending

After the students have been given ample opportunity to carry out investigative play with the materials in this center, their inquiries might be extended in one or more of the following ways:

1. By providing additional materials in the center such as a deck of cards, pattern blocks, a flashlight or candle, and a kaleidoscope.
2. By introducing new activity cards.
3. By asking more challenging questions in later Debriefings, for example:
    - What happens when you move something closer or farther away from a mirror? What observations have you made about that? Do you have any theories about how that works?

- How can a mirror change the way things look? How does that work? Do you have any ideas to explain it?
- What might be some uses for distorting mirrors? What ideas do you have about that?
- Try to think of as many ways to use a mirror as you can.
4. By suggesting background reading about light and reflection from library books and the Internet.

Creating

When the students seem to be coming to an end of their interest in this center, they may enjoy doing other related tasks that emphasize more imagining and creating skills. For example:

1. Work with a partner. Combine two or more mirrors in a way that will allow you to see images around a corner.
2. Work with a partner. Make your own mirror. What materials are better for this? What materials are poor reflectors? How do you explain this?
3. Work with a partner. Design and build a periscope.
4. Write a story, "The Child on the Other Side of the Mirror" (figure 14.1).

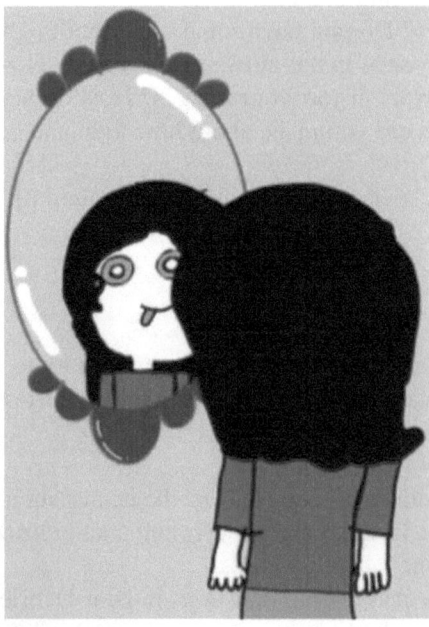

Figure 14.1 *Maya Snow.*

Category B

ACTIVITY 13: THERMOMETERS

In this center, the students work with thermometers to make observations about temperature and the conditions that cause the temperature to change. They are asked to record their observations.

Activity Card

- Use the materials in this center to study temperature.
- What objects are "hot"? What are the temperatures of "hot" objects?
- What objects are "cold"? What are the temperatures of "cold" objects?
- What objects are "warm"? What are the temperatures of "warm" objects?
- How does temperature change?
- Work together to conduct some investigations to see what you can find out. Then write about what you found.

You may have other ideas about investigating temperature. Try out your ideas and see what you can discover.

Materials

A variety of thermometers (indoor, outdoor, body temperature thermometers), a variety of warm, cold, and room-temperature objects (a basin of warm or hot water, ice cubes, a package of frozen food, a container of milk, modeling clay, etc.).

Thinking Operations Emphasized

Observing; comparing; suggesting hypotheses; designing investigations; examining assumptions; gathering and recording data; applying principles; imagining and creating; making decisions; classifying.

Big Ideas

One measure of an object's heat is its temperature. The human body responds to changes in temperature with a variety of physiological processes.

Notes to the Teacher

- You may wish to avoid using any of the breakable types of thermometers, depending on your perception of how carefully the students are able to work with the materials.

Debriefing

Questions to encourage reflection on temperatures are offered below. They should be used selectively and as appropriate.

- What did you observe about objects that are cold? What temperatures did you observe that cold objects have?
- What did you observe about objects that are warm? What temperatures did you observe that warm objects have?
- What did you observe about objects that are hot? What temperatures did you observe that hot objects have?
- What other observations did you make about temperature?
- How do you explain some of the differences in the temperature you found among the various objects?
- How does the temperature change? How do you know that is true?
- What makes an object cold? Hot? Warm? How do you explain it?
- What other investigations did you carry out with these materials?

Extending

After the students have had sufficient time to conduct their initial investigations, their inquiries may be extended in one or more of the following ways:

1. By introducing new activity cards to the center to give new focus to the inquiries, for example:
   - Make a chart of twenty objects and their temperatures. Classify the objects by arranging them into groups.
   - Using pans of quite hot, warm, and quite cold water, conduct investigations to find out how certain temperatures feel on your hands. What observations can you make?
   - How can warm be made cold? How can cold be made warm? Conduct some investigations and write about your findings.
2. By raising more challenging questions in later Debriefing. For example:
   - How come different thermometers give different readings for the same object?
   - How come different parts of the body show different temperature readings?
   - In what ways can you raise the temperature of your hands?
   - In what ways can you lower the temperature of your hands?
   - What is the warmest part of your classroom? How do you explain it?
   - What is the coolest area of the classroom? How do you explain it?

3. By raising questions that call for students to examine some values issues related to the topic. For example:
   - Some people who live in places where it gets quite hot depend on air conditioners to cool their homes, cars, and places of business. Is this a good way to use energy? What do you think?
   - Some people who live in places where it gets quite cold depend on central heating systems using oil, to heat their homes and places of work. Is this a good way to use energy? What do you think?
   - Should we be concerned about the use of energy to heat and cool our homes and places of work? What are your thoughts on this?
4. By suggesting background reading from library books or the Internet.

Creating

When the students seem to have reached the limit of their interest in these investigations, they might be asked to do one or more of the following culminating activities:

1. Make a thermometer that shows temperature in Fahrenheit degrees. Make another that shows temperature in Celsius degrees.
2. Draw a picture of a thermometer that could take the temperature of a volcano when it's erupting.
3. Work with a friend. Think up and list as many uses as you can for thermometers.
4. Write a story about the hottest day on record.
5. Draw some pictures of what ice crystals might look like.
6. Work with a friend. List as many things as you can think of that cold temperature is good for. Make a list of as many things as you can think of that hot temperature is good for.

ACTIVITY 14: ELECTRICITY

In this center, the students work with batteries, wires, and low-wattage bulbs to make observations about electrical energy and electric circuitry.

Activity Card

- Work with the materials in this center to make some observations about electricity and how it works. Talk with each other about what you observed.
- Then write about your observations.

> You may have other ideas about how to use these materials. Try them out and see what you can discover.

Materials

Low-wattage bulbs (flashlight bulbs, twenty-five-watt bulbs); dry cell batteries; wires and clamps; switches; a telegraph key; a bell or buzzer; discarded remote controls (for TV or other remote-controlled appliances); small screwdrivers; toy remote-controlled cars; safety glasses.

Thinking Operations Emphasized

Observing; comparing; designing investigations; generating and testing hypotheses; gathering and recording data; examining assumptions; making decisions; imagining and creating.

Big Ideas

Electricity can be produced by a dry cell to make light, sound, motion, or heat. Electricity can be produced from other sources, such as wind and water, and can be transformed into almost any other forms of energy.

Notes to the Teacher

- The materials in this center should be in two forms: sets that are already assembled and unassembled materials sufficient to create other sets. One assembled set should provide an example of a simple electrical circuit, working on an on-off switch, to light up a bulb. The other set should demonstrate electrical circuitry for a telegraph key. Materials should also be provided for students to assemble their own circuits. Students may also be encouraged to disassemble and reassemble the demonstration sets.

Debriefing

Some questions to promote further reflection during Debriefing are suggested below. They should be used selectively.

- What observations did you make about what electricity can do?
- What did you do to find that out? Do you have some ideas that might explain it?

- How did your electrical model compare with the one that was already assembled?
- In what ways are the electric light model and the telegraph key model alike? How are they different?
- In what ways does electricity create energy? How does that work? How can you explain it?

Extending

After the students have carried out initial investigative play with the materials, their inquiries might be extended in one or more of the following ways:

1. By introducing additional materials to the center, for example, additional electric lights, additional wires, simple electric motors, different types of switches, dead batteries that can be taken apart, other remote-control devices.
2. By adding a new activity card to give the investigations a fresh focus.
3. By raising more challenging questions in later Debriefing. For example:
   - Under what conditions does your model work? When does your model fail to work? How can you explain this? Can you think of some ways to test your theory?
   - In what ways is your model like (different from) the electric light system in this classroom? What ideas do you have about it?
   - What are some other electrical systems that are used in this classroom? In this school? How are they like (different from) the models you built?
   - Where do you suppose our electricity comes from? What ideas do you have about it? How could you explain it? How could you test your ideas?
   - How do water and wind create energy? What theories do you have about that?
   - What can you tell about how remote controls use electricity to operate appliances and other devices? How do you know that is true?
   - Sometimes we experience a "power outage." How do you suppose this happens? What theories do you have about it? What are some consequences of that outage?
   - How, in your view, does electricity enable your work with your tablet, computer, or TV set? How do you know that is true?
   - How, in your view, does electricity enable your use of the telephone or cellphone? How do you know that is true?
4. By raising questions that call for students' examination of values issues related to the topic. For example:

a. Many large metropolitan areas in the United States need and use a great deal of electricity. The more people who live in the area, the more who work in those areas, the more lights are used in the nighttime, the more electricity is needed. In some areas, city officials are running out of resources to supply the demand.

   Canada, the neighboring country to the north, can supply the United States with more electric power. But some Canadians have said, "If you weren't so extravagant in your use of electricity, you wouldn't need so much. Why should we give our precious resources to you?"
   - Are people in the United States wasteful in their use of electricity? Can you give some examples to support your opinion? Should Canadians give the people in the United States this extra power? Where do you stand on these issues?
b. In the early days of the development of electricity, Thomas Edison, inventor of the first electric light, developed a "direct current"—electrical current that runs continually in a single direction. Nikolai Tesla developed an "alternating current"—an electrical current that alternates direction a number of times per second. Edison was very opposed to Tesla's alternating current largely because he was afraid of losing money for his own inventions. Work with a friend and write a short play or story about the "war" between these two inventors.
c. Some people have already bought electric cars instead of gas-driven vehicles. This is part of a plan to reduce carbon emissions into the atmosphere. Should we all be driving electric cars? What is your position on this?
5. By encouraging students to do some background reading from library books and the Internet.

Creating

Investigative play with electricity may be further enriched with one or more of the following:

1. Work with a friend. Use the battery, wires, light bulbs, and switches to design a game that can be played in the classroom.
2. Make a pencil-and-paper design of an electrical current.
3. Create a website to explain how electricity works that can be understood by a primary grader.
4. Create a design for a remote-control operated toy car. What materials would you need to build one?
5. Work with a friend to design a plan to use electricity to produce sound. Draw a diagram or design a website to show how your system would work.

6. Work with a friend and make a list of as many uses of electricity as you can think of.
7. Write a story or a poem titled "The Day the Lights Went Out." Make it as scary as you can.
8. Put your imagination to work and think of how the very first electric light might have been invented. Write a short play about this event.

ACTIVITY 15: AIR AND AERODYNAMICS

In this activity, the students work with balloons to carry out investigations with air. They are asked to record their observations.

Activity Card

- Use the materials in this center to find out what you can about air.
- What observations did you make?
- What does air look like? What are your ideas about that?
- How can you move air from place to place? What theories do you have about that?
- How heavy or light is air? How do you know it's there?
- How can you measure the temperature of air? What are your ideas about it?
- Try as many investigations as you can think of to help you find out about air.
- Then write about what you discovered.

You may have some other ideas for using the materials in this center. Try some of your ideas and see what discoveries you can make.

Materials

Many balloons of different shapes and sizes; string; a balance scale; rubber bands; timer; room thermometer; air pump.

Thinking Operations Emphasized

Observing and comparing; collecting and recording data; suggesting hypotheses; examining assumptions; designing investigations; decision-making; imagining and creating.

Big Ideas

Air exerts pressure and has weight; air pressure can be harnessed to do work. The study of how objects move through the air is called aerodynamics.

Notes to the Teacher

- This is a very safe activity and one for which the materials are easily obtained. It is also a great deal of fun for the students. An activity of this type may be a good "first" for teachers who wish to begin their sciencing program.

Debriefing

Some questions to promote further reflection during Debriefing include the following. They should be used selectively and as appropriate.

- What observations did you make about air?
- What observations did you make about balloons?
- How did balloons help you in your air studies?
- What did you do to find that out? Do you have some ideas to explain that?
- How did you know there was air in the balloon? How could you tell that for sure?
- When the balloon "popped," what happened? Where did the noise come from? How do you explain it?

Extending

When the students have had sufficient time to conduct their initial investigations, their inquiries may be extended in one or more of the following ways:

1. By adding new materials to the center, such as a helium-filled balloon, a pinwheel, a "parachute" made with a handkerchief and string; a deflated bicycle tire, or an old-fashioned "inner tube." More elaborate materials include an air mattress and a life vest.
2. By introducing new activity cards, for example:
    - How many helium-filled balloons might it take to lift a paper clip? A piece of paper? A paper cup? What observations did you make as you did these investigations?
    - How many helium-filled balloons would it take to lift a chair? What are your ideas? Conduct some investigations and try to figure this out.

- Figure out a good way to see how long you can get the air to stay in a balloon, a bicycle tire, an air mattress. Test your idea to see how it works.
3. By raising more challenging questions in later Debriefing. For example:
    - What might be some good ways to get air into a balloon? Into an air mattress? A life vest? A bicycle tire?
    - In what ways do we get air to work for us? How many different ways can you think of?
    - How do we get air to stay in a balloon? A bicycle tire? An air mattress?
    - How might you weigh air? What ideas do you have about that?
    - Where does the air go when you let it out of a balloon? An air mattress? A bicycle tire?
4. By raising questions that call for students to examine some values issues related to the topic. For example:
    - Is our air "clean"? What is clean air? How do you know?
    - What makes the air dirty? What in our own community makes our air dirty? How do you know? What examples can you give to support your ideas?
    - Should we be concerned about clean or dirty air? What are your ideas? What actions should adults be taking on this issue? What actions should we take? What might be some consequences of those actions? What are your ideas?
5. By referring students to library books and the Internet to gather additional information about air.

Creating

Some creative activities that might be used to wind up the air investigations are offered below:

1. Write a story about going to visit a friend in a hot air balloon. Draw a picture of your balloon (figure 14.2).
2. Work with a friend. Try to figure out how large a balloon you would need to lift both of you off the floor.
3. Work with a friend. Make a list of as many ways as you can think of that we can get air to work for us.
4. Write a story about "The Yellow Balloon."
5. Write a poem about "The Balloon Man."
6. Imagine what it would be like to travel around the world in a balloon. Draw some pictures to describe your adventures.

Figure 14.2 *Maya Snow.*

ACTIVITY 16: BALANCES

In this center, the students work either in the classroom or on the playground to make observations about the ways in which balances work.

Activity Card

- Use the materials to carry out some investigations to see how balances work.
- Try out as many ideas as you can think of to show how things balance.
- Talk with each other about your observations. Then write about them.

Perhaps there are other ways to use these materials. Do you have some new ideas for using them? Try out your ideas and see what you can discover.

Materials

Seesaw or teeter-totter on the school playground if available; a 5-foot by 8-inch board; a cement block to serve as a fulcrum; rulers; straight sticks; doweling; children's blocks; assorted objects for balancing.

Thinking Operations Emphasized

Observing; collecting and recording data; designing investigations; suggesting hypotheses; testing hypotheses; examining assumptions; interpreting data.

Big Ideas

The balance between two objects on opposite sides of a fulcrum is determined by each object's weight and its distance from the fulcrum.

Notes to the Teacher

- The concepts involved in this investigative play are basic to many scientific principles studied at both the primary and middle-grade levels. There will be much to investigate with these materials. Therefore, it may be worthwhile to recreate this center several times during the school year.

Debriefing

Here are some questions to stimulate student reflection during Debriefing sessions:

- What observations did you make about balance when you were using the playground equipment?
- When the people (or objects) do not balance, what are some ways you can change the situation? What are your ideas about it?
- What did you do to make the objects balance? How can you explain it?

Extending

After the students have had repeated opportunities to play with balances inside and outside the classroom, their inquiries may be extended in one or more of the following ways:

1. By adding new materials to the center such as balance scales, a variety of weights, ping-pong balls, nuts, bolts, nails, bricks, and blocks.
2. By introducing new activity cards to give the inquiries a new focus.
3. By asking more challenging questions in later Debriefing sessions. For example:
    - In what ways were you able to construct a balance like the one in the schoolyard?

- In what ways were you able to construct small balances?
- How can you balance a very heavy object with a much lighter object? How come that works? How do you explain it?
- What do you need to do in order to make things balance? What are your ideas?
- Why do you suppose it's good to know about how things balance?

4. By suggesting students do some background reading from library books and the Internet.

Creating

When the students' enthusiasms for these activities seem to be ebbing, they may enjoy doing some more creative tasks such as the following:

1. Work with a friend. Draw a picture of a balance that would evenly balance a dinosaur and a cat. What would it look like? How would it work?
2. Work with a friend. Talk together and make a list of as many ways as you can think of in which balances are used in our lives.
3. Draw a picture of a mobile. Then get the materials you need to build it. Make sure that it is fully balanced and hang it up in your classroom.

ACTIVITY 17: PENDULUMS

In this center, the students work with weights and strings to make observations about how pendulums move. They are asked to record their observations.

Activity Card

- Use the materials in the center to make some pendulums.
- Hang them up and make some observations about how they move.
- Try out some investigations by changing the size and weight of the bobs and the length of the string. Observe what happens when you make these changes. Then write about your observations.

You may think of some entirely new ways to use the materials in this center. Try out your new ideas and see what you can find out.

Materials

A variety of weights (different-sized nuts, modeling clay, some bobs, tops, rocks, etc.); different lengths of string; scissors; elastic bands; masking tape.

Thinking Operations Emphasized

Observing; comparing; suggesting hypotheses; collecting, recording, and interpreting data; designing investigations; examining assumptions; and making decisions.

Big Ideas

The time it takes for a pendulum to swing back and forth varies with its length. That time is independent of the weight of the bob.

Notes to the Teacher

- Pendulums may be hung from light fixtures to achieve the best effects. This may require some assistance from the teacher. They may also be hung from tables. There should be sufficient space around the pendulum for it to swing freely.

Debriefing

The following types of questions may be used to promote reflection during the Debriefing:

- What observations did you make about the pendulums?
- What kinds of investigations did you try?
- How did that work? How can you explain it?
- What are some differences you observed in the pendulums? What are some similarities?

Extending

When the students have had sufficient opportunities to conduct their pendulum inquiries, their investigations can be extended in one or more of the following ways:

1. By adding new materials to the center, such as a stopwatch or a clock with a second hand and chart paper to measure and record the observations.

2. By introducing new activity cards.
3. By raising more challenging questions in later Debriefing sessions. For example:
   - What observations did you make when you put heavier weights on your pendulum? How do you explain that?
   - What observations did you make when you changed the length of the string? How do you explain that?
   - What observations did you make when you placed two pendulums side by side? How do you explain what you observed?
   - How might you increase the length of swing time of your pendulum? Why do you think that might work?
   - Why do you suppose it's helpful to know anything about how pendulums work? What ideas do you have about that?
4. By suggesting that students do some background reading in library books or on the Internet about pendulums.

Creating

When the students seem ready to move from their initial investigations, they might enjoy one or more of the following culminating activities:

1. Work with a friend. Think about pendulums and list as many uses as you can for them.
2. Invent a pendulum that will never stop—one that will keep on swinging forever. Draw a picture of it. Then use the materials in the center to build it and test your plan.
3. Think about the work that a pendulum can do. Figure out a way to use a pendulum to open and close a door. Draw a picture of your invention.

ACTIVITY 18: MAGNIFIERS

In this center, the students carry out investigative play with magnifying lenses to examine how images are enlarged to enable us to see things that we can't see with the naked eye. They are asked to record their observations.

Activity Card

- Use the materials in the center to make some observations of what you can see with magnifiers.

- Try as many investigations as you can think of. Talk with each other about your findings.

Then write about your observations.

You may have thought of some other ways to use these materials. Try your ideas and see what you can discover.

Materials

Different kinds of magnifiers, such as hand magnifiers, lenses from old reading glasses, lenses from old cameras or projectors, a telescope, a microscope; a few tall, clear, straight-sided jars; some magazines, pictures, newspapers; a variety of insects: caterpillars, ants, earthworms, flies, and so on (optional); thin skins of vegetables and fruits, for example, onion, potato, carrot, tomato, apple, banana, plum, and peach; a variety of leaves; pond water; glass slides.

Thinking Operations Emphasized

Observing; comparing; classifying and interpreting data; designing investigations; generating hypotheses; examining assumptions; making decisions; and summarizing.

Big Ideas

Magnifiers are specially shaped pieces of glass (lenses) that make images larger. Magnifiers help us to see things we cannot see without them. They make it possible to see that living things are made mostly of cells.

Notes to the Teacher

- Using dead insects may be offensive to some teachers and students and such materials are optional for this center. Should teachers wish to include insects, the students should be cautioned on their handling, since they are fragile, and on their careful return to their containers.
- If teachers wish to capitalize on the use of insects, they may consider using some of the extending activities for further inquiries.

Debriefing

The following are some questions to be used during Debriefing sessions to promote reflection on the big ideas. They should be used as appropriate.

- What observations did you make of objects seen under the magnifying lenses?
- What similarities did you observe among the vegetable and fruit skins? What differences?
- How do you compare what is seen under the magnifying lenses to what is seen without magnification?
- How does a magnifying glass compare to a window glass? What are some similarities? What are some differences?

Extending

After the students have had ample time to carry out investigative play with the materials, their inquiries may be extended in one or more of the following ways:

1. By adding new materials to the center, such as other vegetable and fruit skins; other leaves; other water samples, for example, sink water, raindrops, and teardrops.
2. By adding other materials such as a pair of binoculars and pieces of plain glass.
3. By introducing new activity cards to give a new focus to the inquiries. For example:
   - Which is the best magnifier for studying insects? Skins? Drops of water? How did you figure that out?
   - Make some drawings of the cell structures found in some of the vegetable or fruit skins.
4. By asking more challenging questions in later Debriefing sessions. For example:
   - How do you suppose a magnifying glass works? How do you explain it?
   - What, in your opinion, are magnifiers good for? How do they help in certain medical and technical research?
   - How do magnifiers help with computers, cell phones, and tablets? What are your ideas?
   - How in your view did magnifiers help explain the causes of diseases? What are your ideas about it?
5. By raising questions that call for the examination of some values issues related to the topic. For example:

   The scientist wanted to study the new baby's skin under a microscope. But the baby's father said that it was dangerous for the baby to be examined with the lens and refused permission.

- What are your ideas? Is this a dangerous action for a baby? How do you know? What examples can you give to support your ideas?
- If you think this is dangerous, what do you think might happen?
- If you think it is not dangerous, how might the scientist try to convince the baby's father? What are your ideas?
6. By suggesting that students do some background reading in the library and on the Internet. N.B. The Internet can be especially helpful in viewing human cells seen under magnification.
7. Students may also be interested in reading about the life of Leeuwenhoek, a great deal of which can be found on the Internet.

Creating

When the students seem to be coming to the end of their interest in these investigations, they may be asked to carry out one or more of the following tasks:

1. Study hanging water drops under magnification. (This may be done both indoors and outdoors.) Draw some pictures of what you have observed.
2. Study ice under magnification. Draw some pictures of what you have observed.
3. Study the skin of an onion (other vegetables) under magnification. Draw some pictures of what you have seen.
4. Study one hair from your head under magnification. Draw some pictures of what you have observed.

ACTIVITY 19: LIGHT AND SHADOW

In this center, the students work with various light sources to make observations about light and shadow. They are asked to record their observations.

Activity Card

- Use the materials in the center to make some observations of light and shadow.
- Try as many investigations as you can think of to see how shadows are made.
- Talk with each other about what you have found.
- Then, write about your findings.

You may have thought of different investigations that can be tried with these materials. Try your ideas and see what you can discover.

Materials

Flashlights, overhead projectors, cell phone, screen, video camera, a darkened corner; a white sheet, pieces of black and white construction paper or poster board.

Thinking Operations Emphasized

Observing; comparing; collecting and interpreting data; suggesting hypotheses; examining assumptions; designing investigations; making decisions; summarizing.

Big Ideas

When an opaque body stands in the path of a beam of light a shadow forms. The shadow's size depends on the distance between the object, the light, and the screen.

Notes to the Teacher

- A candle is a popular addition to the center. Before the students study the shadow effects produced by candles, it's important to ensure that appropriate precautions are taken and adult supervision is provided.

Debriefing

Some examples of questions to promote further reflection on the concepts of light and shadow include the following. They should be used as appropriate.

- What observations did you make about shadows?
- What observations did you make about how light makes shadows?
- How do you compare light and shadow? What are some differences? What are some similarities?
- What are the best conditions for creating shadows? How do you explain that?
- How do light and shadow influence what you can see on your cell phone? On the video camera? In the movies? How do you explain it?
- What are some investigations that you tried? What happened when you did that? How do you explain it?

Extending

After the students have had sufficient time to play with the materials in this center, their inquiries may be extended in one or more of the following ways:

1. By adding new materials to the center, for example, a cardboard box open at each end covered by a sheet on one side; a candle; a sundial.
2. By introducing new activity cards to give the inquiries a new focus. For example:
    - In what ways are shadows made by candles different from shadows made by flashlights? Try some investigations and see what observations you can make.
    - How can you send messages using light and shadow? Try some investigations and see what you can discover.
3. By asking more challenging questions in later Debriefing sessions. For example:
    - How are shadows made? How do you know that is true?
    - In what ways can the shapes of shadows be changed? How did you figure that out?
    - Why do you suppose shadows disappear in a very dark room? How do you explain it?
    - Why do you suppose shadows have no colors? How do you explain that?
    - Under what light and shadow conditions do cell phones (tablets, movies, and videos) work best? How do you know that is true?
    - How do movies (films) make use of light and shadow to entertain us? What are your ideas about it?
4. By providing an opportunity for students to extend their inquiries out of doors on a sunny day.
5. By raising questions that call for students to examine some values issues related to the topic. For example:
    Some people believe that you can tell your future by the position of the sun and the planets in our solar system. This is called astrology. What are your ideas about this? Where did you get your information? Should everybody believe this? What do you think?
6. By suggesting that students gather more background information from library books and from the Internet.

Creating

When the students' interest in the materials seems to be ebbing, they may enjoy doing some more creative work to culminate the light and shadow studies. For example:

1. A small group of students may wish to put on a "shadow" play to be shared with the class.
2. Students may make shadow puppets and give a puppet show for the class.

3. Some students may wish to write stories, for example, Scared of My Own Shadow!
4. Students may draw their full shadows using materials available in the center.
5. Shadow profiles of faces (silhouettes) may also be made. Can students identify which person is represented by each shadow profile?
6. Some students may be interested in creating a sundial in the playground of the school.
7. For the more intrepid students, they may create a YouTube video using light and shadow.

ACTIVITY 20: MEASURING

In this center, the students use the materials to gain an increased understanding of measurements. They are asked to record their observations.

Activity Card

- Use the materials in this center to find out what you can about taking measurements.
- Make some measurements using some of the different materials provided.
- Make some observations of how the different measures work and which seem more reliable.
- Talk with each other about your findings. Then write about what you found.

There may be some other investigations to make with these materials. Try your ideas and see what you can discover.

Materials

Rulers of various sizes, both metric and nonmetric; tape measures, both metal and cloth; rubber bands; string; Popsicle sticks; strips of paper; blocks; several sized balls (e.g., ping-pong, tennis, volley, nerf), a cutout tracing of a human foot; a cutout tracing of a human hand; measuring cups of various sizes; measuring spoons.

Thinking Operations Emphasized

Observing; collecting data; comparing and recording data; making decisions; applying principles; designing investigations; examining assumptions.

Big Ideas

Standard units of measurement are an essential part of the mathematical language used to make comparisons, design investigations, and interpret results.

Notes to the Teacher

It may be helpful to add different activity cards to give more than one focus to the students' inquiries. Activity cards might address the following types of investigations:

- How many "foot" lengths is the width of our classroom? Conduct some investigations to see what you can discover.
- How many "hand" lengths is the width of our classroom?
- How many Popsicle stick lengths is the width of our classroom?
- How many inches is the width of our classroom? How many meters?
- What are some differences between metric and nonmetric measures? What are some similarities?
- How would you measure a puddle? What instruments would you use? How would you determine the accuracy of your measurement?
- How would you measure the speed of a ball thrown across the classroom? What factors influence the measurement?

Debriefing

The following types of questions may be used to promote reflection about the big ideas:

- What are some observations you made about measuring?
- What, in your opinion, was the best way to measure a chair? A table? The room? The door? A puddle? What are your reasons for thinking that was the best way?
- In what ways is measuring with a ruler and measuring with a Popsicle stick alike? How are the methods different?
- How does it help us to know what the accurate measurements are of certain things, like the size of a room, the distance to the nearest star, the weight of a dinosaur? What are your ideas?
- How do measures of liquids differ from measures of solids? How are they similar?
- What are some things that are hard to measure? How might we go about measuring them? What are your ideas about it?

Extending

After the students have had sufficient time to carry out investigations with the materials in the center, their inquiries may be extended in one or more of the following ways:

1. By adding new activity cards. For example:
   - Conduct some investigations to discover what you can about: some good ways to measure a hand; some good ways to measure a nose; some good ways to measure a balloon; some good ways to measure amounts of milk or water; some good ways to measure the distance between the earth and one of the nearest stars.
   - How many different answers do you get when four students measure the door? Figure out how to decide who is correct.
   - How can you tell how many kilobytes (kB) are available in your tablet or smartphone? How did you figure that out? What does that measure mean about your tablet or smartphone? What are your ideas about it?
2. By asking more challenging questions in later Debriefing. For example:
   - What instruments give more reliable measures? How did you figure that out?
   - What instruments give less reliable results? How did you figure that out?
   - What happens when two people measuring the same surface get two different results? How do we determine which was more accurate? How do you know?
   - Some forms of energy are measured by BTUs (British Thermal Units). How do you suppose you can measure BTUs? What are your ideas about it?
   - Computer storage and memory are often measured in megabytes (MB) and gigabytes (GB). What do you suppose it means when your computer contains about 1 MB of information? What ideas do you have about that?
   - How are BTUs, gigabytes, megabytes, and kilobytes different from inches, feet, and yards?
3. By suggesting that students do some background reading about measuring from library books and from the Internet.
4. By raising questions that call for the examination of values issues related to the topic. For example:
   - Polls are measurements used to make predictions about future events, like who is favored to win an election. How do polls work? How can we depend on them for accuracy? What are your ideas?

- How can you tell if a measurement is accurate when the carpenters take the measurements for a new garage door? What do you think?
- Why do you suppose we rely on measurements as being accurate? How does that sometimes lead us to make mistakes?
- Should we believe what the "experts" tell us about their measurements? Where do you think we need to be very careful about believing certain measurements to be true? What do you think?
- What good is measuring if there is so much inaccuracy in taking measurements? What do you think about that?
- Design a survey to find out how many students in your class prefer the chocolate ice cream and how many prefer vanilla. How do you know your results are reliable? What assumptions have you made in polling?

Creating

Before the measuring activities are concluded, the students may be invited to do some more creative work with measures. For example:

1. Work with a friend. Try to figure out a way to measure each other's height accurately. Measure and measure again until you are sure your measurement is accurate.
2. Work with a friend. Try to think of as many different ways to measure things as you can. Make a list of those measures.
3. Invent a way to measure the flight of a bird. Write or draw your ideas.
4. Invent a way to measure the depth of the deepest part of the ocean. Write or draw your ideas.
5. Design your own measuring instrument to measure the distance from the earth to the nearest star. Draw some pictures of it.

ACTIVITY 21: GROWING PLANTS FROM SEEDS

In this center, the students study different seeds, plant them, and make some observations about seeds and how they grow. They are asked to record their observations.

Activity Card

- Use the materials in this center to carry out some investigations with seeds.
- Make some observations and decide how these seeds might be classified. Set up some categories and place the seeds into the category where you think they belong. Identify your groups by giving each a name.

- Examine two kinds of seeds and compare them. How are they alike? How are they different? Find as many similarities and differences as you can and record your findings.

You may have some other ideas for conducting investigations with these seeds. Try your ideas and see what you can discover.

Materials

A variety of seeds (fast-growing seeds are preferable, for example, lettuce, lima bean, mung bean, corn, alfalfa, watercress, and radish), paper towels or blotting paper, waxed paper or plastic wrap, saucers, water, sand, potting soil; small pots or other containers such as milk cartons for planting; large spoons for digging.

Thinking Operations Emphasized

Observing; comparing; collecting and recording data; examining assumptions; suggesting hypotheses; designing investigations; making decisions; evaluating; summarizing; applying principles.

Big Ideas

Most plants we know are germinated from seeds. Warmth and water are two important conditions for germinating plants. There is a huge variety of plants. Many of them are edible.

Notes to the Teacher

1. Plastic sheets, newspapers, dustpan, and broom should be available for cleanup, since even when exercising caution, some dirt may sneak onto the floor.
2. It is helpful if the seeds are labeled.

Debriefing

The following types of questions may help to further student's thinking about their investigations.

- What observations did you make about what's in a seed?
- What observations did you make about how seeds grow?

- What differences did you find in the growth of the seeds under different growing conditions? How do you explain it? What are your ideas?
- In what ways were the seeds different? How were they alike?
- What do you suppose are some other things that grow from seeds? How do you know that is true? What examples can you give to support your ideas?

Extending

The seed-growing investigations may be extended in one or more of the following ways:

1. By adding other seeds to the center, for example, flower seeds, herb seeds, and other vegetable seeds (tomato, green beans, squash, and green pepper).
2. By adding growing plants to the center. For example, a potato or sweet potato, the top part of a carrot, the top of a pineapple, an onion, a clove of garlic, and house plants.
3. By adding new activity cards. For example:
   - Take some bean seeds and place them on a very wet paper towel in a saucer, each seed in its own saucer. Cover the saucers with plastic wrap or waxed paper. Place one dish in a warm place and the other in a cool place. Observe what happens for one week. Record your observations. Then suggest some hypotheses to explain any differences you find.
   - Conduct the same investigation using corn seeds. Compare the corn growth with the bean growth. Record your findings. Suggest some hypotheses to explain any differences you find.
   - Conduct the same investigation with alfalfa seeds or mung beans. Compare these seeds with the corn and bean plants. Record your findings. Then suggest some hypotheses to explain any differences you found.
   - Plant some seeds in soil pots. Label them. Put them in different places around the room. Study them every day for a month. Record your findings and suggest some hypotheses to explain any differences you found.
4. By raising more challenging questions at later Debriefings. For example:
   - Some plants grow from seeds, like radishes. Other plants grow from pieces of themselves, like potatoes. How do you explain this? What are your ideas?
   - What did you discover about what plants need to grow? What are your ideas about that? What examples can you give to support your ideas?
   - Why do plants need light in order to grow? How do you explain it? What hypotheses can you suggest?

- Where do you suppose seeds come from? What are your ideas?
- What are some foods that come from plants? Think of as many as you can and classify them.
5. By raising questions that call for the examination of values issues related to the topic. For example:

A scientist has invented a way to destroy the pests that attack corn. Working in her laboratory, she developed a brand-new, genetically engineered microbe, a new form of life that she wants to release into the environment. The scientist claims that this form of life will be perfectly safe for us, that it will only be destructive for cutworms, a common corn pest.

The Environmental Protection Agency (EPA) has a different opinion. The EPA is not sure that the new microbe will be safe. It has told the scientist that she will not be able to release the microbe into the environment. The scientist is very upset. She has spent years and years on her experiments and a great deal of research money has gone into them.

On the one hand, it is a good idea to fight the pests that attack corn. On the other hand, releasing a new form of life into our environment might have serious consequences.

- Whom should we believe? How should we try to figure this out?
- If you could vote, whose side would you be on? What are your ideas?
- Does the way a person votes depend on what that person has "at stake" for him or her? What do you think about that?
  6. By suggesting students do some background reading from library books and the Internet about plants, seeds, and the conditions under which they grow.

Creating

One or more of the following types of activities may bring these studies to a more creative culmination:

The students may:

1. build a large wooden planter to plant their own vegetable garden in the corner of the schoolyard.
2. discover the art in certain vegetables by painting or drawing pictures of vegetables, such as cabbage leaves, eggplants, mushrooms, and a stalk of celery.
3. work in pairs to find out what they can about raisins, drawing a series of pictures to show how raisins start from seeds and wind up in cereal bowls.
4. plan a vegetarian lunch menu or collect recipes for a cookbook featuring vegan dishes.

ACTIVITY 22: SEEDS FROM FRUIT; FRUIT FROM SEEDS

In this center, students collect seeds from different fruits and vegetables, some familiar and some less familiar. They are asked to observe, classify, and interpret data with respect to how plants reproduce and form new plants.

Activity Card

- Use the materials in this center to find out what you can about seeds. For example, where are seeds found? How do they get there? What do they look like?
- How are seeds of different fruits and vegetables similar? How are they different? What are some of their characteristics?
- Observe as many seeds as you can and record your findings.
- Make some more observations and decide how these seeds might be classified. Set up some groups and sort the seeds into the groups. Then give each group a name.

You may have some other ideas for conducting investigations with these seeds. Try your ideas and see what you can discover.

Materials

A variety of locally available fruits and vegetables, such as apple, orange, lemon, grapefruit, grapes, cherries, plum, watermelon, banana, string beans, green pepper, avocado, squash, peas in pods; containers for planting, such as paper cups, aluminum cans, milk cartons, egg cartons, plastic pots; potting soil, water; markers, such as Popsicle sticks or tongue depressors; several knives; paper towels; magnifying lenses; rulers and meter sticks.

Thinking Operations Emphasized

Observing; comparing; classifying; suggesting hypotheses; examining assumptions; interpreting data; designing investigations; making decisions.

Big Ideas

Seeds are produced in the fruit of some plants. New plants are germinated from these seeds. Some fruits of plants (seeds) are edible by humans.

Notes to the Teacher

- This activity would make a good follow-up to Activity 21, Growing Plants from Seeds. Every student working in the center may have his or her own seeds to grow. If sharp knives are to be used in cutting fruits and vegetables, students should be cautioned in advance about their use. In the event that some seeds do not sprout, it's a good idea to examine this in the Debriefing.

Debriefing

Some questions that might be used in Debriefing to advance students' inquiries are suggested below.

- What observations did you make about the seeds you found?
- In what ways were the seeds alike? How were they different?
- In what ways are vegetable seeds similar to fruit seeds? How are they different?
- What do you suppose seeds are for? What hypotheses can you suggest?
- How might you classify these seeds? What kinds of groups could be set up?

Extending

After the students have had ample opportunity to carry out initial investigations with seeds, their inquiries may be extended in one or more of the following ways:

1. By adding other seeds to the center, such as dandelion seed heads, tree seeds (fir cones, chestnuts, "helicopter" seed pods from maple trees), packaged seeds.
2. By adding some starter vegetable plants, such as tomato, green pepper, or squash.
3. By adding new activity cards. For example:
    - Work with a friend. Plant some fruit and vegetable seeds. Label them so that you will have a record of what you planted and when. Observe your plants every day for a month and keep a record of what you did to help them grow and what happened. What differences did you observe in what happened in each of your plants?
    - Work with a friend. Make some predictions about what your plants will look like as they begin to grow. Draw some pictures or diagrams that show shape, color, texture, and size.
4. By raising more challenging questions at later Debriefings. For example:
    - What observations did you make about where seeds come from? What examples can you give?

Category B 165

- What observations did you make about the conditions under which seeds grow? What examples can you give?
- What observations did you make about the length of time it takes for seeds to germinate? What examples can you give?
- Some seeds do not grow after they are planted. How do you explain this? What hypotheses can you suggest?
- Some fruits and vegetables have seeds that are clearly visible. What about fruits and vegetables where the seeds are not visible, like some grapes, eggplants, and carrots? How do new plants grow from them? What are your ideas about that?
- What did you find out about the best way for growing seeds? About planting seeds?
- Some trees, like redwoods, live very long lives. Some plants live very short lives. How do you explain those differences in the length of lives of plants? What hypotheses can you suggest?

5. By suggesting students do some background reading in library books and on the Internet.
6. By raising questions that call for the examination of values issues related to the topic. For example:
   - To what extent should farmers be permitted to use pesticides in controlling the pests that attack fruits and vegetables in their growing stages?
   - What might be some consequences to the farmer (storekeeper, consumer, and children) of a ban on pesticides?
   - If you wanted to avoid eating fruits and vegetables that have been sprayed with pesticides, what might you do? What are your ideas about this? What examples can you give to support your ideas?
   - Some areas have their own organic farms. But the prices for the fruits and vegetables grown organically are higher than those in the supermarket. Despite that, should we buy only organic foods? Where do you stand on those issues?
   - Some builders want to cut down very old trees that are still healthy, to make room for new housing. Should they be allowed to do that? What do you see as both sides of the argument? Whose side are you on?

Creating

When the investigations with seeds have come to their natural conclusion, the students may culminate these studies with some more creative endeavors. For example, they may:

1. Work with partners using seeds gathered from fruits and vegetables to create seed mosaics. This can be done by painting and gluing them to construction paper to create original designs.
2. Work singly or in pairs to create jewelry from seeds. Necklaces, rings, bracelets, headdresses, and belts can be created with string, needle, thread, and painted seeds.
3. Work together to build a planter (see Activity 21) and grow a vegetable garden. This can be a very "fruitful" activity with rich potential for many additional investigations.
4. Work in small groups to plan, prepare, and cook a vegetarian and or fruitarian lunch.

ACTIVITY 23: TINY PLANTS (1): MOLDS

In this activity, the students carry out inquiries into the world of the fungus family, specifically molds. They are asked to record their observations.

Activity Card

- Use the materials in this center to make some observations of mold.
- Try some investigations to see what you can discover about what mold is, how it grows, what it looks like, what it smells like.
- Talk with each other about your observations and then write about them.

Materials

Slices of bread, some cheese, a half container of plain yogurt; containers or plastic bags to keep samples moist; slices of tomato, string beans, green pepper; magnifying lenses; sugar; water. (A flat plastic pan with a layer of soil on which to lay fresh, unmoldy samples could also be used for growing molds as soil already contains the spores of molds. To keep the soil moist, the pan should be covered with plastic wrap.)

Thinking Operations Emphasized

Observing and recording; comparing; suggesting hypotheses; identifying assumptions; designing investigations; making decisions; creating and inventing.

Big Ideas

Molds are plant-like organisms of the fungus family. They are colonies of single-celled microorganisms that usually need dark and damp conditions to grow.

Notes to the Teacher

- This will need some advance preparation to provide samples of items that have already begun to mold as well as items likely to grow mold during the investigations. To encourage mold formation, keep items moist, as drying inhibits mold growth. Good candidates for growing mold are foods without preservatives—breads, dairy products, fruits, and vegetables. Place in plastic bags (to keep moisture in), outside of the refrigerator, and mold should begin to form in a few days. Students should be cautioned about washing their hands after their work with molds and to keep their hands away from the mouth when handling mold.

Debriefing

Some questions that might be raised during Debriefing to encourage reflection include the following:

- What observations did you make about mold? About how it looks? About how it smells?
- What observations did you make about how mold grows?
- What differences did you observe in the different molds? What were some similarities?
- Where do you suppose mold comes from? What hypotheses can you suggest to explain it?
- What kinds of foods are more likely to grow mold? What makes you think that's true?
- What kinds of foods are less likely to grow mold? What makes you think that's true?
- What do you suppose helps mold grow? What in your inquiries led you to that idea?
- What do you suppose would prevent mold from growing? What examples can you give to support those ideas?

Extending

The initial investigations might be extended in one or more of the following ways:

1. By introducing new foods that depend on special varieties of mold for flavor and texture, such as blue cheese, Gorgonzola, and Camembert.
2. By introducing several dried foods, such as dried mushrooms, tomatoes, prunes, raisins, and apricots.

3. By introducing a microscope so that molds can be examined much more closely. Microscopes are usually available among the science supplies of most elementary schools. If not, try borrowing one from a neighboring high school.
4. By introducing new activity cards to the center. For example:
   - Design an investigation that will allow you to observe the effects of moisture and dryness on the growth of molds.
   - Design an investigation that will allow you to observe the effects of darkness and light on the growth of molds.
   - Design an investigation that will allow you to observe the effects of temperature on the growth of molds.
   - Design an investigation that will allow you to observe the life cycle of a mold. Record your observations.
5. By suggesting background readings from the library or the Internet about mold and other microorganisms.
6. By raising new questions in later Debriefings. For example:
   - What observations of mold did you make under the microscope? How did these differ from the observations made with the naked eye?
   - How do these organisms compare with plants? How are they alike? What are some differences?
   - How are these organisms affected by the changes in growth conditions? What examples can you give to support your ideas?
   - What examples can you give of how microorganisms are useful to us? How are they harmful to us?
   - Why do you suppose the dried foods did not develop mold? What hypotheses can you suggest to explain it? How might you test those ideas?

Creating

Some of the following activities may be used to bring these inquiries to a more creative conclusion:

1. Students may be asked to find molds at home and bring them to class. They should be cautioned about handling them.
2. Students may work in small groups to design investigations in which mold may be grown more quickly.
3. Students may work cooperatively or alone to illustrate the molds they have observed through the microscope.
4. Students may work cooperatively or alone to write stories about mold, for example, Slime and Mold; The Mold that Took Over the Breadbox; The Mold that Nobody Loved; The Mold that Was Afraid of Sunlight.

ACTIVITY 24: TINY PLANTS (2): YEAST

In this investigative play, students carry out inquiries in the world of microorganisms—specifically yeast. They are asked to record their observations.

Activity Card

- Use the materials in this center to find out what you can about this microorganism called yeast.
- Try some investigations to see what you can discover about what yeast is, what it looks like, how it grows, and what it smells like. Talk together and then write about your observations.

Materials

Slices of bread of several different varieties; yeast cakes, packets of dried yeast; sugar, honey, molasses, water, apple juice; containers and bowls of various sizes; flour (whole wheat, white enriched, rye), magnifying lenses.

Thinking Operations Emphasized

Observing and recording; comparing; examining assumptions; suggesting hypotheses; making decisions; designing investigations.

Big Ideas

Yeast is a microorganism (structure that cannot be seen with the naked eye) that needs a temperate climate (not too hot or too cold) to grow. Yeast feeds on sugar.

Notes to the Teacher

- Cakes of live yeast can generally be purchased at a local bakery, although a special request must usually be made of the baker. While packets of dried yeast are found on the shelves of most supermarkets, it is considerably cheaper to buy dry yeast in bulk, at a neighborhood health food shop or granary. Dry yeast is best kept for long periods in the refrigerator, and it's a good idea to check the "expiration date" on packets as these tiny organisms do not live forever.

Debriefing

Some questions that might be used during Debriefing to promote student reflection include the following:

- What observations did you make about yeast?
- What are some differences between the cakes of yeast and dry yeast?
- What are some differences you found in the way yeast grows?
- Why do you suppose these microorganisms are called "tiny plants"? What ideas do you have about it?
- How is yeast like other fungi? How is it different?
- How is yeast like other plants? How is it different?

Extending

After the students have had opportunities to carry out investigative play with yeast, their inquiries may be extended in one or more of the following ways:

1. By adding new materials to the center such as a microscope, and some sourdough.
2. By introducing new activity cards that call for designing new projects or investigations. For example, Design an investigation:
   - that will allow you to observe the best conditions for growing yeast
   - that will allow you to observe the effect of heat and cold on yeast growth
   - that will allow you to observe the effect of light and darkness on yeast growth
   - that will allow you to observe the kinds of foods yeast eats
   - that will allow you to observe the life cycle of yeast
   - that will allow you to observe the way yeast works in our food
   - that will allow you to observe the gas bubbles produced by growing yeast
3. By asking more challenging questions in later Debriefing. For example:
   - What observations did you make about the best conditions for growing yeast? What examples can you give to support these ideas?
   - What observations did you make about the effect of heat and cold on yeast growth? What hypotheses can you suggest to explain why yeast does not grow in cold water?
   - Under what conditions does yeast die? How do you know that is true?
   - How is the life cycle of yeast different from and similar to the life cycle of other plants?

- How is it possible for yeast to be brought back to life from its dry state? What are your ideas?
- What other living things can be dried and reconstituted? What examples can you think of?
- What do we have to know about yeast in order to make it work for us in our food?

4. By suggesting students do background reading about yeast and other microorganisms in library books and the Internet.
5. By raising questions that call for the examination of values issues related to the topic. For example:

Yeast is a wonderful organism. It can be dried out, preserved for a long time, and then reconstituted. One day, there may be a way to dry out other forms of life and reconstitute them later on.

- Should we try to do this? If so, what forms of life would benefit from this treatment? What forms of life should be exempt? What are your thoughts on this? What do you see as some potential consequences of your ideas?

Creating

When the students' interest in the investigations seems to be nearing an end, some culminating activities in more creative realms might be enjoyed. For example:

1. Baking bread is natural! If the students begin early in the day, you can have warm bread for lunch. Several cookbooks provide dozens of excellent recipes as does the Internet.
2. The students can make their own sourdough. Some bread books include a sourdough starter recipe. Starters can be purchased (dry) from health food stores, but it is probably more interesting for students to discover that these spores already exist in the air.
3. Making sourdough pancakes.
4. Writing stories: My Microorganism Garden; The Yeast That Saved the World; Yeasties Beasties and Other Tiny Critters.

ACTIVITY 25: FLOWERS

In this activity, students examine flowers and study their parts and their structures.

Activity Card

> - Study the flowers in the center and talk with each other about what you have observed.
> - Make a list of your observations.
>
> You may have some other ideas for carrying out investigations with these flowers. Try your ideas and see what you can discover.

Materials

At least four different kinds of flowers (e.g., daisy, chrysanthemum, carnation, rose—whatever can be easily acquired in the neighborhood market or garden); several pairs of scissors; a knife; several magnifying lenses; white paper.

Thinking Operations Emphasized

Observing and recording; comparing; classifying and interpreting data; imagining and creating; making decisions; identifying assumptions.

Big Ideas

Flowers are parts of plants and come in a variety of shapes, colors, and smells. Flowers become "fruit bodies" that produce the seeds used to create new plants.

Notes to the Teacher

- Inexpensive bunches of assorted flowers may be found in many supermarkets. Supermarket managers may be willing to unload yesterday's wilted posies at reduced rates for school use.

Debriefing

Questions to promote students' reflection about flowers asked during Debriefing include the following:

- What observations did you make about these flowers?
- What observations did you make about the different parts of flowers?
- What were some of the differences you observed about the different flowers?
- What were some of the similarities?

- In what ways might these flowers be classified? What kinds of groups might be set up?

Extending

There are many ways in which the flower studies may be extended. For example:

1. Other flowers can be brought in and examined and compared.
2. Flowers can be compared with nonflowering plants.
3. Scents of flowers can be compared.
4. Illustrations of different flowers can be collected from old calendars, magazines, newspapers, and a scrapbook made of flowers that have been classified according to students' criteria.
5. Students can do background reading about flowers from the library and the Internet.
6. More challenging questions may be raised in later Debriefing. For example:
   - Why do you suppose some flowers have a pleasant smell and others have no smell?
   - What do you suppose is the purpose of the scent of flowers? What hypotheses can you suggest?
   - Suppose you wanted to grow some flowers. How would you go about doing that?
   - What have you observed about the life cycles of some flowers?
   - Why do you suppose flowers need bees? What theories do you have about that?
7. Questions that call for students to examine values issues related to the topic may also be included. For example:
   - Is it more important to use our land to grow flowers or food? What are your thoughts?
   - In a part of Washington state called Skagit Valley, acres and acres of land are devoted to the growing of tulips. During tulip season, many tourists drive down to see the fields of tulips. What, in your opinion, is so cool about looking at fields of tulips?
   - The local park is trying to raise money to build a large flower garden. Some parents are opposed to this, saying that the park is supposed to be for children to play. Other people say that flowers are so beautiful, a big flower garden should be created for everyone's pleasure. What is your view of this? What are your opinions?
   - How come we take flowers to people who are sick? How do flowers cheer them up? What are your thoughts on it?

Creating

As the students move from their investigations into more creative activities, they may be asked to try one or more of the following:

- Growing flowers from seeds, including building or finding materials to serve as flowerpots; purchasing or otherwise acquiring seeds; planting seeds; providing hospitable growing conditions, including sunlight, water, and warmth; observing and recording growth; hypothesizing about the lack of germination of some seeds.
- Drying and pressing flowers.
- Collecting pictures of flowers and classifying them.
- Drawing pictures of flowers and labeling parts.
- Writing poems about flowers.
- Making artificial flowers with colored tissue paper and pipe cleaners.
- Visiting a nursery or greenhouse to study mass production of flowers.

ACTIVITY 26: FOODS: HOW FOODS CHANGE

In this center, the students study food, especially the conditions under which food changes and how the changes occur. They are asked to record their observations.

Activity Card

- Use the materials in this center to conduct some investigations to see how foods change.
- Make some observations of what happens to certain foods over certain intervals of time.
- Talk with each other about your observations and write what you discovered.

You may have some other ideas for investigating the changes that take place in foods. Try out your ideas and see what discoveries you can make.

Materials

Small quantities of some of the following foods: butter, apple, salt, egg, milk, bread, potato, tomato, orange, sugar, corn flakes, dry legumes, rice crackers, flour, tea, coffee beans, cheese; pot or pan; hot plate; scales; magnifying lens; spoons, jars.

Thinking Operations Emphasized

Observing and recording; classifying; comparing; designing investigations; making decisions; summarizing; evaluating; imagining and creating; suggesting hypotheses; identifying assumptions.

Big Ideas

Certain foods undergo change when they are heated, dried, processed, preserved, combined with other foods, cooked, fermented, allowed to decay.

Notes to the Teacher

- No specific food is mandatory for these inquiries—practically whatever is easily available in one's refrigerator or cupboard may be used. Several food groups should, however, be represented. There might be a small amount of mess in handling the food, and newspaper on the tables is a good precaution. Students should also be cautioned about the proper use of the hot plate and warned not to ingest any of the food samples.

Debriefing

The following questions may be helpful in promoting thoughtful reflection about the changes seen in foods. For example:

- What observations did you make about the foods?
- What observations did you make about how the foods could change? How did some of the changes occur?
- What kinds of changes did you see in the apple? Potato? Orange?
- How were these changes alike? How were they different?
- How do you explain these changes? What hypotheses can you suggest?
- What kinds of changes did you see in the rice? beans? How can that be explained?
- In what ways could you change the egg? the salt? the flour? the bread? the tea? the sugar? What are your ideas about this?
- What observations did you make about some of the conditions that change foods? How does that work? What hypotheses can you suggest to explain it?
- Why do you suppose an apple, left overnight on the table, changes, but rice does not? How can that be explained? What hypotheses can you suggest?

Extending

The students' inquiry into the conditions under which foods change may be extended in one of several ways. For example:

1. By adding new foods to the center: yogurt, bean sprouts, mushrooms, yeast, fish, tofu, lettuce leaves, banana, and onion.
2. By introducing new activity cards. For example:
   - What happens to bread (apple, potato, egg, fish, etc.) if left on a plate, on the table, for three days? Observe and record your findings. How do you explain what happened? How do you explain the differences seen among the foods you studied?
   - What happens to bread (apple, potato, egg, fish, etc.) if left on a plate in the refrigerator for three days? Observe and record your findings. How do you explain what happened? How do you account for the differences between the changes in the food outside and inside the refrigerator?
   - Figure out as many ways as you can to change the composition of these foods. Conduct some investigations to test some of your ideas.
   - What happens to bread (apple, potato, egg, fish, etc.) when it is heated or cooked? Conduct some investigations and record your findings.
3. By raising more challenging questions in later Debriefings. For example:
   - What observations did you make about foods that change rapidly? What theories can you suggest that might explain those rapid changes?
   - What observations did you make about foods that change slowly? What theories can you suggest that might explain the slowness of the changes?
   - What observations did you make about foods that hardly changed at all? What theories can you suggest that might explain this?
   - What different kinds of changes did you observe? How do these changes occur?
   - In what ways could these foods be grouped? What categories could be set up? What other foods might be added to each of the groups in your classification?
   - In what ways could changes in food be speeded up? How might they be slowed down? What are your ideas about this?
   - What do you suppose causes the brown spots in banana? apple? potato? What hypotheses can you suggest?
   - What makes mold? Where does it come from? What is it made of? What are your ideas?

- What makes food smell bad? What are your ideas about how this happens?
- What other things change their compositions besides food? What examples can you give of other things that change?
4. By suggesting students do some background reading in library books or the Internet.
5. By raising questions that call for the examination of value issues related to the topic. For example:

Some foods are packaged so that they will have a longer shelf life. It means that certain chemicals are added to the food to preserve them for longer periods. Many processed foods contain small amounts of these chemical additives.

Some people believe that these additives are bad for you and that you should stay away from them. Other people claim that the amounts of chemicals are so small that you couldn't really be harmed by eating them.

- Where do you stand on this issue? What foods do you eat that contain chemical additives? What foods contain no additives? How do you know that is true?
- What are your beliefs about the kinds of foods that are good for you? What data support your ideas?

Creating

The following types of creative activities showing how foods change may be used to culminate the food inquiries.

- Making butter
- Making peanut butter (Caution! Check to see if any students have peanut allergies!)
- Making noodles
- Making bread
- Making popcorn
- Making ice cream

ACTIVITY 27: SKINS

In this center, the students carry out investigative play with a variety of skins in order to make observations of their properties and functions.

Activity Card

- Use the materials in this center to conduct some investigations about skin.
- In what ways are the skins alike? How are they different?
- Make some observations about strength, texture, hardness, or softness, edibility, color, shape, smell, and function.
- Talk with each other about your observations, and write your observations.

You may have other ideas about how these skins may be studied. Try out your ideas and see what you can find out.

Materials

A variety of skins, including fruit skins (apple, banana, orange, grape, mango, coconut, pear, melon), vegetable skins (potato, onion, carrot, squash, tomato), nut skins (peanut, almond, sunflower seeds, filberts), and animal skins (pieces of leather, molted reptile skins, pieces of fur); small knives; magnifying lenses; microscope.

Thinking Operations Emphasized

Observing; comparing; classifying and interpreting data; examining assumptions; suggesting hypotheses; designing investigations; making decisions; evaluating.

Big Ideas

Animal skins function primarily for protection. Skin is a growing organ. It has color (pigmentation) and comes in layers; it may have hair, feathers, or scales.

Notes to the Teacher

- A few simple precautions will avoid any messy residue from this activity. Newspaper spread on the table prior to investigative play should be all that is needed. Discarded food skins can be stored in a large plastic container for use in Replay (though the skins may be the worse for wear) or to recycle as compost.
- Acquiring molted reptile skins may prove more challenging, unless your school is in or near a desert area, where such molting is a fairly common occurrence. The high-school science teacher might be helpful. Failing such acquisition, the play will not seriously suffer.

- ONCE AGAIN CAUTION SHOULD BE TAKEN TO DISCOVER IF ANY STUDENT HAS ANY ALLERGIES RELATED TO ANY OF THESE MATERIALS.

Debriefing

The following questions are examples of what might be asked during Debriefing to promote further reflection about skins:

- What observations did you make about skin in general?
- More specifically, what observations did you make about the strength of skin? The texture? Hardness or softness? Color? Edibility? Shape? Smell?
- What kinds of living things have no skin? Can you give some examples?
- In what ways might these skins be grouped?
- What do you suppose skin is good for? What hypotheses can you suggest?
- What differences did you find between animal skins and plant skins?
- Why do you suppose some animals shed their skins? How is this done? What are your ideas about it?
- Which skins are more attractive? What is there about them that makes them attractive? What are your ideas about it?

Extending

The investigative play with skins might be extended in one or more of the following ways:

1. By adding new material to the center. For example: feathers; hair; fish skins (smelly!); chicken skin, chicken feet (available in Chinese markets where chickens are sold); coconut skin; crab, shrimp, oyster, or mussel shells.
2. By introducing new activity cards. For example:
   - Compare feathers and leathers. How are they alike? How are they different?
   - Conduct some investigations to see what differences can be found in hair and skin.
   - Compare the shells of marine animals with skin. How are these coverings alike? How are they different?
   - Conduct some investigations to see how your skin is different from or similar to chicken skin, banana skin, and onion skin. Record your findings.
3. By raising more challenging questions during later Debriefings. For example:
   - What do you suppose skin is made of? What examples can you give to support your ideas?
   - Why do you suppose you find moisture on your skin? How do you explain how it gets there?

- Why do you suppose human and some animal skins have hair? What theories do you have about it?
- Why do you suppose human skins come in different colors? How do you explain it? What are your ideas?
- What makes the skin wrinkle? How do you explain this? What are your ideas?
- How does skin heal when it is cut? How do you explain it? What are your ideas?

4. By suggesting that students do some background reading about skins in library books and on the Internet.
5. By raising questions that allow for the examination of values issues. For example:

Some merchants carry out a very lucrative business trading in animal skins. They find out which skins are the most desirable—that is, which ones will be worth the most money—and then they find ways to acquire those skins. Some of this trading is illegal, but much of it is a legal business. Look at some of the smart shops in town. You will see shoes made of alligator skins, ladies purses made of eel skins, coats made of fox skins, and jackets made of seal skins. You can even buy skins on eBay.

- Every one of these articles costs an animal a life. Is it worth it? Where do you stand on this issue?
- What clothing of your own comes from animal skins?
- Are there alternatives? What would be some consequences if we decided not to use animal skins to keep us warm? What are your ideas?

Creating

Some suggestions for ways in which the investigations with skin might be creatively concluded include asking the students to:

1. Work in pairs and think of twenty good uses for animal skins.
2. Write some idioms about skin ("the skin of my nose," the "skin of my teeth," etc.)
3. Work in pairs to create ten metaphors about skin, for example, "skin as smooth as silk" or "a skin as wrinkled as an old eggplant."

ACTIVITY 28: BONES AND SHELLS

In this activity, the students carry out investigative play with bones and shells to observe and compare the properties and structures of internal and external skeletal structures.

Activity Card

- Use the materials in this center to make some observations about bones and shells.
- What differences do you see in the bone samples? What similarities?
- What differences do you see between the bones and the shells? What similarities?
- Conduct some investigations to find out about the differences in hardness, texture, smoothness, flexibility, weight, strength, breakability, and size.
- Talk with each other about what you have found and write about your observations.

Materials

A variety of bone samples (chicken, fish, beef, pork, lamb); models or photographs of skeletal structures (dog, cat, lizard, fish, etc.); photographs or models of human skeletons; a variety of shells from assorted shellfish (crab, lobster, clam, oyster, scallops, mussels); a turtle shell; magnifying lenses; scales; rulers.

Thinking Operations Emphasized

Observing and recording; comparing; suggesting hypotheses; gathering and interpreting data; designing investigations; making decisions; evaluating; identifying assumptions.

Big Ideas

The function of an internal skeleton is to maintain structure and stability and provide for motility. External skeletons function to protect the animal as well.

Notes to the Teacher

- Collecting an assortment of bones and shells may require some thought, advance planning, and legwork. Try the local butcher for animal bones (beef, lamb, and pork). Or simply save the bones from a meat or fish meal. If you do not live in a coastal area, mollusks and crustaceans are perhaps better acquired through the local fishmonger. The Internet and the local and school libraries are good sources for photographs of human and animal

skeletons. Try the high-school biology teacher for bone loans. As a last resort, these items can be purchased from biological supply companies, if your school has a budget for such extravagance.
- Check to see if any student has shellfish allergies before including these samples in the center.

Debriefing

The following types of questions contribute to a more thoughtful examination of skeletal structures. They should, however, be used as appropriate.

- What observations did you make of these bones and shells?
- What observations did you make about the properties of bones (hardness, texture, flexibility, weight, size, etc.)?
- What differences did you observe between bones and shells? What similarities?
- What differences did you observe among the bone samples?
- What observations did you make about the properties of shells?
- What observations did you make about how bones are connected? About how shells are connected?
- What do you suppose are some functions of bones? Of shells? How do you know that is true?

Extending

After the students have had sufficient opportunities to engage in investigative play with these materials, their inquiries may be extended in one or more of the following ways:

1. By adding new materials to the center, such as photographs of skeletons. Photographs of crustaceans and mollusks in natural habitats may also be included.
2. By introducing new activity cards.
3. By raising more challenging questions in later Debriefing. For example:
   - In what ways might these bones and shells be classified?
   - How might you tell about the kind of animal this was? What evidence are you using to figure that out?
   - How do bones mend themselves when they are broken? What are some theories that you have to explain?
   - What kinds of animals have no bones? In what ways are they different from animals with bones?
   - How are bones different from (like) the skeletal frameworks of buildings?

4. By suggesting students do some background reading from library books and the Internet.
   5. By raising questions that call for students to examine some values issues related to the topic. For example:

Margaret wears a bone from a rabbit's foot around her neck. She says that it is her good luck charm and that whenever she wears it, she is bound to have good luck. What's more, if she should forget her lucky charm, she is bound to get into trouble.

- What are your ideas about this? Do bones make good luck charms? Do you have other ideas about lucky pieces?
- What is your opinion of how good luck comes to you? What examples can you give to support your ideas?

Creating

There are several ways to bring this investigative play to a creative culmination. For example:

1. Whole fish skeletons, in particular, make very good rubbings and students can work in pairs to do this art activity. Rubbings can be made by placing lightweight paper over a well-cleaned fish skeleton, then rubbing gently with charcoal or very soft pencil.
2. Students may work in teams to draw pictures of the skeletons of cats, rabbits, frogs, snakes, and other animals.
3. Students may work together to draw pictures of the external skeletal structures of lobsters, crabs, shrimps, and crayfish.
4. Students may invent poems, songs, or write stories about bones. For example: The Skeleton in My Closet; My Broken Bone; The Case of the Missing Bone.

ACTIVITY 29: SKELETONS

In this center, the students work with fish skeletons to make some observations about skeletal structures.

Activity Card

- Use the materials in this center to make some observations about skeletons.
- Look sharply. Try to notice everything you can about these bones.

> - Talk with each other about what you observe and then write your observations.
>
> You may have some other ideas for investigations with these materials. Try them and see what you can discover.

Materials

Three or four whole fish skeletons (salmon, flounder, carp, sole—any available local fish is appropriate); parts of fish skeletons; newspaper; paper towels.

Thinking Operations Emphasized

Observing; comparing; classifying and interpreting data; summarizing; applying principles; making decisions; imagining and creating; suggesting hypotheses.

Big Ideas

Internal skeletons are made up of arrangements of bones that vary among different animals. They maintain structure and stability and help mobility.

Notes to the Teacher

- Acquiring fish skeletons requires personal ingenuity and the cooperation of fish-eating friends. Ask your local fish store for the discards of filleted fish. Soaking the bones in a mild soap and water solution dilutes strong odors.

Debriefing

The following types of questions are more likely to promote thoughtful reflection about the big ideas. They should be used as appropriate.

- What observations did you make about skeletons?
- What observations did you make about the locations of the larger bones?
- What observations did you make about the locations of the smaller bones?
- What observations did you make about how the bones are connected?
- How is one particular skeletal structure like or different from another?
- What observations did you make about the texture of the bones?
- What do you suppose bones are made of? How do you know that is true?

Extending

After the students have had ample time to work with the materials, their inquiries may be extended in one or more of the following ways:

1. By adding new materials to the center, such as other kinds of skeletal structures or photographs of skeletons.
2. By introducing new activity cards.
3. By raising more challenging questions in later Debriefings. For example:
   - What kinds of animals have skeletal structures? How do you know that is true?
   - What kinds of animals do not have skeletal structures? How do you know that is true?
   - How do you suppose bones help us move? What are your ideas?
   - How do bones break? How do they mend? How do you know that is true?
4. By suggesting students do some background reading about skeletons in library books and on the Internet.

Creating

When interest in the investigations seems to be diminishing, it might be helpful to integrate these studies with other areas of the curriculum. For example:

1. Prepare some fish and chicken dishes for an impromptu class lunch. After boiling all the bones with bleach for a few hours and drying them thoroughly, the students may work in small groups to try to reconstruct the skeletons.
2. The students may use clay to create carapaces of turtles.
3. The students may try to feel the bones in their arms, legs, and heads and draw some pictures of those bones.
4. The students may feel the way the bones in their fingers move and draw some pictures of how those bones are connected in their hands.
5. The students may try to imagine what their own skeletons might look like and draw some pictures of how they envision their own skeletons.

ACTIVITY 30: BIRDS

The investigative play in this center emphasizes extensive observations of birds in their natural habitat and the recording of those observations. To do this requires the construction of a bird feeder and so this activity has two parts.

Activity Card (1)

- Use the materials in this center to design and build a bird feeder that can hang outside your classroom window. When the feeder is finished and hung in place with a supply of birdseed, you will be able to observe and study the birds that come to feed.
- You will need to decide what type of feeder will allow you to see the birds easily, and that you can take down when necessary to refill the birdseed.

Activity Card (2)

- Place your feeder in a position so that you may observe the birds easily.
- Work together as you watch the feeder for a long time. What observations can you make about the birds that come? Their distinctive markings? How they feed? When they come? Their individual and group behavior? The shape of head and beak? Their sizes? Their different sounds? How they communicate with each other? When they come to the feeder?
- Talk to each other about your observations and keep a record of what you have found.

Materials

Several good size pieces of wood (redwood, cedar, pine—or whatever is easily available and not too hard for students to saw through); nails, hammer, saw, pliers, screwdriver; thin wire; sturdy cord or rope; three or four lengths of ½-inch doweling; illustrations of bird feeders; binoculars; birdseed.

Thinking Operations Emphasized

Designing projects; making decisions; observing; comparing; classifying; collecting and organizing data; suggesting hypotheses; evaluating; making decisions; creating and imagining.

Big Ideas

Birds are generally characterized by their wings, feathers, two feet, and ability to fly. There are many different types of birds; they differ in color, shape, size, their songs, and ways of flight. Birds may live on land or water.

Notes to the Teacher

- At first glance, this activity is likely to seem more suited to suburban or rural school settings, where a greater variety of birds is likely to be found. But there are birds in cities too, and there is a good chance that they will come to the feeder once they have discovered its existence. This may take some time.
- Note that the activity is carried out in two parts. There is hands-on science involved in the construction of the feeder. A library book may be included showing different types of feeders. Students may, of course, wish to create their own designs and this should be encouraged. There is much to be learned from any creative attempt.
- There is also the observation part of the activity. Binoculars are important but not imperative. Once birds start to come there will be much for students to do in observing and recording what they see.
- Birdseed, available in hardware stores, pet shops, and dollar stores, is inexpensive. Students may earn money or do some fundraising to buy birdseed.
- Once the birds have discovered the feeder, it is important that students continue to stock it with feed, as the birds may become dependent on it, especially in very cold seasons.

Debriefing

The following types of questions are offered as examples of what may be asked during Debriefing to promote thoughtful inquiry. They address both the building and observation stages of the activity.

- What kind of feeder did you decide to build? Why do you think that was a good design?
- Where will it be placed? What makes that a good location?
- How will it be refilled when it is empty? What plans are being made for that?
- How will birds get access to the feeder? How will that work?
- What kinds of birds have you observed? How does this differ at different times of the day?
- What observations have you made about their colors? Size? Feathers? Shape of their heads? Beaks? The way they feed? Their sounds? Their individual and group behavior?
- Which birds have you observed feeding together? How would you describe their behavior?
- How do birds communicate with each other? What theories do you have about that?

- What are some differences you have observed in birds of different species?
- What observations have you made about how they see? Hear?
- What observations have you made about how they fly?
- How do you suppose the birds found out about the feeder? What hypotheses can you suggest?

Extending

The study of birds may be extended in one or more of the following ways:

1. By introducing photos of water birds for observation and comparison.
2. By introducing new activity cards that extend the study of birds to outside the school.
3. By raising more challenging questions in later Debriefing. For example:
   - Are birds smart? How do you know?
   - What are birds good for? How do you know this? Can you give some examples?
   - How do land birds compare with water birds? What are some similarities? differences?
   - How do birds learn to fly? What are your ideas about this?
   - How do birds learn to build a nest? How do you explain this?
   - Do birds have feelings? How do you know? What examples can you give?
   - How are birds born? How do you know? How are they looked after when they are very young? How do you know that is true?
   - Is it better for birds to be pets in cages, or to be in the wild? What are your ideas? Tell why you have those beliefs.
   - When do birds sing? What theories do you have about that?
   - What different kinds of foods do different birds eat? How do you know this? What accounts for those differences? What hypotheses can you suggest to explain it?
   - What do you know about birds that can talk, like parrots, parakeets, and macaws? How do birds learn to talk? What ideas do you have about that?
4. By raising questions that allow for the examination of some values issues related to the topic. For example:
   a. The zoo in Honolulu has a bald eagle, America's national bird, in a cage, on view for all visitors. The eagle has had its wings clipped, so that it may not fly. In any case, it would not be able to fly because the cage is too small.

      What are your views on birds in cages? Should we keep them in cages so that we may have the pleasure of seeing them? Or shall we let them go free to fly as they wish? What is your opinion of this? Do you have some data to support your opinions?

b. The gull comes to her window every morning. It taps on the window with its beak until she relents and gives it some bread. Then it flies away and returns the next morning for more.

   She is troubled. On the one hand, she wants to give the gull a treat. On the other hand, she worries that the gull will become dependent on her and stop looking for food on its own.

   Where do you stand on humans feeding wild animals? What do you see as some benefits of doing this? What do you see as some negatives?
5. By suggesting that students do some background reading about birds in library books and watching YouTube videos of birds on the Internet.

Creating

There are many creative ways of culminating the study of birds. The students may:

1. Draw illustrations of the birds that have come to the feeder and put them together in a book.
2. Gather and classify pictures of birds.
3. Make papier-mâché birds mounted on a string and suspend them from the ceiling.
4. Make a bird mobile.
5. Learn to imitate bird sounds.

ACTIVITY 31: THE WORLD WIDE WEB

This activity asks students to investigate the many functions of the Internet, how it is used, how it may be used, and its many positive and negative features.

Activity Card

- Use the tablets (and/or laptop or desktop computers) to find out what you can about the Internet.
- What can you discover about how to access information? What can you discover about where information can be located?
- What can you discover about how people can share information with each other?
- What did you discover about how people can communicate with each other from anywhere in the world?

- What other functions does the Internet offer?
- Talk with each other about your discoveries and make some notes about what you found.

Materials

Tablets; desktop computers; laptop computers.

Thinking Operations Emphasized

Observing and recording; suggesting hypotheses; gathering and interpreting data; designing investigations; evaluating; identifying assumptions.

Big Ideas

The Internet is a vast network that connects computers all over the world. Through the Internet people can share information and communicate from anywhere with an Internet connection. It supports communication via social media, electronic e-mail, "chat rooms," newsgroups, and audio and video transmissions. It is also the source of a great deal of misinformation.

Notes to the Teacher

- Obviously these investigations require access to and use of computers—either tablets or desktop or laptop computers. Many students might have their own tablets and they might be encouraged to bring them to class. Some schools have computer labs that might lend their tablets for these inquiries. Although at first glance this may seem more appropriate for middle graders, many younger students already have knowledge and use of their own tablets.

Debriefing

The following questions may serve to promote students' increased awareness of the many uses for computers as well as some of the downsides of promoting disinformation and the abuse of social media.

- What did you find as some of the many ways in which computers can be and are used?
- What, in your view, enables your computer to link up with computers all over the world? What hypotheses can you suggest that enable this to happen?

- What are some of the benefits of the Internet? What are some negative features?
- In what ways does the Internet allow for gathering a lot of information? Which search engines, in your opinion, are better at doing this?
- How, in your view, did computers help us to learn during the months when schools were closed? How effective did you consider online learning to be for you? What were some of the advantages? disadvantages?
- When you discover something on the Internet, like advice, or information about a topic, how do you know what you find is true? How do you determine the accuracy of that information? What are your ideas about it?

Extending

After the students have had sufficient opportunities to carry out investigations with their computers and tablets, their inquiries may be extended in one or more of the following ways:

1. By adding new activity cards to the center. For example:
   - Use your computer or tablet to locate information about any topic that you choose. Work together and try to determine how accurate that information is.
   - Working together, make a list of some of the worst examples of bad information that is found on the Internet.
   - Use your computer to locate the ways in which social media is used to publish blog posts, videos, and photos. Talk together and try to determine the advantages and disadvantages of how social media is being used.
2. By raising more challenging questions in later Debriefing. For example:
   - How, in your view, might we prevent the spread of disinformation on computer networks? What would you suggest?
   - How might we enable people to be more discriminating about whether information spread on computers is false? What ideas do you have about that?
   - Of what use is Twitter? Tik Tok? What's good about it? What's not so good?
   - Should there be some controls for the spread of harmful videos, photos, and false information? What is your opinion about that?
   - How do you suppose you can use your computer or tablet to control your TV? What ideas do you have about that?
3. By suggesting students do some background reading from library books and from the Internet about its many useful applications and its downsides.
4. By raising questions that call for students to examine some values issues related to the topic. For example:

Cynthia's boyfriend asked her to post some nude photos of her on the Internet. He promised that they would be for him alone and they would be private. She didn't want to disappoint him, so she did that. And her photos went viral.

- What is your opinion of what she did?
- Why do you suppose people can be persuaded to do something that puts them at risk?
- How does a computer serve this kind of function? Who would be interested in seeking out such photos? What are your ideas about that?
- What should Cynthia do now? What would you suggest to her?

Creating

Below are several suggestions offering students opportunities to use their computers in more creative ways. For example:

1. Design a website for your class that describes the work you have been doing with science investigations.
2. Use your tablets to create some "op art" posters.
3. Design an app that will allow you to map the streets you take to go from home to school.
4. Use your computer or tablet to make some photos of a favorite pet and create a photo album of your pet.

ACTIVITY 32: PARACHUTES

In this center, the students work with fabric, string, and weights to make their own parachutes and observe how air creates pressure to keep parachutes afloat.

Activity Card

- Use the materials in the center to make some parachutes.
- Play with the parachutes and make some observations of how they work.
- Talk with each other about what you have observed.

You may have some other ideas for using these materials. Try them and see what happens.

Materials

An assortment of fabrics or other materials (plastic, old bedsheets, gauze, burlap, etc.) cut into squares of various sizes; an assortment of "weights" (clothespins, pieces of wood, nuts, and bolts), string, scissors.

Thinking Operations Emphasized

Observing; collecting and recording data; comparing and interpreting data; suggesting hypotheses; designing investigations; identifying assumptions; applying principles; making decisions; imagining and creating.

Big Ideas

Air is a substance that surrounds us and takes up space. Air exerts pressure, which creates resistance on the surface of a parachute to slow its descent.

Notes to the Teacher

- It may be a good idea to spend time scouting out a safe, high place from which parachutes may be dropped. Discussing some safety rules and reminding students of them before they begin their work is probably a good beginning step.

Debriefing

Some questions that might be raised to promote more thoughtful reflection during Debriefing include some of the following:

- What observations did you make about the parachutes?
- How did you discover that?
- What observations did you make about the parachutes that stayed up in the air longer?
- How do you explain that? What hypotheses can you suggest?
- What observations did you make about the parachutes that fell more quickly? How do you explain that?
- What did you observe about the air in the parachute? How did that work?

Extending

When the students have had sufficient opportunities to conduct their inquiries, their investigations might be extended in one or more of the following ways:

1. By providing new materials in the center, such as much larger pieces of cloth, much heavier "weights," cloths of heavier weight (such as cottons, muslins, and plastic sheeting).
2. By introducing new activity cards. For example:

- Conduct some investigations to see which fabrics make the best parachutes. Record your findings.
  - What kind of work can parachutes do? Try some investigations and see how many things you can discover.
3. By raising more challenging types of questions in later Debriefing. For example:
   - What fabric, in your opinion, makes for better parachutes? How can you tell?
   - What fabric, in your opinion, makes for less successful parachutes? How can you tell?
   - Suppose you wanted to make a parachute to hold a very heavy weight. What would you have to do? How do you know that would work?
   - What makes a parachute work? Where did you get that idea from? How do you know it's true?
   - Based on your work in this center, what are some discoveries you made about air? How did you find that out? How do you know it's true?
   - What other devices work like parachutes? What examples can you give of how they work?
4. By suggesting students do some background reading about parachutes and air pressure in library books and on the Internet.

Creating

When the students have exploited their enthusiasm for making and testing parachutes, they may culminate these investigations with one or more creative tasks. For example:

1. Work with a friend and try to think of as many ways as you can to show how air pressure helps us to do work. Draw some pictures or diagrams of how this happens.
2. Use a half-inch dowel, a piece of sturdy paper, and a straight pin to make a pinwheel. Compare the way your pinwheel works to the way a parachute works.
3. Write a story, "My First Parachute Drop." Imagine how it would feel and write about it.

ACTIVITY 33: TOOLS AND MACHINES

In this center, students examine a variety of small tools and machines to see how they work.

Activity Card

> - Make some observations of the small machines and tools in the center.
> - Work with your group to see if you can figure out how they work. What are some of the important parts?
> - Take one or two of them apart and see if you can put them back together again.
> - What do you suppose they are used for? What are your ideas about that?

Materials

Hammers, screwdrivers, clamps, rulers and tape measures, scissors, saw, can opener, hand magnifiers, calculator, analog and digital clocks, cell phone, grinder, egg beater, room thermometer, pencil sharpener, remote control for TV, bulb baster, timer, toy cars and trucks, other toys that consist of different moveable parts.

Thinking Operations Emphasized

Observing and comparing; suggesting hypotheses; examining assumptions; designing investigations; classifying; applying principles.

Big Ideas

Tools have been invented and designed to aid humans in doing their work. They make it possible for people to move things beyond their strength, move faster and farther than their legs can carry them, and store and analyze more information than their brains can cope with. Tools can, of course, be used for good purposes as well as for evil.

Notes to the Teacher

- The tools listed in the materials section can, of course, be varied, omitted, added to—in other words, include what's easily available to carry out some inquiries about these simple machines. No tool in these inquires is more essential than others. If students are to take things apart, the tools should be disposable, in case things go awry. If some tools of value are included, students should be cautioned that these are not dispensable and need to be treated with care.

Debriefing

Some questions that can be used to promote students' thoughtful reflection about simple machines include some of the following:

- What observations did you make about these tools and simple machines?
- What observations did you make about how they work?
- What observations did you make about how a _____ makes our work easier?
- What did you discover about which parts of the tools were essential? Nonessential? How did you figure that out?
- Which of them do you consider of greater importance to your home? Which of less importance? What makes you think that is true?
- How do you suppose people managed before these tools were invented? What are your ideas about that?

Extending

When students have had sufficient time to carry out initial investigations with these simple tools, their inquiries might be extended in one or more of the following ways:

1. By adding new and different tools to the center. For example: wedge, wheel and axle, pulley, screws, and inclined plane.
2. By introducing new activity cards. For example:
   - How do wedges work? How do they make our work easier? Try some investigations and see what you can discover.
   - How do wheels and axles work? How do they make our work easier? Try some investigations and see what you can discover.
   - How do pulleys work? How do they make our work easier? Try some investigations and see what you can discover.
3. By raising more challenging questions in later Debriefings. For example:
   - Which of these tools do you consider more useful? Less useful? How did you figure that out?
   - Which of these tools are useful in construction work? How did you figure that out?
   - Which of these tools are useful in laboratories? How did you figure that out?
   - How might you classify these tools? What kinds of groups can you set up?
   - What are some other tools that you can think of that are essential to our lives? What examples can you give of their importance?
4. By raising questions that ask students to consider some values issues related to tools. For example:
     A leaf blower is a tool that is used in many communities to gather and collect fallen leaves and bin them to be used in compost. It is an

extremely noisy tool and makes not only a lot of noise but also creates a lot of fumes that smell bad and add pollutants to the air.

But they save a lot of work for those whose job it is to collect the leaves. How should this issue be resolved? Should leaf blowers be banned? What are your ideas about it?
5. By suggesting students do some background reading about tools and machines that work for us, from library books and from the Internet. See, especially, references that provide information about the Industrial Revolution and the invention of the steam engine—examples of tools and machines that changed the world.

Creating

When the students' interest in these initial investigations is winding down, adding some creative activities might be a way to bring this set of inquiries to culmination. For example:

1. Work with a friend and design a tool that will tell you the way the wind is blowing.
2. Work with a partner and design a tool that will add fresh food to your dog's dish in the morning when you want to sleep late.
3. Work with a friend to design a dog exercise machine to use when you don't want to take your dog out. Draw some diagrams of how you think this works.

ACTIVITY 34: WIND SOUNDS

In this center the students work with the materials and use their breath, trying to create and vary sounds. IN CASE OF THE RISK OF CONTAMINATION, THIS ACTIVITY SHOULD BE OMITTED.

Activity Card

- Use the materials in this center to make some musical instruments. Try to make instruments that make different kinds of sounds when you use your breath.
- See how many different kinds of sounds your instruments can make.

You may have other ideas for using the materials in this center. Try them and see what you can discover.

Materials

Cardboard tubing from various paper products; narrow-necked bottles, such as pop bottles, vinegar bottles, syrup bottles, salad dressing bottles; straws, both paper and plastic.

Thinking Operations Emphasized

Observing; comparing, classifying and interpreting data; suggesting hypotheses; applying principles; designing investigations; making decisions; evaluating; inventing and creating.

Big Ideas

Vibrations produce sound. You can make vibrations in a column of air. The sound can be varied by changing the size and shape of the air column.

Notes to the Teacher

- **Students should be cautioned about passing the tubes they have used to each other. If there is a risk of contamination, this activity should be omitted.**

Debriefing

The following types of questions might be raised during initial Debriefing sessions to promote student reflection.

- What observations did you make about the instruments you created?
- What observations did you make about how sounds were created?
- In what ways did your instruments compare with each other? How were they alike? How were they different?
- What observations did you make about how you could vary the sounds on your instruments? What observations did you make about how pitch could be changed? Volume?

Extending

After the students have had ample opportunities to conduct their initial investigations, their inquiries might be extended in one or more of the following ways:

1. By adding new materials to the center. For example: real wind instruments such as simple whistles, recorders, and flutes. Any wind instrument that may be obtained easily can be added.
2. By adding new activity cards.
3. By raising more challenging questions in later Debriefing sessions. For example:
   - How are sounds produced? How do you explain it?
   - What materials contributed to the production of the sounds? How do you know?
   - What materials make better sounds? How do you know?
   - How do these wind instruments compare with stringed instruments? How are they alike? How are they different?
   - How are the "real" instruments like (different from) the ones you made?
4. By suggesting students do some background reading about the history of wind instruments from library books and the Internet.

Creating

When the students seem to have exhausted their interest in these materials, they may enjoy winding up these inquires in more creative ways. For example:

1. Work with one or two friends and using the same instruments you made, form a band. Prepare a piece of music to perform for the class.
2. Work with one or two friends. Sing a song that you have learned in school and try to play it on your instruments.
3. Have a look at some photos of a Didgeridoo. Work with a friend and see if you can make one.

ACTIVITY 35: WIND ENERGY

In this center, the students make pinwheels and observe how they work.

Activity Card

- Use the materials in the center to make some pinwheels.
- Conduct some investigations to find out how pinwheels work.
- How does the design of your pinwheel make it work better? Talk with each other about your ideas. Then write what you observed.

Materials

Heavy bond paper cut in squares measuring 8 × 8 and 12 × 12 inches; ¼-inch dowels cut into 12-inch lengths or pencils with eraser tips; crayons; scissors; straight pins; a model of a pinwheel.

Thinking Operations Emphasized

Observing; comparing and interpreting data; applying principles; suggesting hypotheses; examining assumptions; summarizing; making decisions; imagining and creating.

Big Ideas

Air is a substance that surrounds us and takes up space. When air moves, we feel it as wind. Wind may be used as a source of energy.

Notes to the Teacher

- This is an activity in which limited teacher effort yields major results in promoting conceptual understanding. It is safe, clean, and a lot of fun.
- Crayons or felt-tip pens can be used to make more colorful pinwheels. Several different pinwheels may be made in advance to serve as models for this center.

Debriefing

Questions such as the following may be raised at initial Debriefing sessions to promote further reflection about wind power:

- What observations did you make about how to make a pinwheel turn?
- What observations did you make about the direction in which the pinwheel turned? How do you explain it?
- Suppose you wanted to make it turn in the other direction. How might you arrange for that to happen?
- What observations did you make about the shape of the pinwheel?
- What other shapes could it have and still turn? What do you think about it?

Extending

There are several ways to extend students' inquiries into wind power. For example:

1. By introducing new activity cards. For example:
   - How does the shape of a pinwheel make it turn? Try out different shapes and make some observations of what happens.
   - How does the size of a pinwheel help it turn? Try out different sizes and observe and record what happens.
   - How does the strength of the wind affect the way the pinwheel turns? Try out different wind strengths and observe what happens.
   - In what other ways does wind power work for us? Working in pairs, list the ways in which wind power is used in our lives.
   - In what ways can a pinwheel be made to help something else to work? Invent ways to show how the pinwheel's action may contribute to the working of another machine.
2. By raising more challenging questions in later Debriefing. For example:
   - What other examples can you think of to show how wind can be used as a source of energy?
   - Where do you suppose wind comes from? How do you know that is true?
   - There may be times when the power of the wind can be destructive. What examples can you give of this?
3. By raising questions that allow for the examination of values issues related to the topic. For example:

   Wind can exert a powerful force and this power can be used to generate energy. Some people have been using wind power as an alternative to fossil fuels.
   - What are your views on such an alternative?
   - If wind power is so good and so cheap, why don't more people use it?
   - What are some of its limitations, in your opinion? What are some of its good features? What data back up your ideas?
4. By suggesting students do some background reading on wind power from library books and from the Internet.

Creating

Before leaving this set of inquiries, students may enjoy engaging in more creative tasks, such as:

1. Designing and building a large windmill that will use wind power to do some other work.
2. Designing and building a kite that uses wind power to fly.
3. Inventing a wind-making machine that will create a force of wind when the natural wind dies down.
4. Designing and building a sailboat or a trireme to show how wind power moves boats.

5. Writing a poem about the terrifying power of the wind in a hurricane or tornado.

ACTIVITY 36: SOUNDS WITH STRINGS

In this center, the students work with string and other materials to make observations about vibration and sound.

Activity Card

- Use the materials in this center to make some stringed instruments.
- What different kinds of instruments can be made?
- How are the sounds made on each?
- Try out your ideas and see what happens. Talk together and then write what you observed.

There may be other ways to use the materials in this center. Do you have some other ideas? Try them out and see what you can discover.

Materials

Rubber bands, string, scissors, fine wire, wire cutters, a few cans, several sturdy cardboard containers, wood strips (approximately ¼ × 1¼ inches), stapler.

Thinking Operations Emphasized

Observing; comparing and interpreting data; suggesting hypotheses; examining assumptions; making decisions; creating and imagining; designing investigations.

Big Ideas

Vibrating objects produce sound. Changing the vibrations by using different objects and/or changing their dimensions changes the sound.

Notes to the Teacher

- This is a very safe activity, one that might be implemented at the very beginning of a sciencing program. If wood strips cannot be obtained easily a 12-inch ruler may be substituted for the soundboard to which string or rubber bands may be attached with a stapler.

Debriefing

The following are some questions that might be used during the Debriefing sessions to promote student reflection on the big ideas:

- What kinds of instruments did you make in this center?
- What observations did you make about the way each of your instruments produced sound?
- In what ways did the sounds obtained from the rubber-band instruments and the sounds from the stringed instruments compare? How were they alike? How were they different?
- In what ways were the sounds produced by the wire instruments like the other instruments? How were they different?
- What observations did you make about how the sounds could be changed?

Extending

When the students have had sufficient time to carry out initial investigations, their inquiries might be extended in one or more of the following ways:

1. By adding to the materials in the center, for example: actual musical instruments such as the dulcimer, autoharp, guitar, or ukulele.
2. By introducing new activity cards. For example:
    - Conduct some investigations to show how you might change the sounds that are made.
    - Conduct some investigations to try to figure out how the sounds are made.
3. By raising more challenging questions in later Debriefing. For example:
    - Which of these materials, in your opinion, makes a more beautiful sound? What materials help to produce this sound? How do you explain it?
    - Compare two of the instruments that you made in this center. In what ways are they alike? How are they different?
    - Compare one of the instruments you made with one of the "real" instruments. How are these alike? How are they different?
    - What observations did you make about how pitch is raised or lowered? What observations did you make about how volume is raised or lowered?
    - What observations did you make about what happens to the string, wire, or rubber band when the instrument is played?

4. By raising questions that ask students to examine some values issues related to the topic. For example:

    Roy uses his tablet to listen to some of his favorite music. But he loves to play it so loud, you can hear the music from way down the block. His mother keeps telling him that he is going to make himself deaf and hurt his ears. But Roy loves the loud sounds.

    What are your ideas about kids and grown-ups who enjoy listening to very, very loud music? Is this something we should be worried about? What do you think?

5. By suggesting that students do some background reading about stringed musical instruments in library books or the Internet.

Creating

When the students' interest in these inquiries seems to be exhausted, they may engage in some more creative tasks. For example:

1. Use one or more of the instruments you made to make up a song. Play it for the class.
2. Using any materials you can find for yourself, make your own violin or cello. Use pictures from a library book or the Internet to study the design of the instrument and see if you can create your own version.
3. Form your own band with the various instruments created in this center.

ACTIVITY 37: STATIC ELECTRICITY

In this center, the students work with the materials provided to make observations about static electricity. They are asked to record their observations.

Activity Card

- Use the materials in this center to conduct some investigations about how materials stick together.
- How can you get them to stick together? Which materials are better at this? Which are less good? What observations can you make about how this works?
- Talk with each other about what you have found and then write about your observations.

You may have some other ideas for using these materials. Try your ideas and see what you can discover.

Materials

Small pieces of tissue paper; a rubber comb or a resin rod; a few pieces of fabric (wool, nylon, other synthetics, cotton, silk, fur); balloons.

Thinking Operations Emphasized

Observing; comparing; classifying; interpreting data; designing investigations; suggesting hypotheses; examining assumptions; applying principles; making decisions; imagining and inventing; evaluating.

Big Ideas

Friction produced by rubbing two objects together may create a static charge. Different combinations of materials produce a greater or smaller static charge.

Notes to the Teacher

- This is another safe, clean, and dry activity with a productive yield in terms of student learning. Materials needed are easily found, and teachers who are just beginning their sciencing programs may wish to consider this among their first choices.

Debriefing

Some questions that might be raised at initial Debriefing sessions to promote reflection about the big ideas include the following:

- What observations did you make about the materials in this center?
- What observations did you make about the materials that stuck together? In the ways they stuck together? How do you explain it? What are your ideas?
- What did you have to do to make them stick together? How can you explain how that works?

Extending

The static electricity study may be extended in several ways. For example:

1. By introducing new activity cards. For example:
    - What happens when you rub a piece of wood against an inflated balloon and then place the balloon next to a wall? Does it always work? How do you explain it?

206   *Chapter 14*

- What happens when you rub a comb with a piece of wool and then place your hand over the comb? Does it always work? How do you explain that?
2. By raising more challenging questions in later Debriefing sessions. For example:
    - What are some observations you made about static electricity?
    - What can you do to create static electricity?
    - What kinds of materials help to make static electricity? How does that work?
    - What kinds of materials are useless in making static electricity? How do you explain it?
    - How do you explain the magnetic attraction of the balloon when it is charged? What do you think?
3. By suggesting students do some background reading about static electricity in library books and on the Internet.

Creating

As the students move from their investigations into more creative types of activities, they might like to try one or more of the following:

1. Make a drawing showing how static electricity was produced in your investigations (figure 14.3).

Figure 14.3 *Maya Snow.*

2. Design an investigation to show that static electricity can repel as well as attract.
3. Design an investigation to demonstrate that there is electricity built up in the materials.
4. Write a story about "The Charged Cat."

ACTIVITY 38: KITES

In this center, the students build their own kites and make some observations of how they are constructed and made to fly. They are asked to record their observations.

Activity Card

- Use the materials in the center to design and build your own kite.
- Ask your teacher's permission to take your kites outside to fly. Conduct some investigations and make some observations of how kites fly.
- What helps a kite fly better? What are your ideas? Talk about your observations and write them down.

Materials

Strips of balsa wood or wooden dowels of two lengths (some of 2 feet, others of 1 ½ feet) large sheets of colored tissue paper or light plastic sheeting; string; stapler; glue (nontoxic).

Thinking Operations Emphasized

Observing; collecting and recording data; comparing and interpreting data; examining assumptions; suggesting hypotheses; applying principles; making decisions; creating.

Big Ideas

Many children's toys demonstrate scientific principles. Kites, for example, make use of the wind as an aerodynamic force.

Notes to the Teacher

- Thin strips of wood or dowels can be purchased inexpensively at a local lumber yard or hardware store and cut to specification.

- The glue used should be the firmer-bonding and nontoxic kind rather than the rubber cement or white paste normally found in school supplies. STUDENTS SHOULD BE CAUTIONED ABOUT INHALING GLUE FUMES!
- One or two models of kites may be made or commercially obtained and placed in the center as examples.
- Students should, of course, have the opportunity of taking their kites outside to fly and observe and record what occurs. This activity is probably best done during a windier season.

Debriefing

During initial Debriefing sessions, the following types of questions can be raised to promote reflection about kite construction and kite flying. For example:

- What are some observations you made about building kites?
- What observations were made about the kinds of shapes that kites may have? What did you observe about the materials used in kite building?
- What observations did you make about the relationship between the shape of a kite and the way it flies?
- What do you suppose keeps a kite up in the air? How do you explain it?
- What do you suppose makes a kite fall? How do you explain it?

Extending

When the students have completed their kite building and have had a chance to fly them, their inquiries might be extended in one or more of the following ways:

1. By introducing kites of other shapes (box kites, Japanese wind-sock kites; fish kites) and observing how these fly.
2. By introducing other wind-powered toys (paper airplanes, pinwheels, sailboats, balloon-borne baskets) for making comparisons.
3. By raising more challenging questions following more extensive investigations. For example:
    - Why do you suppose some kites fly better with tails and others do not? How do you explain it?
    - What observations did you make about the purpose of a tail on a kite?
    - How might you measure how high your kite can fly? What are your predictions? How might you test your ideas?
    - How are kites different from (similar to) pinwheels? Windmills? Sailboats? Airplanes?

4. By raising questions that allow for the examination of values issues related to the topic. For example:
   - Are kites safe toys? What makes them safe or unsafe? What are your ideas about this? What data back up your opinions? Can you give some examples to support your ideas?
5. By suggesting students do some background reading about kites and aerodynamics in library books and on the Internet.

Creating

When the students have exhausted their interest in their kite investigations, they might culminate these inquiries in one or more of the following ways:

1. Hold a kite flying contest.
2. Make a classroom or hall display of students' kites.
3. Have the students design a machine to determine the force or speed of the wind.
4. Have the students design and build a wind vane.
5. Have the students write stories about kites, for example: The Greatest Kite Flying Disaster in the History of Kites.

ACTIVITY 39: BOUNCING BALLS

In this center, the students carry out investigations with a variety of balls. They are asked to record their findings.

Activity Card

- Use the materials in the center to conduct some investigations about bouncing balls.
- How high do the balls bounce? Which ones bounce higher?
- Make some observations and record your findings.

You may have some other ideas about conducting investigations with these balls. Try out your ideas and see what you can learn.

Materials

A collection of balls of different sizes, weights, and compositions, for example, rubber balls, clay balls, ball bearings, volleyballs, polyethylene balls, a ball of yarn, rubber-band balls, tennis balls, ping-pong balls, footballs, basketballs, plastic balls, ball of string, golf ball, billiard ball, marble, balloon; different surfaces on which to bounce the balls, for example, pieces of wood, tile, foam rubber, pieces of metal sheeting, sand, a pan of water, corrugated paper, plastic sheeting.

Thinking Operations Emphasized

Observing; comparing; classifying and interpreting data; designing investigations; applying principles; making decisions; summarizing; evaluating; suggesting hypotheses; identifying assumptions; imagining and inventing.

Big Ideas

Elasticity of balls causes them to bounce. The extent to which a ball can bounce against a hard surface is a measure of its elasticity.

Notes to the Teacher

- Balls may, of course, be found in the school's recreational equipment storage area. Students may also be encouraged to bring balls from home to add variety to the materials in the center.

Debriefing

During initial Debriefing sessions, student's thinking about the inquiries may be further stimulated by asking some of the following types of questions:

- What observations did you make about bouncing balls?
- What differences did you notice? What were some similarities?
- If you wanted to classify these balls, what kinds of groups could you make? In what group would each ball belong? Tell your reason for putting it in that group.
- What observations did you make about dropping balls on different surfaces? How do you explain what happened? What ideas do you have about it?
- What ways did you invent to measure how high balls bounce? How did you decide that would be a good way to do it?
- What makes a ball bounce? What are your ideas about it?

Extending

When the students have had sufficient opportunities to carry out their initial investigations with the balls, their inquiries might be extended in one or more of the following ways:

1. By adding some new activity cards to the center. For example:
   - What are some good ways to measure the bounce of a ball? Conduct some investigations and record your findings.
   - What happens when you drop a ball from different heights? Conduct some investigations and record your findings.
   - What happens when you drop a ball on different surfaces? Conduct some investigations and record your findings.
   - What are some differences you observed in the different balls? Set up a classification system and place each ball in the group where it belongs.
   - What can you do to change the way a ball bounces? Conduct some investigations and record your findings.
   - What other things bounce? Conduct some investigations and record your findings.
   - Make a chart to show how different balls bounce.
2. By raising more challenging questions following additional investigations. For example:
   - What theories can you suggest to explain why some things bounce and others do not? How could you test those theories?
   - What theories can you suggest to explain why some balls bounce better on some surfaces than on other surfaces?
   - What theories can you suggest to explain why some balls bounce higher?
3. By suggesting students do some background reading about elasticity in library books and on the Internet.

Creating

Before leaving the investigations on bouncing balls, the students may enjoy engaging in one or more of the following culminating activities:

1. Work with a friend. Invent a brand-new game using a small ball and a large ball. Invent a scoring system for your game.
2. Work with a friend. Figure out a good way to measure the path a ball takes when you throw it.
3. Work with a friend and think of twenty different uses for balls. Make a list of them.
4. Write a story, "The Magic Ball."

ACTIVITY 40: FRICTION AND INERTIA

In this center, the students carry out investigative play with tops, yo-yos, gyroscopes, and flywheels. They are asked to record their observations.

Activity Card

- Use the materials in the center to study how these toys work.
- What makes the top spin? What makes the top stop spinning?
- What makes the yo-yos work? What makes them stop?
- How do the other toys work? What makes them stop working?
- Conduct some investigations and make some observations. Talk with each other and then write your observations.

You may have some other ideas for using these materials. Try out your ideas and see what you can discover.

Materials

Several tops of different sizes and shapes; several yo-yos; one or two gyroscopes; one or two flywheels; one or two Frisbees.

Thinking Operations Emphasized

Observing and recording; comparing; classifying and interpreting data; suggesting hypotheses; examining assumptions; designing investigations; making decisions imaging and creating; evaluating and criticizing.

Big Ideas

Things in motion tend to stay in motion as long as no external force interferes. Friction causes things to slow and stop. Things at rest tend to stay at rest. These tendencies are known as inertia.

Notes to the Teacher

- The tops in this center should be both the whip-spun kind and the twirled kind. They may be commercially obtained or homemade.
- Students may also be asked to bring some of these items from home.

Debriefing

The following types of questions may promote reflection about the ways these toys work:

- What observations did you make about how tops spin? About what makes them stop?

- In what ways are tops like yo-yos? How are they different?
- What observations did you make about gyroscopes? How are they like tops?
- What keeps a top spinning? What makes it stop? How do you explain it?
- What observations did you make about flywheels? How are flywheels like Frisbees?

Extending

The students' thinking on this inquiry may be extended in one or more of the following ways:

1. By adding new toys to the center such as a ball, a wheel or set of wheels, toy cars.
2. By adding new activity cards. For example:
   - How long can you make a top spin? Conduct some investigations and record your findings.
   - How long can you make a gyroscope spin? Conduct some investigations and record your findings.
   - Study tops and yo-yos. Find as many similarities as you can.
   - Carry out some investigations with the Frisbee. Record your findings.
3. By raising more challenging questions in later Debriefings. For example:
   - What are the properties of a good top? Why do you think that those properties will make the top work better?
   - How are Frisbees like tops or yo-yos? How are they different?
   - What other kinds of toys operate on the same principles as tops and yo-yos? What makes you think that is true?
   - What kinds of toys depend on a gyroscope for their action? What makes you think that is true?
   - If you wanted to keep a top spinning for a very long time, what might you do? What makes you think that would work?
4. By suggesting students do some background reading about friction and inertia in library books and on the Internet.

Creating

The students may enjoy participating in one or more of the following culminating activities to wind up their investigations with friction and inertia:

1. Work with a friend. Make up a game using a yo-yo.
2. Work with a friend. Using any materials available, build your own flywheel.

3. Work with a friend. Make a list of as many toys as you can think of that operate in the same ways as yo-yos, tops, and Frisbees.
4. Using whatever materials are available, make your own gyroscope.

ACTIVITY 41: MAGNETS

In this center, students carry out investigative play with magnets. They are asked to record their observations.

Activity Card

- Use the materials in the center to conduct some investigations with magnets.
- What can magnets do? Test as many ideas as you can think of.
- What materials work best with magnets? Talk with each other about your ideas.
- Then write about your observations.

You may have some other ideas for investigations with magnets. Try them and see what discoveries you can make.

Materials

Different kinds of magnets (horseshoe magnets, bar magnets of different sizes and strengths); various small objects containing metal (straight pins, paper clips, metal filings, thumbtacks, staples, nails, screws, coins); various larger objects containing metal (scissors, stapler, hammer, screwdriver, pliers, wrench, can opener, spoon, fork); various nonmetal objects (plastic spoons, plastic cups, plastic pens, paper products, glass objects, ceramic objects, cloth, cork objects).

Thinking Operations Emphasized

Observing and recording; comparing; classifying and interpreting data; applying principles; making decisions; designing investigations; suggesting hypotheses; examining assumptions; imagining and inventing.

Big Ideas

Some materials have magnetic properties. Magnets attract or repel each other, depending on their positions.

Notes to the Teacher

- If possible, try to obtain metal objects containing cobalt, nickel, and iron, as these are strongly attracted to magnets. A Canadian nickel should be included, if possible, as well as a US nickel. Try coins from any other country, if available. Iron filings are usually available in science equipment storage areas. If not available in your school, try the local high-school physics department.

Debriefing

The following types of questions might be raised during initial Debriefing sessions to promote reflection about magnetism:

- What observations did you make about the materials in this center?
- What observations did you make about the objects that were attracted by the magnets? How did you explain this?
- What observations did you make about the objects that were not attracted by the magnets? How do you explain it?
- What differences did you observe between the horseshoe and the bar magnets? What similarities did you observe?
- What observations did you make about the ends of the bar magnet? How do you explain this?

Extending

When the students appear ready to have their play extended, consider the following options:

1. Adding new materials to the center. For example, small pins stuck in corks in a small basin of water, bar magnets hung from a frame, and objects that contain combinations of metal and nonmetal parts.
2. Introducing new activity cards. For example:
   - How can these objects be classified? Set up some categories and place each item in the category you think it belongs.
   - What work can magnets do? Try some investigations and record your findings.
3. Raising more challenging questions in later Debriefing sessions. For example:
   - How do you use a magnet to make an object move? How do you explain its working?
   - How could you group the objects in this center? How would you decide to which group each object belongs?

- What theories can you suggest to explain why some items are attracted to magnets and some are not?
- What theories can you suggest to explain how a magnet gets its power?
- How do you make a magnet? What are your ideas?
- What are magnets good for? What are your ideas?

4. By suggesting students do some background reading about magnets in library books and on the Internet.

Creating

To culminate the investigations, the students may enjoy doing one or more of the following:

1. Work with a friend. Make a magnet.
2. Work with a friend. Figure out a way to find out the strength of a magnet. Conduct some investigations and record your findings.
3. Work with a friend. Place a bar magnet under a piece of paper. Sprinkle some iron filings on the paper. Observe what happens. Draw some pictures of what you see. Then suggest some hypotheses to explain it.
4. Try to imagine what kind of magnet you could use to lift a car. Draw a picture of it.
5. Write a story about "The Magnet That Wouldn't Let Go!"

ACTIVITY 42: WHEELS AND AXLES

In this center, the students carry out investigations with wheels and axles to make observations about simple machines.

Activity Card

- Use the materials in this center to conduct some investigations with wheels.
- What observations can you make about wheels?
- What observations can you make about how wheels are made to turn?
- What observations can you make about how wheels make our work easier?
- Talk with each other about your ideas and then write your observations.

You may have some other ideas for using the materials in this center. Try them out and see what discoveries you can make.

Materials

A supply of wheels of various sizes and constructions (e.g., plastic wheels, wheels from children's toy trucks and cars, wagon wheels, rubber wheels from children's toys, an old automobile tire, metal wheels with axles, a bicycle wheel, a steering wheel); wheels from household appliances (for example, pencil sharpener, meat grinder, egg beaters); spring scale; bricks, concrete blocks, large pieces of timber, and/or other weights; large plastic tubs or large cartons.

Thinking Operations Emphasized

Observing and recording; comparing; interpreting data; suggesting hypotheses; examining assumptions; designing investigations; making decisions; evaluating; applying principles; imagining and inventing.

Big Ideas

A wheel is a simple machine with several different functions. In one function it allows us to move things more easily. Axles conduct the power that turns wheels; every wheeled vehicle needs axles in order to enable the wheels to turn.

Notes to the Teacher

- In acquiring a collection of wheels, begin first with what is available in the science storage room. Then, try your own basement, attic, kitchen, storage closet, or garage. If your collection is still meager, visit "second-hand" stores in the neighborhood. Ask the students to bring in broken toys with wheels. Finally, there is the local, reliable hardware store.

Debriefing

More thoughtful inquiry about the concepts underlying how wheels and axles work may be generated with the following types of questions during initial Debriefing:

- What observations did you make about wheels?
- What observations did you make about how wheels are made to turn?
- What did you see as the purpose of the axles? How did you figure that out?
- In what ways do wheels make our work easier? How do you explain this?

Extending

To extend students' inquiries about wheels, some of the following may be tried:

1. Adding a doorknob and a screwdriver to the center and introducing new activity cards that focus inquiry on these new materials. For example:
   - Where is the wheel function in these tools? What are your ideas about it? How are these like other wheels? Conduct some investigations and make some notes of what you found.
   - Use a scale and figure out how much force is required to turn wheels of different sizes. Conduct some investigations and make some notes of what you found.
   - Use a scale to figure out how much force is required to move a concrete block with and without wheels. Conduct some investigations and make some notes of what you found.
2. Raising more challenging questions in later Debriefing. For example:
   - Think of some ways in which wheels work for you. What examples can you give?
   - What makes a wheel move more easily? What makes a wheel move more slowly? What examples can you give?
   - In what different ways can wheels be made to move? What examples can you give?
3. By raising questions that allow for the examination of values issues related to the topic. For example:
   - It takes energy to drive wheels, but wheels make life easier for us. If you had to conserve energy, what wheel-driven machines would you be able to do without? What are your thoughts?
   - What wheel-driven machines would you not be able to give up? What are your views?
4. By suggesting students do some background reading from library books and the Internet.

Creating

The students may be asked to participate in some of the following tasks to bring to a close the work in this center:

1. Work with a friend. Take a trip throughout the school. Observe the many ways in which wheels are used in the school to do work. Make some notes of what you observed.
2. Work with a friend. Using any materials available in the room, construct a machine that operates with one or more wheels. Make some illustrations of it.

3. Invent a machine that uses wheels to dial a telephone. Draw a picture of it.
4. Invent a machine that uses wheels to give an elephant a bath. Draw some pictures of it.
5. Write a story about the day the wheel was invented.

ACTIVITY 43: LEVERS

In this center, students carry out investigations with a variety of levers, inclined planes, and weights. They are asked to record their observations.

Activity Card

- Use the materials in the center to find out what you can about how levers work.
- How can levers lift heavy things? What are your ideas about it?
- What are some differences when you lift heavy weights with and without a lever? Make some observations and record your findings.

Try some other investigations with these materials and see what you can discover.

Materials

A variety of small boards, for example: a ruler, a yardstick or meterstick, several shelves of different lengths and widths; bricks, concrete blocks and other materials that may serve as a fulcrum; materials of different weights, for example: metallics, heavy books, bricks, firewood, a bag of soil; a spring scale.

Thinking Operations Emphasized

Observing and recording; comparing; classifying and interpreting data; examining assumptions; suggesting hypotheses; designing investigations; applying principles; evaluating; making decisions; summarizing; imagining and inventing.

Big Ideas

Levers are simple machines that make work easier. They allow us to lift heavy loads. The human forearm is sometimes used as a lever.

Notes to the Teacher

- The school storage room or basement may turn up discarded shelves that would make ideal material for the levers center.
- There should be several objects that are quite heavy along with objects that weigh less.

Debriefing

The following are some questions that may be used during initial Debriefing to promote reflection about how levers work:

- What observations have you made about how levers work?
- How can you explain how they work? What are your ideas?
- In what ways is a lever like your arm? How is it different? In what ways does your foot work like a lever?
- What observations have you made about how levers and inclined planes make our work easier?

Extending

The investigative play with levers may be extended in one or more of the following ways:

1. By adding new materials to the center. For example: nutcrackers, wheelbarrow, bottle opener, crowbar, ice tongs, tweezers, and scissors.
2. By adding some new activity cards to give a different focus to the inquiries. For example:
    - Design some investigations to show how you use a lever to lift some very heavy weights. Record your findings.
    - Design some investigations to show how you would balance lightweights against heavy weights. Record your findings.
    - Design some investigations to show how much force you need to lift a 25-pound weight. You will need a spring scale for this. Record your findings.
    - Design some investigations to show how the amount of force necessary to move an object up an inclined plane changes with the slope of the incline. Record your findings.
3. By raising more challenging questions in later Debriefing. For example:
    - What are some differences between an inclined plane and a lever? What are some similarities?
    - In what ways is a wheelbarrow like a nutcracker? How are they different?

- How much force does it take to lift a 25-pound weight without a lever? How much with a lever? How do you explain the difference?
- What observations did you make about how the lever works when you move the fulcrum to different positions?
4. By suggesting students do some background reading about levers in library books and on the Internet.

Creating

Some of the following may serve as culminating activities for the lever studies:

1. Work with a friend. Think up as many ways as you can to show how your arm works as a lever. Make some illustrations of those examples.
2. Work with a friend. Draw a diagram to show how two people would use an inclined plane or a lever to move a piano into an apartment on the top floor of a building with no elevator.
3. Work with a friend. Design an investigation to find out how much energy it takes to climb a flight of stairs or go up a ramp, each going the same distance from the main floor to the second floor. Figure out a way to measure your findings.

ACTIVITY 44: GERMS

In this center, the students conduct inquiries into the role of germs in spreading disease.

Activity Card

- Work with two partners and make a survey of everyone in the class who has had one or more of the following symptoms of illness in the last month: fever, sore throat, cough, sneezing, rash, vomiting, bellyache, or other illness that caused absence from school.
- Create a graph to show which classmates have had one or more of these symptoms of illness.
- Create a graph to show how classmates believed they contracted their illness.
- Find out what these students did for their illnesses. Working together write a summary of the different remedies they used to help them get well.

Materials

No materials are needed for this center.

Thinking Operations Emphasized

Observing and recording; comparing; examining assumptions; suggesting hypotheses; summarizing; collecting, organizing and interpreting data; classifying; creating and inventing.

Big Ideas

Most diseases are caused by microbes that invade the body. A more familiar term for these microbes is "germs." Germs can enter the body through the air we breathe; through eating food or drinking water; through breaks in the skin, through the bite of a carrier. Unwashed hands often carry germs to the mouth or to your eyes. When we understand more about how germs are spread, it helps us to prevent the spread of disease.

Notes to the Teacher

- There's very little preparation that needs to be done for this investigative play. Just ensure that students who do not wish to reveal any previous onset of illness may choose not to participate in the inquiries.

Debriefing

The following are some questions that may be raised during Debriefing to promote further reflection on the big ideas:

- What observations did you make about the different kinds of illnesses that have been going around in your classroom last month?
- What observations did you make about the illnesses that occurred more frequently?
- What observations did you make about the numbers of students in your class affected by those illnesses?
- What observations did you make about the reasons your classmates gave for how they got sick?
- What observations did you make about what students did to help themselves get well again?

Extending

The investigative play may be extended in one or more of the following ways:

1. Work with two partners and use the Internet or library to find out what you can about diseases that are caused by germs.
2. Work with a partner and use the library or the Internet to find out what you can about these two scientists who played major roles in identifying germs as the cause of disease: Semmelweis and Lister. Working together, write a summary that describes the contributions of each man.
3. Work with two partners and use the library or the Internet to find out what you can about the Black Plague or the Spanish Flu. Working together, write a summary about the causes of this disease, how it spread, what happened to the people who got sick from it, and what was done to prevent the disease from spreading.
4. Work with two partners and use the library or the Internet to find out what you can about the most recent epidemic of COVID-19. Working as a team, write a summary about the causes of this disease, how it spreads, what happened to the people who got sick from it, and what steps the government took to prevent the disease from spreading.
5. Work with two partners and use the library or the Internet to find out what you can about the people who claimed that COVID-19 was a hoax and refused to get a vaccination. Working as a team, write a summary about what you consider some of the reasons behind such thinking, and what you see as some consequences of their beliefs.
6. By raising more challenging questions during later Debriefing. For example:
   - What do you see as the role of germs in spreading disease? What have you discovered in your investigations that support those ideas?
   - What is your understanding of germs—what they are and what they do to make you sick?
   - What is your understanding of how germs are spread?
   - Where do you suppose germs come from? What are your theories about it?
   - What do you know about how germs come into our bodies? What assumptions have you made?
   - How do people try to prevent catching a sickness caused by germs? What ideas do you have about it?
   - How does washing hands help in the prevention of germs being passed from one to another? What are your theories about it?
7. By raising questions that address some values issues related to the big ideas. For example:

In some states and provinces, having a vaccine passport permits you to get on a plane, go into a restaurant, and enter a large arena to watch a sports event. A large group of people have marched in protest against such a rule. They don't want to get vaccinated. They want their freedom to ignore the steps you need to take to prevent the spread of COVID-19.

Where do you stand on these issues? Should all people be required to get vaccinated? Should we allow people their freedom to refuse getting vaccinated? What do you see as some consequences of either of these positions? What do you suppose is behind some of their beliefs?

Creating

To culminate the studies of germs, some of the following more creative tasks may be suggested:

1. Work with a partner. Use the library or the Internet to gather the information you need for this activity. Create a poster of your own design that describes four different kinds of germs: virus, bacterium, fungi, and protozoa.
2. Work with a partner. Create a poster or a web page that describes how our classmates can take precautions against spreading germs. Give your poster a catchy title.
3. Work with a friend and write a short biography of Ludwig Semmelweiss.

ACTIVITY 45: TIME

In this center, the students carry out investigations around the concept of time, using clocks and other timing devices. They are asked to record their observations.

Activity Card

- Use the materials in this center to make some studies of time.
- In what ways is time measured?
- What other kinds of instruments besides clocks measure time?
- How are clocks and other timers alike? How are they different?
- Conduct some investigations and see what you can find out. Then write about your findings.

You may have other ideas for conducting investigations about time. Try your ideas and see what discoveries you can make.

Materials

Two or three clocks (e.g., a wind-up wristwatch, a quartz watch, a digital clock, a wall clock, an alarm clock, a clock radio, a clock with a sweep second hand) and several timers (e.g., a stopwatch, hourglass, egg timer).

Thinking Operations Emphasized

Observing and recording; comparing and interpreting data; suggesting hypotheses; identifying assumptions; designing investigations; making decisions; applying principles; evaluating and criticizing; classifying; imagining and creating.

Big Ideas

Clocks are used in the accurate measurement of time. It is the measured or measurable period during which an activity, action, process exists or occurs.

Notes to the Teacher

The materials in this center may be somewhat more difficult to acquire without relying on personal resources. However, the student inquiry that results may be worth the extra effort involved in getting them. Here are some ideas for getting the materials:

- Ask parents to donate materials. Make sure they understand that the materials may not necessarily be returned in the same condition. (It's probably not a good idea to donate the priceless grandfather clock handed down through the generations.)
- Ask personal friends and teaching colleagues for donations of old clocks. They may be happy to unload relics that are just taking up space knowing the materials will be put to good use.
- Check the local second-hand store or flea market. These resources might yield just enough materials to get the investigations started. Make sure, however, that at least one of the clocks may be taken apart.

Debriefing

The following are some examples of questions that might be used during initial Debriefing to promote reflection about time and timing devices:

- What observations did you make about how clocks work?
- In what ways are digital clocks like analog clocks? How are they different?

- What are some assumptions that are being made when we time an activity? What are your ideas?
- How are timers like clocks? How are they different? What are your ideas?
- What inaccuracies did you observe among the clocks and timers? How do you explain them?
- Why do you suppose it's important to know how much time an activity takes? What ideas do you have about that?

Extending

The investigations may be extended in one or more of the following ways:

1. By adding new activity cards. For example:
    - How long does it take to tie a shoelace? Make a paper airplane? Blow up a balloon? Jump 100 times? Fill a glass of water? Fill a gallon bucket? Bounce a ball 100 times? Grow a tooth? Read a page of a book? Walk to school? Write your name? Eat your lunch? Grow a flower? Bake a cake? Sew a button on a shirt? Conduct some investigations and make some observations about the time it takes to do some of these things. Record your findings.
2. By raising more challenging questions during later Debriefing. For example:
    - How long did it take (name of student) to do 100 bounces? How long did it take (name of another student)? How do you explain the difference?
    - How long does it take (name of student) to walk to school? How long does it take (name of other student)? How do you explain the difference?
    - How long does it take to grow a new tooth? What's your prediction? Why do you think that's true?
    - Why do you suppose it's important to be able to measure time accurately? What are your ideas about that?
    - What do you suppose people did in early days before they were able to measure time?
    - When (student's name) said it took him/her 15 minutes to jump 100 times, what assumptions were being made about the timing of this activity?
    - What do you suppose it means when people say "time flies"? What are your ideas about it?
3. By raising questions that call for the examination of some values issues related to the topic. For example:

Some tests you take in school are "timed." That is, you have a certain amount of time to finish the test. If you don't finish on time, you are penalized or lose points.
- What is your opinion of tests that must be finished in a certain time? What do you see as some disadvantages of timed tests? If you were the teacher, how would you change it?

4. By suggesting students do some background reading about time and timing devices in library books and on the Internet.

Creating and Imagining

Before leaving the studies on time, the students may engage in one or more of the following creative tasks:

1. Work with a friend. Make a timing device using a glass of water.
2. Work with a friend. Make a timing device using the sun.
3. Work with a friend. Make a timer using a candle.
4. Write a poem about how you feel when time "drags its feet" or when "time flies."
5. Draw a picture of how it might look when "time flies."
6. The painter Salvatore Dali created a painting of a melting clock. What do you suppose he meant in that painting? What are your ideas about it?

ACTIVITY 46: OURSELVES (1): HANDS AND FEET

In this activity, the students examine their own and each other's hands and feet and make some observations about themselves and the differences observed in the group. They are asked to record their findings.

Activity Card

- Use the materials in this center to study your hands and feet.
- What observations can you make about your hands? Study them and write what you find.
- Compare each other's hands. How are they alike? How are they different?
- What observations can you make about your feet? Study them and write what you see.
- Compare each other's feet. How are they alike? How are they different? Record your findings.

Materials

Large sheets of paper, magnifying glass, mirrors, crayons, pencils.

Thinking Operations Emphasized

Observing and recording; comparing; collecting, classifying and interpreting data; suggesting hypotheses; identifying assumptions; designing investigations; making decisions; applying principles; evaluating and criticizing; imagining and creating.

Big Ideas

Human hands and feet serve important functions in the human organism. There is a wide range of differences among hands and feet. Handprints and footprints are unique.

Notes to the Teacher

- If you choose to extend this activity into the realm of handprinting and footprinting, the task can become quite messy. So it is probably a good idea to anticipate this, to talk with the students beforehand about carrying out simple precautionary measures and to provide sponge, soap, water, and paper towels in the center. Some students may be shy about removing their shoes and socks and perhaps that may be addressed prior to beginning this activity.

Debriefing

The following types of questions may be raised to promote reflection about the big ideas underlying these investigations:

- What observations were made about your hands? What are some functions of hands?
- What observations were made about your feet? What are some functions of feet?
- In what ways are hands different among the people in your group? How do you explain those differences? What do you see as some advantages of such differences?
- In what ways are feet different among the people in your group? How do you explain those differences? What do you see as some advantages of such differences?

Extending

The investigative play with hands and feet may be extended in one or more of the following ways:

1. By adding new materials to the center (this is the messy part). For example: ink pads, watercolor paints, and additional paper for fingerprinting, handprinting, and footprinting.
2. By adding new activity cards. For example:
   - Study the fingerprints of all the people in the group. Record your findings.
   - Study the footprints of all the people in your group. Record your findings.
   - Compare each other's fingerprints, handprints, and footprints. What similarities can be found? What differences? Record your findings.
   - What are some different functions of fingers and toes? What did you discover when you studied them?
3. By raising more challenging questions in later Debriefings. For example:
   - Why do you suppose everyone has a distinctly different set of fingerprints? Handprints? Footprints? How do you explain it?
   - In what ways are hands like feet? How are they different?
   - In what ways are human hands and feet different from and similar to the feet of a chimp? A rabbit? A cat?
   - Why do you suppose fingernails and toenails can grow back when they are cut but not fingers and toes? How do you explain this? What are your ideas?
   - What did you discover about the many functions of fingers and toes?
   - What did you discover about how wrists and ankles serve the purposes of hands and feet?
4. By raising questions that call for examination of some values issues related to the topic. For example:

   People are different in very many ways. Some of them are small and some grow to be quite tall. Some have large hands and feet and some have small limbs. Some are quite thin and others are not so thin. Some have curly hair, some straight hair, and some have no hair at all!
   - Have you heard people shame the appearance of others? Have you heard people call each other rude names to highlight the way in which they are different? What are your views about that?
   - Should such behavior be laughed at? Ignored? Punished?
   - If you saw this happening in your group, what action might you be willing to take? Where do you stand on this issue?

5. By suggesting that students do some background reading in library books and on the Internet about individual differences and the implications of those differences on our appreciation and respect for others.

Creating

Several types of activities may bring these studies to culmination. For example:

1. The students may do a handprint or footprint collage of all students in the class.
2. The hands of persons over sixty years old may be studied and pictures drawn of them.
3. Stories may be written about hands and/or feet. For example: Footprint in the Sand; The Grotesque Toe; Girl with the Purple Nails; Twinkle Toes; Magic Fingers.

ACTIVITY 47: OURSELVES (2): PULSE AND HEARTBEAT

In this center, the students carry out investigations with pulses and heartbeats, making observations about the relationship of heartbeat to activity level. They are asked to record their findings.

Activity Card

- Use the materials in the center to conduct some investigations about each other's heartbeat.
- Conduct some investigations to find out about each other's pulse.
- Make a chart and record your observations about the heartbeats of the students in your group.
- Conduct some investigations to find out under what conditions the heartbeat and pulse rate change. How does it change? Record your findings.

Materials

One or two stethoscopes, graph paper, a watch with a sweep second hand.

Thinking Operations Emphasized

Observing and recording; comparing; classifying and interpreting data; collecting and organizing data; suggesting hypotheses; examining assumptions;

summarizing; applying principles; evaluating; making decisions; designing investigations.

Big Ideas

Pulse is created by the heart pumping blood through the arteries and can be found in different parts of the body. Exercise and rest can change heartbeat (and pulse).

Notes to the Teacher

- This activity cannot be carried out without the use of stethoscopes, but students' toy stethoscopes are perfectly adequate. The school nurse may be willing to lend a stethoscope for these investigations.

Debriefing

Questions in the initial Debriefing sessions may follow closely along the lines of the activity card. For example:

- What observations did you make about your own heartbeat?
- What were some similarities you noticed among the members of the group? What were some differences?
- What observations did you make about your pulse? What were some similarities you observed among members of the group? What were some differences?
- What observations did you make about how the beat increased or decreased? How do you explain these changes?
- What observations did you make about the sound of the beat? How do you explain it?
- What do you see as the connection between what you feel in the pulse and what you hear in the heartbeat? What makes you think that is true?

Extending

The heartbeat and pulse investigations may be extended in one or more of the following ways:

1. By introducing new activity cards. For example:
    - Jump up and down twenty times. What observations can you make about the change in your heartbeat before and after the jumping exercise? Make a chart or graph showing this information.

- Jump up and down twenty times. What observations can you make about the changes in your pulse before and after the jumping? Make a chart or graph showing this information.
- Design 3 exercises. Check your heartbeat and pulse before and after each exercise. Record your findings on a chart or graph.
2. By raising more challenging questions at later Debriefing sessions. For example:
    - What observations did you make about the effect of exercise on heartbeat? On pulse? How do you explain it?
    - What is the relationship of the heartbeat to the pulse? What are your ideas? What information in your charts helps you to make this observation?
    - What do you suppose might happen to the heartbeat and pulse during a long sleep? What are your ideas? What data allow you to make that assumption?
    - Where do you suppose the noise comes from when you hear your heartbeat? What are your ideas?
    - What do you suppose makes the heart beat? What are your ideas?
3. By suggesting students do some background reading in library books and on the Internet about the human heart.

Creating

The heartbeat and pulse studies may be culminated in one or more of the following ways:

1. Work with a friend and draw some pictures of how you both think the heart works.
2. Write a poem about a person with a "loving heart."
3. Work with a partner and write a mystery story called The Heart Machine; or, The Transplanted Heart.
4. Work with two partners and using whatever materials are available, make a model of a human heart, showing how the heart works.

ACTIVITY 48: OURSELVES (3): HUMANS AND THE ENVIRONMENT

In this center, the students carry on investigations to examine the effects of certain environmental conditions on aspects of personal well-being. They are asked to record their findings.

Activity Card

- Use the materials in the center to find out how sounds, light and darkness, space, and climate affect how you feel.
- Carry out some investigations that show how certain sounds affect you.
- Carry out some investigations that show how light and darkness affect you.
- Carry out some investigations that show how the space you are in affects you.
- Talk with each other about what you experienced and what you found. Then record your ideas.

Materials

Hammer, nails, chalk, small blackboard (if these are still available in schools), saw, scraps of felt, plush, or velvet fabric, scissors, voice recording device, recordings of different kinds of music, earphones, electric motor, flashlight, 150-watt light bulb, lamp, eyeshades, dark glasses, small chair, one or two timers, small cardboard carton, big enough to squeeze a student into.

Thinking Operations Emphasized

Designing investigations; observing and recording; collecting and interpreting data; examining assumptions; suggesting hypotheses; applying principles; making decisions; evaluating and criticizing; summarizing; imagining and inventing.

Big Ideas

Environmental conditions affect living organisms. Living organisms in turn affect the environment. The study of this relationship is called ecology.

Notes to the Teacher

- This activity is probably more suitable for students who have had some background with the Play-Debrief-Replay sciencing program, since it calls for greater independent functioning.
- It is conceivable that students may attempt investigations that are potentially hazardous in this center (e.g., playing music of excessively loud volume) so teachers should ensure that safety procedures and rules about what investigations may or may not be carried out are strictly enforced.

Debriefing

The following types of questions are suggested to promote students' thoughtful reflection about the big ideas:

- What observations did you make of the effect of certain sounds on how you feel?
- What sounds made you feel more comfortable? What hypotheses might explain that?
- What sounds made you feel uncomfortable? How would you explain that?
- What observations did you make of the effect of light and darkness on how you feel? What conditions made you feel comfortable or uncomfortable? How do you explain that?
- How does the space you occupy affect how you feel? What space conditions made you feel comfortable or uncomfortable? What examples can you give to support your ideas?
- What other environmental conditions affect your sense of well-being? What examples can you give of how that works?

Extending

When students' interest in their inquiries with light, space, and sound appear to be diminishing, their investigations may be extended in one or more of the following ways:

1. By adding new materials to the center that would lead to new investigations. For example: items with pleasing and noxious smells (flowers, perfumes, certain spices, nontoxic cleaning fluid, decaying fish, or eggs), "beautiful" and "ugly" examples of artwork or sculpture.
2. By introducing new activity cards that invite investigations with these new materials.
3. By raising more challenging questions in later Debriefing. For example:
    - What observations have you made about the kinds of environmental conditions that affect the way we feel? What list of conditions can be generated? How might these be classified?
    - How do these conditions affect the way we live? What examples can you give to support those ideas?
    - How do we in turn affect the environment? What observations have you made about how this occurs? What examples can you give?
    - In what ways are we affected by temperature? sound? light? aesthetics? food? The air we breathe? How do you know this? What data support your ideas?

- What kind of an environment do we need in order to live comfortably? safely? How do you know this? What data support your ideas?
- In what ways do we change our environment? What examples can you give? What are some consequences of this? How do you know that is true?
- Adrian says that colors also affect the way we feel. Does that idea have any credibility? If so, what examples can you give to support that idea?

4. By raising questions that call for the examination of some values issues related to the topic. For example:

    Arthur told his classmates that sitting in a very hot classroom during June makes him sweat and that is why it is hard for him to learn his lessons. He thinks that either the school should get some air conditioners or else start summer holidays in May.
    - What is your view of Arthur's position about how environment affects how we learn?
    - Do you agree with him? If you do, can you give some examples to support your view?
    - What other environmental conditions might affect the way we learn?

5. By suggesting students do some background reading about how environmental conditions affect us and how we humans affect our environment from library books and the Internet.

Creating

One or more of the following might be enjoyed by students to culminate the inquiries in this area:

1. Work with a partner. Together, design and draw an illustration of the "perfect environment to learn in." Explain how this perfect space makes for more comfortable learning.
2. Work with a partner. Imagine a town in which the water was no longer fit to drink. Write a story about it. How did it happen? What was the effect of such a condition on the lives of the people?
3. Work with a partner. Create a plan for improving the school environment. Share your plan with the others in your class and find out what you would need to do to put it into operation.[1]

---

[1] Adapted by permission of the Publisher. From Selma Wassermann, *Teaching for Thinking Today: Strategies, and Activities for the K-8 Classroom.* New York: Teachers College Press. Copyright, © 2009 by Teachers College, Columbia University. All rights reserved

Chapter 15

Category C

Who's Afraid of Spiders? Activities 49–58

Activities for the intrepid teacher involving greater mess and perhaps the need for greater management of personal distaste.

Activity 49: Squids
Activity 50: Spiders
Activity 51: Minibeasts
Activity 52: Live Animals
Activity 53: Earthworms
Activity 54: Eggs
Activity 55: Colors
Activity 56: Metals
Activity 57: Plastic
Activity 58: Garbage (Midden Heap)

ACTIVITY 49: SQUIDS

In this activity, the students examine squids and make some observations about this marine animal. They are asked to record their observations.

Activity Card

> Use the materials in this center to make some observations of squids.
>
> - What can you observe about their shape? What observations can you make about some of the parts of this marine animal?

- What do you suppose the different parts are used for?
- Talk with each other and discuss your ideas. Then make some illustrations showing what you found.

Materials

One squid for each pair of students working in the center; scissors, magnifying lenses, paper towels, newspapers to cover tables.

Thinking Operations Emphasized

Observing and recording; collecting, comparing, classifying, and interpreting data; suggesting hypotheses; examining assumptions; designing investigations; making decisions; imagining and creating.

Big Ideas

Squids are sea animals. Eight of the ten tentacles surround the mouth. The skeleton is like a shell but located inside the body. It is called a pen!

Notes to the Teacher

- Gentle and benign creatures of the deep, squids may be purchased fresh, if you live in coastal areas, or frozen, in many fish stores, or large, well-equipped supermarkets. They are an inexpensive source of protein and make for quite wonderful sciencing activities.
- Instead of scissors, sharper dissecting tools may be used. This will depend on your judgment of student responsibility to work with these more advanced tools.

Debriefing

After the students have had ample opportunity to dissect and study squids, the following questions may be raised to promote further reflection on the big ideas:

- What observations did you make about the shape of the squid?
- What observations did you make about some of its parts?
- What do you suppose all those tentacles are for?
- What observations did you make about the mouth?
- What observations did you make about the inner parts of the animal?

- What do you suppose is the function of that part of the animal?
- How are squids different from fish? How are they like fish?

Extending

It is entirely likely that the squid supply will be exhausted well before the students' enthusiasm for this dissection has waned. Their inquiries may then be extended in one or more of the following ways:

1. By introducing other marine animals for dissection and comparison. For example: shellfish, mollusks, and fish with backbones.
2. By creating new activity cards that reflect the newly introduced materials.
3. By raising more challenging questions in later Debriefing. For example:
    - What observations did you make about squids that suggest how this animal moves in water?
    - What observations did you make about the squids that suggest how this animal might take in food? What kind of food it might take in?
    - What observations did you make about how it lives in water?
    - What other animals that live in the sea are like the squid? What are some similarities? What other sea animals are very different? What are some differences?
4. By raising questions that call for the examination of some values issues related to the topic. For example:

    "Squids are just dumb animals," said Mickey. "It doesn't matter if we cut them up. They don't feel anything anyway."
    - What's your view on this? Is Mickey right? How do you know? What examples can you give to support your ideas?
5. By suggesting students do some background reading about squids in library books and on the Internet.

Creating

As a culmination to the squid dissections, the students might undertake one or more of the following creative tasks:

1. Find out some good ways of cooking squid. Collect the materials you need and make a squid lunch for the class.
2. Work with a friend. Draw some illustrations of squids in their natural habitat.
3. Work with a friend. Make a model of a squid from paper or clay.
4. Write a poem, "The Loneliest Squid in the Sea."
5. Write a story, "My Friend, the Squid."

ACTIVITY 50: SPIDERS

In this center, the students are asked to collect spiders as their contribution to setting up the center. They will then observe the spiders and record their observations.

Activity Card

- Spend some time observing the spiders in the jars.
- What observations can you make about spiders? What do they look like?
- What kinds of parts does a spider's body have?
- What are these parts used for?
- What observations can you make about what the spiders do?
- Talk with each other about your observations. Then write about what you found.

You may have made other observations. Write about what you have learned or draw some pictures.

Materials

A few large glass jars or an aquarium to house the spiders so that they may be easily observed; smaller containers, either plastic or glass, for the students' spider hunt; protective gloves for collecting; magnifying lenses.

Thinking Operations Emphasized

Observing and recording; collecting, comparing, classifying, and interpreting data; suggesting hypotheses; examining assumptions; making decisions; designing investigations; summarizing; imagining and creating.

Big Ideas

There are many different kinds of spiders, but all spiders have similar body parts and structures that contribute to their being able to get food and reproduce. Most spiders must eat other living things to survive.

Notes to the Teacher

- Prior to beginning work on this center, it may be helpful to revisit the introductory material that deals with ethical concerns about studying living

things in the classroom. It may also be helpful to review the discussion about collecting and caring for living creatures. See, for example, Notes to the Teacher in Activity #51.
- To the question, "How do I tell students where to find spiders?" the answer is "Everywhere." In a nonurban location, the possibilities are endless. In more urban settings, the students may search around flower beds, in parks, and in and around trees and gardens, as well as in the corners of homes and the school.
- What makes containers suitable for collecting live trophies should be explained to the students. For example, they should have ample room and secure lids, so that the spiders will not be tempted to wander off to more hospitable territory.
- Spiders are very fragile and can easily be damaged if students do not exercise extreme caution in collecting and containing them. Collected spiders may be transferred to large glass jars or a large aquarium complete with "furnishings." Spiders can be fed flies and must have a supply of water, lest they die. Spiders need air; poke a couple of holes in the lid of the jar!
- Students should be alerted to not touch the spiders with their hands; protective gloves would be a good idea to use for their collections.
- Consider releasing the spiders into their natural environment once the investigations are over.

Debriefing

The following types of questions may be raised to promote students' thoughtful reflection about their spiders' observations:

- What observations have you made about spiders?
- What observations did you make about their shapes? About the structure of their bodies?
- What did you observe about the spiders' behavior?
- In what ways are spiders different from ants? Caterpillars? How are they alike?
- In what ways were the spiders you collected alike? How were they different?

Extending

The students' interest in spiders may be extended in one or more of the following ways:

1. By introducing new activity cards. For example:
    - What observations can be made about how and what a spider eats? Study the spiders and record your findings.

- What observations can be made about the behavior of different kinds of spiders? Study the spiders and record your findings.
- What observations can be made when two or more spiders are in the same habitat? Observe the spiders and record your findings.
- How does the spider know there is danger present? Make some observations and write about some examples that support your ideas.
2. By raising more challenging questions in later Debriefing sessions. For example:
    - What observations can be made about how and what a spider eats? Why do you suppose that food is particularly good for a spider?
    - How does a spider spin a web? What are your ideas about this?
    - What are webs made of? What do you think?
    - What do you suppose is the purpose of a web? What are your hypotheses?
    - What happens when a web gets a hole in it? How do you explain what happens?
    - What similarities and differences do you find in spider webs? How do you explain them?
    - In what ways are spiders like humans? How are they different?
    - Why do you suppose people are afraid of spiders? What are your ideas?
3. By raising questions that call for the examination of values issues related to the topic. For example:

    Every time Jack sees a spider, he stomps on it. When Bruno asked him why he did that, he said, "They're poisonous and they can kill you. It's better if we kill them all."
    - How do you suppose Jack got those ideas? Is he right? Do you believe this too?
    - Where did your ideas about spiders come from? What data do you have to support them?
    - If Bruno disagrees with Jack, what should he say to him?
    - If Jack managed to kill all the spiders in his garden, what do you believe might be some consequences? What do you think about that?
4. By suggesting students do some background reading about spiders in library books and on the Internet.

Creating

The sciencing activity on spiders may be concluded in one or more of the following ways:

1. Make a book that tells the most interesting things learned about spiders.
2. Look for spiders in their natural habitat and observe them without disturbing them. Then record, either in writing or in drawing, what was observed.

3. Find some spider webs to study and record what was observed.
4. Work with a partner and design and build a spider web.
5. Write a poem called "The Giant Spider."
6. Work in pairs to plan a program that would help people overcome their fear of spiders.

ACTIVITY 51: MINIBEASTS

In this activity, the students collect minibeasts (insects) of all kinds, bring them to the center, observe them, and record their findings.

Activity Card

- Spend some time observing the insects in the jars.
- What observations can you make about these insects?
- What observations can you make about their size? Shape? Colors? How they move? How they eat? What they eat?
- How do they protect themselves? What observations can you make about the ways in which different insects do that?
- Study two different insects closely. How are they alike? What kinds of differences do you find? Write about what you have found.

You may wish to make some other observations. Study the insects and see what you can learn.

Materials

For collecting: small strainers, small plastic containers for carrying the animals back to school; for keeping in the classroom: some large glass jars with cheesecloth covering or an aquarium; leaves and twigs to form a "natural" habitat; protective gloves for collecting.

Thinking Operations Emphasized

Observing and recording; collecting, comparing, classifying, and interpreting data; examining assumptions; suggesting hypotheses; summarizing; making decisions; evaluating; applying principles; imagining and creating.

Big Ideas

There is great biological diversity in the insect world. Insects have a large variety of body parts and internal structures that help them find food and reproduce.

Notes to the Teacher

Before beginning work in this center the students will first be involved in the collection of insects for study. Certain procedures should be made explicit for this part of the activity. For example:

1. *Where to look for minibeasts*: If the school is in a suburban or rural area, minibeasts will be abundant, in ditches, ponds, fields, woods, orchards, and the like. If the school is in an urban area, the students may look in corners of attics and basements, in parks and gardens, on beaches or riverbanks, at construction sites, in trees, and under rocks.
2. *Safety precautions*: If the students are to be looking near deep water, instructions about water safety are very important. If they are to be looking in and around ponds of stagnant water, thorough hand washing is essential. Plastic or heavy cloth gloves are advised for collections.
3. *Precautions that should be taken in the collection of live animals*: Some guidelines should be established that would help students develop sensitivity to the need to give living things proper care and respect. For example:
   - A good collector searches carefully.
   - A good collector does not destroy the insect's environment.
   - A good collector handles the animals carefully, taking care not to hurt or damage them.
   - A good collector replaces any part of the animals' habitat that he or she has disturbed.
   - Good collectors do not collect animals indiscriminately. They take only what they need for study.
   - Good collectors do not aim for the biggest collection. They collect carefully and selectively.
4. *Guidelines for keeping living things healthfully and safely in the classroom*: These guidelines would include the following:
   - Minibeasts need "homes" where they can live comfortably, with adequate food, air, and, water.
   - Minibeasts need homes in which they can be observed with a minimum of disruption to their lives.
   - Insect homes should be secure so that they are discouraged from departing on their own (School Council Publications, 1973, pp. 11–12).
5. *Guidelines for keeping minibeasts in perpetuity*: If the students want to keep the insects in the classroom after the activity is over, it is important that they commit to caring for them by insuring they are fed and have water. If they are to be returned to their natural habitats, students should be advised on how to carry these procedures out safely.

Debriefing

The following types of questions may promote further reflection about the big ideas:

- What observations did you make about these insects?
- What observations did you make about shapes? Sizes? Colors? The way they move? What they eat? Their behavior?
- In what ways are these insects alike? How are they different?
- How might they be classified? What kinds of groups might be set up?
- How do you suppose insects see? How do they hear? What makes you think that is true?
- How do insects protect themselves from danger? How do you know that is true? What examples can you give to support your ideas?

Extending

Students' interest in the minibeast inquiries may be extended in one or more of the following ways:

1. By adding new insects to the center. For example: caterpillars, earthworms, slugs, moths, beetles, flies, ants, and grasshoppers.
2. By introducing new activity cards.
3. By raising more challenging questions in later Debriefing sessions. For example:
   - What do you suppose this animal's natural "home" is like? What makes you think that is true?
   - How do you think this animal is born? What are your ideas about it?
   - How does this animal communicate with others of the species? What are your ideas?
   - What do you suppose the antennae are for? What makes you think that is true?
   - What do you suppose this animal is useful for? What are your ideas?
   - How do you suppose this animal reproduces? What are your ideas about it?
4. By raising questions that call for the examination of values issues related to the topic. For example:

    Alice was in her garden observing some ants. She had put a piece of apple out. First, one ant found it. Then, in a short while, there were swarms of ants on the apple. Alice thought that there had to be some way in which the ants, even though tiny animals, had "intelligence."
   - Where do you stand on this issue? Do ants have intelligence?

- Where do your ideas about this come from? What supporting data have you gathered?
5. By suggesting that students do some background reading about insects in library books and on the Internet.

Creating

There are many ways to wind up this minibeast inquiry in more creative endeavors. The students may work with a friend and:

1. choose one animal, study it carefully, and draw some illustrations of it.
2. make a large model of any animal in your collection.
3. collaborate to write a story: "The Bug That Nobody Liked."
4. find out how to build a "wormarium" (worm farm). Gather the materials you need to build it.

ACTIVITY 52: LIVE ANIMALS

In this center, the students make extensive observations of the behavior of a live animal in captivity. They are asked to record their findings.

Activity Card

STUDY THE ANIMAL FOR A LONG PERIOD OF TIME.

- What observations can you make about its shape? Color? Skin or fur? Legs? Tail? The way it moves? Its hearing? How it sees? How it makes sounds?
- What observations can you make about how this animal protects itself from danger? What examples can be seen of this behavior?
- Talk to each other about your observations. Then write about what you found.

You may have other ideas for studying the animal. Try your ideas and write or tell what you learned.

Materials

One or more animals that can easily be kept in a cage in the classroom; for example, guinea pig, rabbit, lizard, hamster, snake, white mouse, bird, tropical fish; an appropriate cage or tank; food and water supply; other materials to create a "natural" habitat for the animal selected.

Thinking Operations Emphasized

Observing and recording; collecting, comparing, classifying, and interpreting data; suggesting hypotheses; identifying assumptions; designing investigations; making decisions; summarizing; applying principles; evaluating; imagining and creating.

Big Ideas

Some animals are alike in the way they live and in their behavior. Others are very different from one another. Animals have certain features that help them live in different environments.

Notes to the Teacher

- Live animals should not come into the classroom until the students have developed sufficiently responsible behavior about their care and protection. Although guinea pigs, rabbits, and hamsters are the more usual classroom guests, there may be more fun in having Sam the Snake or Leapin' Lizard as classroom guests.
- These pets are generally found in a local pet shop, where instructions for their care and feeding are part of the purchase.
- Animals from the wild should not be brought in for study. In fact, certain states and provinces strictly forbid this.
- Students should be involved in the care and feeding of the animal, cleaning the cage, and other responsibilities as part of this study. Guidelines for carrying out these duties should be explicit.
- Ethical considerations for the care and keeping of live animals in the classroom should be carefully reviewed. These are made explicit in Activity #51.

Debriefing

The following types of questions may be helpful in promoting reflection about animal behavior:

- What observations did you make about the animal? What observations did you make about the animal's sleeping and waking behavior? its exercise? its feeding habits? How it sets up a burrow? How it responds when students interact with it?

- What observations did you make about the structure of the animal? Its skin or fur? Its legs? Its tail? The way it moves? How it breathes? How it sees? How it hears? How it makes sounds?
- In what ways is this animal like other animals of that species? How is it different?
- Why do you suppose this animal would make a good pet? What are your ideas? What are the attributes of a good pet?
- How do you suppose this animal lives outside of captivity? What are your ideas?
- How does the animal protect itself from danger? How do you know? What examples can you give to support your ideas?
- How do you suppose the animal feels about living in this classroom? What makes you think that is true? What behavior did you see that supports that assumption?

Extending

The live-animal study may be extended in one or more of the following ways:

1. By introducing another animal, of a different species, into the classroom. For example: chicks, parakeet, and turtle.
2. By introducing new activity cards.
3. By raising more challenging questions in later Debriefing. For example:
   - In what ways is this animal like (another animal)? How are they different?
   - What other animals may be grouped in the same category as this animal? Why do you think they should be grouped together?
   - How smart is this animal? How do you know? What did you see in the animal's behavior that supports that assumption?
   - What kinds of feelings did the animal show in its behavior? What examples can you give?
   - How is this animal born? What are your ideas about that? How are its young like human babies? How are they different?
   - If you wanted to teach this animal something, how might you do that? In what ways is your teaching method different from or similar to the teaching you see at school?
   - Is it better for an animal to live in the wild or to live in a protected environment in the care of humans? What are your ideas about this?
4. By raising questions that call for the examination of some values issues related to the topic. For example:
   - Do animals have feelings? What are your ideas about this? Where did they come from?

- Can animals be trained to communicate with humans? What are your ideas about this? What examples can you give to support your ideas?
- Do animals have intelligence? What are your ideas about this? Where did those ideas come from? What examples can you give to support them?
- Should wild elephants be captured and taken to work in the circus? What are your views on this? What do you see as some downsides of doing this? What are some positives?

5. By suggesting students do some background reading about certain animals in library books and on the Internet.

Creating

The live-animal studies may be brought to conclusion by having students undertake one or more of the following:

1. Work in pairs and collect pictures of animals, set up a classification system for their collection, and create a scrapbook organized by category.
2. Work with a friend to make papier-mâché models of any animals of their choice.
3. Write poetry about a favorite animal.
4. Write about what it would be like to live the life of a tiger in a zoo.
5. Create a website about protecting animals in the wild from poachers.

ACTIVITY 53: EARTHWORMS

In this center, the students work with the common earthworm and a number of different surfaces—hard and soft, dark and light, smooth and rough, wet and dry—to determine the effects of environment on behavior. They are asked to make observations and record their findings.

Activity Card

- Study the earthworms for a long time. Then, one at a time, using the materials in the center, change the surfaces on which you place the earthworms.
- What observations can be made about the effect of changing the environment on the earthworm's behavior?
- Talk with each other about what you observed and write about what you found.

Materials

Earthworms (found in the school yard or a park or, if necessary, purchased from a biological supply house); a variety of items with flat surfaces, such as pieces of cloth with different textures, wood, aluminum foil, plastic wrap, some earth, some sand, water, sandpaper; several magnifying lenses.

Thinking Operations Emphasized

Observing and recording; collecting, comparing, classifying and interpreting data; suggesting hypotheses; examining assumptions; evaluating and criticizing; making decisions; designing investigations; imagining and inventing.

Big Ideas

Earthworms are simple animals that live in the soil. They help aerate the soil and aid plant growth. Changing their environment results in a change of behavior.

Notes to the Teacher

- Water should be used only to dampen the surfaces of the soil or sand. Earthworms can drown! Several magnifying lenses are essential for this center, since closer study will yield considerably more data and aid in generating hypotheses.
- Worms can be kept in a plastic pan filled with about 3 or 4 inches of soil, kept moist but not sodden. Students may feed worms by sprinkling fine cuttings of grass, lettuce, or other greens on top of the soil, and covered with a fresh layer of soil. This procedure should be repeated every two or three days.

Debriefing

Questions such as the following promote students' reflection on the big ideas:

- What observations did you make about the body of the earthworms?
- What observations did you make about the motion of the earthworm as it moves across a surface? What differences in moving behavior were you able to notice?
- Which kinds of surfaces seem to be the preferred environments of the earthworm? How did you figure this out?

- What other surfaces might be tried? Why do you think that surface would be good to try?

Extending

When the students have had ample time to investigate the characteristics of earthworms and their behavior under several different environmental conditions, their inquiries might be extended in some of the following ways:

1. By adding new materials with different surfaces to the center.
2. By adding materials that would create different environmental effects, such as a large light bulb; a bag of ice cubes.
3. By introducing new activity cards to reflect the new materials.
4. By including more challenging questions in later Debriefing, such as the following:
    - What hypotheses can you suggest for the observed effects of different conditions?
    - What other environmental conditions might be investigated? What might you expect to observe? What makes you think that is true?
    - What does this study tell you about the relationship of environment to behavior? How is this true with other animals? What examples can you give? What investigations might be set up to test those ideas?
5. By raising questions that call for the examination of values issues related to the topic. For example:
    - How does the earthworm feel about participating in these experiments? How do you know that? Do earthworms have feelings? How do you know that is true?
    - What is your opinion about experimenting with live animals? Should this be done? Under what circumstances? What, if anything, might lead you to change your mind?
6. By suggesting that students do some background reading about earthworms in library books and on the Internet.

Creating

When the limits of these investigations have been reached, it might be useful to culminate the inquiries with one or more of the following tasks:

1. Ask the students to work in trios to gather the materials for a "worm farm." They will have to remember to keep the soil moist. A small piece of wood or a rock on the soil surface for the worms to crawl beneath is

a good idea. Worms need privacy too! Worms can be fed with greens, cornmeal, or even particles of food from the family table. About once a week, the contents of the "farm" can be spread on a table and examined closely with a magnifying lens. The students may record any changes in the physical characteristics of the worms themselves and describe changes in the soil or in the contents of the farm.
2. The students may work in pairs to draw pictures of the earthworm based on their observations with both the naked eye and with the magnifying lenses.
3. The students may work in pairs to write a story called, "Marvin, My Pet Earthworm."
5. The students may wish to collect data about animal experimentation. Reports may be presented with at least two points of view: benefits to humankind and excesses of animal experimentation.

ACTIVITY 54: EGGS

In this center, the students work with hen's eggs to observe some of their general characteristics. They are asked to record their observations.

Activity Card

- Use the materials in this center to make some studies of eggs.
- What observations can you make of the outside of eggs? Of the inside?
- What observations can be made about texture? Size? Weight? Color? The different parts? Smell? Shape?
- What observations can be made about the thickness of the shell? Strength?
- What differences do you find among the eggs in the center? What similarities?
- Try some investigations and see what you can discover. Talk with each other about what you found and record your observations.

Materials

Several hen's eggs, preferably brown and white (one egg for each pair of students working in the center); bright light; paper or aluminum foil plates; paper towels or newspaper; blunt knife; probing sticks (toothpicks or tongue depressors); magnifying lenses.

Thinking Operations Emphasized

Observing and recording; comparing, classifying, and interpreting data; suggesting hypotheses; designing investigations; applying principles; making decisions; evaluating; imagining and creating.

Big Ideas

Hens (and many other animals) lay eggs as a means of reproducing their young. The inside of a fertilized hen's egg contains an embryo that develops into a chick.

Notes to the Teacher

- This activity is definitely messy. It is important, however, that each pair of students be allowed to break their own egg and carefully examine its contents. Do not discard the shells, as there is much to observe about them as well.
- If you are going to extend the activity into the hatching stage, such a move requires some prior consideration. For example, what will happen to the young chicks? Has a home for them been gotten ready? Have steps been taken to convey the chicks to that home? Will the chicks be disposed of? If so, how will this be handled? In what ways will students' feelings about this be dealt with? A review of the ethical considerations for the care and keeping of live animals found in Activity #51 is suggested.

Here are some points that you will want to know about hatching:

- Eggs will require about twenty-one days to hatch.
- They must be kept warm (102–104°F) in an incubator.
- They must be kept moist (sprinkle them with water early in the morning and before leaving school and keep the incubator water well full.)
- They must be rotated, especially for the first eight or nine days. Turn them over early in the morning, at noon, and upon leaving school.
- Do not help the chick to escape the shell.
- About an hour after the chick is hatched, move it to a brooder. (A brooder can be a small box kept warm, but not hot, with a small light bulb close by or directly inside.)
- Feed the chicks with starter mash, but don't handle them too much.

Debriefing

The following examples of questions may help to promote further reflection about eggs and stimulate additional investigations.

- What observations did you make about the shell?
- What hypotheses can you suggest to explain its shape? Its thickness?
- What differences did you observe when you examined the shell under bright light? With your magnifier?

- How do you explain the differences in the colors of the shells? What hypotheses can you suggest to explain them?
- What observations did you make about the inside of the egg? What observation did you make about the different parts of the inside of the egg?
- What other observations did you make with your magnifying glass?
- In what ways were the eggs alike? How were they different?
- From what part of the egg does the chick develop? What makes you think that is true? What data are you using to support your idea?
- What other animals lay eggs? Make a list of animals that lay eggs. How can this list be classified?
- What are eggs good for? How do you know that is true?

Extending

When the students seem to have exhausted their initial investigations, their inquiries may be extended in one or more of the following ways:

1. By introducing new materials. For example, asking the students to collect other kinds of eggs (quail, duck, goose, turkey, fish, insect) for study and investigative play. Of course, students should be cautioned NOT to remove eggs from nests that are being hatched.
2. By introducing new activity cards reflecting the additional materials.
3. By hatching eggs in the classroom. (See Notes to the Teacher above.)
4. By raising more challenging questions in later Debriefing. For example:
   - How are fish eggs like poultry eggs? How are they different?
   - How are insect eggs similar to and different from poultry eggs? Fish eggs?
   - Where do eggs come from? How are they formed? How do you know that is true?
   - What happens in the cases of animals that do not lay eggs? How are young born?
   - What are some differences between fertilized and unfertilized eggs? What are some similarities?
   - How do chickens hatch? How is this different from other birthing? How do you know that?
5. By raising questions that call for the examination of some value issues related to the topic. For example:

   Rapunzel said "I never eat eggs. Eating eggs is the same as murdering baby chickens."
   - What are your views on this? Is this true? Should we never eat eggs? What do you believe about this? Where did your ideas come from?

6. By suggesting students do some background reading about eggs in library books and on the Internet.

Creating

When the students have exhausted their interest in investigations with eggs, opportunities may be offered to extend their thinking into more creative realms. For example, ask the students to:

1. work in pairs to draw detailed illustrations of eggs of chickens, fish, insects, and other animals.
2. undertake the care of a baby chick to observe and record the stages of development.
3. write a story describing what it is like to be in a shell, narrating the hatching process.

ACTIVITY 55: COLORS

In this center, the students use paints, dyes, and prisms to study colors. They are asked to record their observations.

Activity Card

USE THE MATERIALS IN THIS CENTER TO CONDUCT SOME INVESTIGATIONS WITH COLORS.

- What observations did you make? What observations did you make about how colors change?
- What observations did you make about how colors mix?
- Talk with each other about your observations and then write what you found.

You may have some other ideas for using the materials in this center. Try them out and see what new discoveries you can make.

Materials

Several prisms; watercolor paints: reds, yellows, blues, whites; food coloring or other nontoxic dyes; white paper; several transparent containers; eyedroppers, straws, spoons.

Thinking Operations Emphasized

Observing and recording; gathering, comparing, and interpreting data; examining assumptions; suggesting hypotheses; applying principles; evaluating; summarizing; designing investigations; making decisions; creating and imagining.

Big Ideas

Sunlight is a mixture of many different-colored rays, even though it looks almost white. White light separates into several colors (red, orange, yellow, green, blue, indigo, and violet) when it goes through a prism.

Notes to the Teacher

- You may want to remind students that food coloring will stain. It may be a good idea to provide sponges, soap, and paper towels for cleanup, as well as plastic coverings for the table and floors and possibly smocks for the students.

Debriefing

The following types of questions may be useful in promoting students' reflection about color:

- What observations did you make about colors?
- What observations did you make about how colors change?
- What observations did you make about the colors seen from the prism?
- How are the colors made by the paint different from the colors made by the dyes?
- What observations did you make about the way the colors come from the prism? How are the colors from the prism different from the paint colors?
- What observations did you make about how colors mix?
- Why do you suppose red and yellow together make orange? How do you explain it?

Extending

After the students have had sufficient time to carry out investigations with the colors, their inquiries may be extended in one or more of the following ways:

1. By adding materials to the center. For example: mirrors, crayons, oil paints, pastels, additional paper of different textures and colors, pieces of fabric of different types and textures, pieces of plastic sheeting.

2. By introducing new activity cards that reflect the new materials.
3. By raising more challenging questions in later Debriefing. For example:
   - In what ways is the color yellow made by the paint different from the color yellow seen in the prism? How do you explain the differences?
   - Why do you suppose the prism needs the sun or other light sources to make color? What are your ideas?
   - Where do you suppose colors come from? What are your ideas?
   - How do you suppose a prism disperses color? What is there about it that allows it to do that? How come mirrors can't do the same thing?
   - How come you can't see colors in the dark? How do you explain it?
   - When (student) sees red, does he/she see the same color as (student)? How do you know that is true?
   - What relationship does color have to feelings? How do you know that is true?
4. By raising questions that call for the examination of value issues related to the topic. For example:

   Some people believe that people with dark skin are less smart, less capable, less deserving than those with white skin.
   - Where do you suppose these ideas come from? How do you explain it?
   - What does skin color have to do with intelligence? What ideas do you have about that?
   - How, in your opinion, can people with racist views about skin color be taught that skin color has nothing to do with anything other than skin color? How might that be done?
5. By suggesting that students do some background reading about color in library books and the Internet. This may be a good opportunity for them to read about racism deriving from skin color.

Creating

Some of the following types of more creative activities may be used to bring these inquiries to a close. For example, have the students:

1. do tie-dying and other textile dying.
2. collect materials to make natural dyes, for example, onion skins, marigolds, lichen, raspberries, blueberries.
3. make batik.
4. write poetry about rainbows.
5. write stories about colors, for example: "Red Makes Me Mad!" "The Skin I'm In," "The End of the Rainbow."

ACTIVITY 56: METALS

In this center, the students carry out investigative play with a variety of metals in order to make observations about properties of metals. They are asked to record their observations.

Activity Card

- Use the materials in the center to conduct some investigations with metals.
- How are these metals alike? How are they different?
- Make some observations about the differences in strength, hardness, texture, and flexibility.
- Talk with each other about what you have found. Then write about your findings.

You may have some other ideas for conducting investigations with the materials. Try out your ideas and see what discoveries you can make.

Materials

A variety of pieces of different types of metal (e.g., copper, tin, brass, lead, steel, aluminum, nickel, cast iron); a variety of types of metal wire (e.g., solder, copper, aluminum); hammer, steel wool, bolts, sandpaper, water, nails, screws, staples, candle (or other source of heat), heavy-duty shears, soldering iron, safety glasses.

Thinking Operations Emphasized

Observing and recording; collecting, comparing, and classifying; examining assumptions; suggesting hypotheses; designing investigations; applying principles; summarizing; evaluating; making decisions; imagining and creating.

Big Ideas

Metals can be described by what they are made of, their color, weight, texture, strength, flexibility. Metals can be changed under certain conditions, such as heating or combining them. Different metals are suitable for different purposes.

Notes to the Teacher

- Scraps of metal may be acquired through one or more of the following sources: the high-school metalworking shop, a local construction site, a machine shop, an auto-body shop, a building supply outlet.
- Metal products may also be included in this center, for example, aluminum foil, pots and pans, aluminum cans, cake tins, and other cooking utensils, toy cars and airplanes, can openers, ball bearings, magnets, coins, springs, marine propeller or shaft, automobile parts, bicycle chain, machine parts.
- If students are to be allowed to use heat (flame or soldering iron) in their investigations, you might wish to enlist the aid of a parent to supervise the activities from a reasonable but attentive distance.
- Safety glasses are recommended for these metal investigations—just as a precaution.

Debriefing

The following types of questions are suggested for the initial Debriefing to promote reflection about the metal investigations.

- What observations were you able to make about the metals in the center?
- In what ways were the metals different? How were they alike?
- In what ways might these metals be classified? What kinds of groups could you set up? In which group would each piece of metal belong?
- What observations did you make about the strength of the different metals? What kinds of tests did you do to find that out?
- What observations did you make about the hardness of metals? What tests did you do to figure that out?
- What observations did you make about how easily the metals break? How did you determine that?
- What do you suppose are some good uses for soft metals? for hard metals? What examples can you give to support your ideas?

Extending

The investigative play with metals can be extended in one or more of the following ways:

1. By adding new materials to the center, for example, metal tools, children's toys made with metal, other metal cooking utensils, metal garden tools.
2. By introducing new activity cards that reflect the added materials.
3. By raising more challenging questions in later Debriefing. For example:

- How are metals made? What theories do you have?
- How do you make a bicycle chain? What theories do you have about that?
- Suppose you wanted to combine two different metals. How could you do that?
- In what ways are metals important in your life? What are some important things that are made with metals? What do you suppose they could be made of instead?
- Can you imagine what life was like before metals were discovered? What do you think?

4. By raising questions that call for the examination of some value issues. For example:

    Sarah's mother has a set of large aluminum pots. She has just read an article in the newspaper that aluminum pots may give off bits of aluminum in the cooking process, which would then be absorbed in the food that has been cooked in those pots. Sarah's mom is worried. She does not want to harm her family, but she does not have the money to replace them.
    - What should Sarah's mom do? Where do you stand on this issue?
    - Is it true about aluminum pots? How might you find out the truth about this issue?
    - If this was true what advice would you give Sarah's mom?

5. By suggesting students do background reading about metals, their discovery, their multiple uses, in library books and on the Internet.

Creating

Some examples of more creative activities are suggested below.

1. Work with a partner and use some of the materials to create a metal sculpture.
2. Work with a partner and use scraps of metal to design a necklace or other jewelry.

ACTIVITY 57: PLASTIC

In this center, the students carry out investigative play with a variety of plastic products to make observations about the properties of plastic. They are asked to record their findings.

Activity Card

- Use the materials in this center to make some observations about plastic.

- What differences do you see in the different pieces of plastic?
- Conduct some investigations to find out about the differences in hardness, texture, smoothness, strength, weight and flexibility. Talk with each other about what you found and record your ideas.

You may have some of your own ideas about investigating with these materials. Try them and see what new discoveries you can make.

Materials

A variety of plastic products: plastic toys, dishes, cups, forks, spoons, jugs, beakers, other utensils; food containers; ballpoint pens; felt-tip pens; plastic baggies; plastic clothing, such as rainwear, boots, jackets; plastic tubing, such as hoses; garden tools; packing cases; storage cases; buckets; pail; dish drain; comb; toothbrush; baby pants; egg cartons; Styrofoam cups, Styrofoam chips; hammer, string, nails, saw, scales, sources of heat, scissors, staples, pieces of wood, heavy-duty rope, weights, sandpaper; glue; safety glasses.

Thinking Operations Emphasized

Observing and recording; collecting, comparing, classifying, and interpreting data; examining assumptions; suggesting hypotheses; designing investigations; applying principles; making decisions; evaluating and criticizing; imagining and creating.

Big Ideas

Plastics can be described by their different properties, such as color, weight, texture, flexibility, and strength. Most plastic is not biodegradable.

Notes to the Teacher

- Plastics can be found virtually everywhere. One quick tour around the school and home should yield a more than adequate collection for this center. Students may also be asked to bring in samples of plastics from home. However, parents should be alerted that plastics may be damaged in students' investigations and should not expect to have the materials returned intact.
- A precaution about working with plastic: Students should not use a heat source to conduct their investigations with plastic since the fumes may be toxic and some plastics are flammable.

Debriefing

The following types of questions are suggested for the initial Debriefing to promote reflection about the properties of plastic:

- What observations did you make about the plastic materials?
- In what ways are these plastic materials alike? How are they different?
- What observations did you make about hardness? Stiffness? Toughness? Strength? Smoothness? Flexibility? Color? How easily the plastic breaks or tears? How much weight it can hold?
- How might these plastic materials be classified? What kinds of categories could be set up? In what group would each piece of plastic belong?
- Some plastics break very easily. Others are very tough. How do you explain that?

Extending

The students' inquiries with plastic may be extended in one or more of the following ways:

1. By adding new plastic materials to the center.
2. By adding new activity cards. For example:
   - Try to find out which plastic container is the best for packaging food. Conduct some investigations and record your findings.
   - Try to find out which plastic container is the most breakable. Conduct some investigations and record your findings.
   - Try to find out which plastics can hold the most weight. Conduct some investigations and record your findings.
   - What happens when you stretch plastic? Conduct some investigations and record your findings.
   - Compare some pieces of plastic with some pieces of metal. How are these materials alike? How are they different? Try to find as many differences and similarities as you can.
   - What happens to plastic when we are finished using it? Where does it go? How does it get disposed of? Design some investigations to find this out and record your findings.
3. By raising more challenging questions in later Debriefing. For example:
   - What, in your opinion, are some advantages of using plastic? What are some disadvantages? What work did you do in this center that helped you form those opinions?
   - What, in your opinion, are some properties of plastics that make it a valuable material? What work did you do in this center that helped you to figure that out?
   - How do you suppose plastics are made? What theories do you have about it?

- In what ways do you use plastic products in your life? Think of as many ways as you can.
- How might these plastic products be classified? In which group would each belong?
- Can you imagine a time before plastics were invented? What did we use before we had these plastic products?
- How are plastics disposed of? How do you know this? Is this good? What are your opinions about it?
- Is it better to use a plastic cup or a ceramic cup? What makes you think that is true? What examples can you give to support your ideas?

4. By raising questions that call for the examination of some value issues related to the topic. For example:

Plastics are very useful in our lives. They are used to make all kinds of products, from tools to machinery to equipment to toys to office supplies. In many ways plastics are an improvement over metals. They are cheaper, lighter, and easier to handle. In some instances, they are stronger. Yet all is not wonderful in the use of plastics. Plastic products are nonbiodegradable—that is, they do not decompose, so they stay with us, in our garbage virtually forever. When they are dumped into the ocean, they are a menace to fish and other marine life.

- What are your views on the use of plastics and the environmental effects of their use? Where do you stand on these issues?

5. By suggesting students do background reading about plastic use and their environmental impact in library books and on the Internet.

Creating

There are several creative ways in which students may wind up their investigations with plastics. For example:

1. Work with a friend and design a mobile using only plastic products as weights. For this activity you will need several lengths of ¼-inch doweling or a wire hanger.
2. Work with a friend. Think together to invent a brand-new way of using plastic material.
3. Work with a friend. Design and build a plastic boat that will hold a 5-pound weight and remain afloat.

ACTIVITY 58: GARBAGE (MIDDEN HEAP)

In this center, the students examine the contents of a waste disposal bin and make observations about the nature and amount of waste material that is an adjunct to contemporary life. They are asked to record their findings.

Activity Card

> **USE THE MATERIALS IN THIS CENTER TO MAKE SOME STUDIES OF GARBAGE.**
>
> - What observations can be made about this garbage?
> - How could it be classified? Set up some groups and show where each item would belong.
> - Record your findings.
>
> You may have some other ideas for conducting investigations with the materials in this center. Try out your ideas and see what discoveries you can make.

Materials

Garbage (See Notes to the Teacher); disposable plastic gloves.

Thinking Operations Emphasized

Observing and recording; collecting, comparing, classifying, and interpreting data; applying principles; designing investigations; examining assumptions; suggesting hypotheses; evaluating and criticizing; summarizing; making decisions; imagining and inventing.

Notes to the Teacher

- The collection of garbage for this center should be selective. Garbage can be "cleaner" or "messier," and teachers have some choices with respect to how far they want to go on that continuum. But whatever trash is to be studied, it should not contain anything that might be harmful for students to handle, such as sharp pieces of glass, broken shards, toxic materials, or waste matter that might cause other problems, such as hygienic or sanitary waste. In any event, protective gloves are essential in handling these materials.
- The classroom wastebasket or the school office basket might be good starting points.
- Selected garbage brought from home in a large plastic bag may also be used even though it is likely to cause some smirks from colleagues in the staff room.
- Disposable plastic gloves are generally available in large quantity packages in supermarkets or dollar stores.

- A supply of newspapers to spread out over the tables on which the garbage is to be studied is highly recommended.

Debriefing

Some questions that advance students' thinking about their garbage studies:

- What observations did you make about this garbage? What observations did you make about the items found?
- In what ways might the items in the garbage be classified? What groups can be set up?
- If you were a visitor from another planet and had only this garbage to examine, what would it tell you about the people who lived here?
- Where does the smell of garbage come from? How do you explain it?
- What do you know about how garbage is collected? Where is it taken? What happens to it when it is dumped? What are your ideas? How might you go about finding that out?

Extending

The inquiries into garbage may be extended in several ways:

1. By introducing other garbage collections into the center, for example, from the school office, from the local supermarket, from a nearby factory or business, from a nearby park or playground.
2. By introducing new activity cards that reflect the additions to the center.
3. By raising more challenging questions and questions that raise values issues in later Debriefing. For example:
   - We generally have some unpleasant feelings about garbage. Where do these come from? What are your ideas?
   - How are these feelings translated into the way we treat garbage in our homes?
   - How are these feelings translated into the ways we think about the people who collect trash?
   - Where are the garbage dumps in our own community? Why do you suppose they are located in those areas? What are your ideas about it?
   - Sometimes there is a lot of garbage littering the street or the playground. Why do you suppose people throw their trash around? What are your ideas about it?
   - What do you suppose might happen if all the garbage dumps became full? Where might we put the garbage then? What are your ideas about it?
   - Some towns and cities have laws that require people to recycle their garbage. Why should this be done? What's good about it? What are your ideas?

- Some towns and cities encourage people to create compost that is collected to be used in fertilizing the soil for plant and flower growth. What is compost? What kinds of garbage can be used for compost? What are your ideas about it?
- By raising questions that address some values issues. For example:
- In some countries, very poor people search the garbage dumps to look for waste food because they are hungry. How does it happen that people get to be so poor they need to find food from garbage? What are your thoughts about this?
4. By suggesting that students do background reading about garbage, recycling, waste, midden heaps, and composting, in library books and the Internet.

Creating

The studies of trash may be brought to conclusion by having students engage in one or more of the following activities:

1. Work with a friend. Plan an investigation to figure out how much garbage each of you produces in a single day. Create a graph to record your findings.
2. Work with a friend. Plan an investigation to see what happens to the following types of garbage after a one-month period: an eggshell, a metal can, a plastic food container, a piece of bread, some potato skins, some scraps of paper, and a plastic cup. Make some illustrations that show the data you have gathered.
3. Work with a friend. Organize a program for your classroom that would collect paper for recycling. Plan an advertising campaign to persuade other students in the school about the reasons for contributing their paper trash to the recycling program.
4. Work with a friend. Conduct some inquiries to find out how much food is wasted during a period of one week in the school cafeteria. Think of some good ways to organize the data from your investigations.

Section IV

JOURNEY INTO THE UNKNOWN

Chapter 16

Evaluating Student Growth

Evaluation practices have a funny way of taking over and shaping all the educational experiences of a school. No matter what goal statements have been identified by the school district, it is the procedures we choose to evaluate with that shape what students, and consequently parents, will see as "what's really important." That is why evaluation practices must be of a piece with the program's goals if the goals have any chance of success. In a program where goals and evaluation practices are at war, it is inevitable that "will it be on the test?" will eclipse everything else.

A discussion of evaluation cannot take place in the absence of prior consideration of a program's learning goals. Although the following list of goal statements for sciencing has been grouped into several categories, each overlaps with the others, and all are blended into a common core of what are considered those educationally sound and accepted academic, social, and intellectual outcomes in teaching and learning science. (See, for example, Rowe, 1973; Goldberg, 1970; Carin and Sund, 1984; Beichner and Dobey, 1994; Jacobsen and Bergman; 1991; Martin, Sexton, Wagner and Gerlovich, 1994; Advancement of Science, 1993; Hazen and Trefil, 1990; Duckworth, 1990.)

GOALS FOR A SCIENCING PROGRAM

Social: Increased Growth in:

1. Responsible classroom behavior
2. Ability to make reasoned, thoughtful choices
3. Ability to accept consequences of one's actions
4. Becoming a responsible and cooperative participant of a group

5. Assuming responsibility for the classroom learning environment
6. Becoming a cooperative and productive group member

Personal: Increased Growth in:

1. Sense of personal autonomy
2. Sense of self-worth

Cognitive and Intellectual: Increased Growth in:

1. Making thoughtful, accurate observations
2. Forming reasoned and appropriate hypotheses
3. Identifying assumptions and differentiating assumptions from fact
4. Making comparisons and identifying similarities and differences
5. Classifying objects and creating categories in which items may be ordered
6. Gathering data and making meaningful interpretations of the data
7. Making decisions based on reasoned deliberations and thoughtful consideration of alternatives
8. Creating, imagining, and inventing
9. Becoming more tolerant of uncertainty
10. Ability to design experiments to test hypotheses
11. Ability to formulate and raise questions about phenomena
12. Developing a knowledge base with respect to scientific information
13. Increased skill as a problem solver

Appreciations and Attitudes: Increased Growth in:

1. Appreciation for science as means of acquiring information and understanding the world
2. Appreciation for science and scientific explorations
3. Appreciation for exploration, for searching, for experimentation to find out more
4. Ability to recognize science as a process of discovering rather than a body of information with accepted "truths"

EVALUATING STUDENTS' WORK IN SCIENCING

With the goals identified it becomes apparent that such outcomes cannot be measured with any single pencil-and-paper test, no matter how sophisticated. Nor can such a comprehensive view of student growth be reflected in a single numerical score. Even the most ardent test advocates recognize the fallacy of such practice.

The evaluation practices being proposed in this chapter meet several criteria for effective evaluation. They enable teachers to make informed and accurate assessments of student growth toward specified learning outcomes. They provide diagnostic information, pointing to ways of remediating difficulties. They allow for students' growth as self-evaluators. Finally, they provide a sound base of information from which reports to parents about student learning can be made.

CLASSROOM OBSERVATIONS

No pencil-and-paper classroom test is likely to be more effective in diagnosing student performance than the day-to-day observations of a professionally trained teacher. Close scrutiny of student behavior, in a variety of tasks, over an extended period of time, such as observing the student's interactions in a group, observing their problem-solving abilities on a given task, and noting where and how difficulties arise for that student, will uncover valuable data about student ability and student learning (AAAS, 1989).

Teachers' professional observations need to be recognized and appreciated as the source of the richest data for diagnostic work. In spite of the potential for built-in personal bias, the wealth of data from this source is likely to be infinitely more reliable to the classroom teacher in promoting student learning than a numerical score on a single examination (AAAS, 1993).

Systematic focused observations. In using so broad a screen as classroom observations, it is helpful to use some kind of "screening device"—a tool that can focus classroom observations on specific behaviors related to the goals of sciencing. Such a tool allows the teacher to gather data that point to areas of difficulty and areas of strength, allowing for diagnostic evaluation and leading to suggestions for teaching.

The checklist below is one such tool, and it is offered here for the teacher's use. Of course, teachers should feel free to modify such a list and reshape it to reflect the learning goals in their individual classrooms.

Profile of Student Performance on Sciencing Tasks

(*Diagnostic Checklist*)

Student's Name
Date of Observations: (1st)   (2nd)   (3rd)

KEY

1 = consistently   2 = frequently   3 = occasionally   4 = rarely

	Observations		
	1st	2nd	3rd

Social Group Behavior

The student:

1. Can work independently, that is, he/she does not depend on me for help with every step of every problem.
2. Can make reasonable, thoughtful choices and accept the consequences of those decisions.
3. Is a responsible and cooperative member of the group.
4. Is helpful in caring for the classroom environment.
5. Works purposefully and productively in the group.

Personal Behavior

The student:

1. Shows awareness of his/her strengths and limitations in learning tasks.
6. Shows awareness of self as a capable problem solver.
7. Shows confidence in self as a problem solver.
3. Shows ability to deal effectively with new situations.
4. Shows a sense of personal pride in self and work.
5. Shows confidence in self as a creator and innovator.
6. Shows growth in self-esteem.
7. Shows growth in self-initiating behavior.

Cognitive and Intellectual Behavior

The student:

1. Is able to make thoughtful, accurate observations.
2. Is able to suggest reasonable and appropriate hypotheses.
3. Can identify assumptions and differentiate these from facts.
4. Is able to identify similarities and differences of significance when making comparisons.
5. Is able to classify objects and create related categories.
6. Is able to gather data and make meaningful interpretations of that data.

7. Is able to make decisions based on data.
8. Is able to be creative, imaginative, and inventive in working on sciencing tasks.
9. Is able to design experiments to test hypotheses.
10. Is able to suspend judgment and be more tolerant of uncertainty.
11. Is able to formulate and raise intelligent questions about scientific phenomena.
12. Shows growing understanding of major scientific concepts.
13. Reveals increased knowledge with respect to scientific information.

Attitudes and Appreciations

The student:

1. Has enthusiasm for exploration, experimentation.
2. Shows a love for science and scientific exploration.
3. Shows an appreciation of science as a means of acquiring information and understanding of our world.
4. Shows increased interest in finding out and a decreased need to know "the answer."

SELF-EVALUATION

The importance of involving students in the evaluative process has long been advocated by many in the academy and in the field. These professionals believe that such involvement is critical not only in the promotion of student learning but also in the realm of self-awareness.

Self-evaluation shifts the locus of evaluation onto the learner. Such a shift requires that learners assume more responsibility for their choices, their actions, and the consequences of those actions. Learners thus decrease their dependence on outside authorities for judging their actions, for deciding whether what they do is "good" or "less than good."

What distinguishes the most creative and innovative scientists of our time is their confidence in themselves and in their ability to undertake experimentation with the most far-reaching, mind-boggling problems that confront them. Their inner strength imbues them with courage, drive, inspiration to create and invent, and the freedom to live with risk and uncertainty. Such attributes cannot emerge in an individual who has been intimidated by the judgments of others, one who must always turn to others to know, "Is my work good?"

Persons whose locus of evaluation is far outside themselves have become crippled in their own independent functioning. Perhaps worse, they are likely to fall prey to the manipulations and coercions of others to whom they have transferred the power of judgment over their lives.

Can elementary school students play a role in self-evaluation? The data from both elementary and middle-grade teachers suggest that not only can they do so but that they learn to do so thoughtfully, intelligently, sensitively, and with much wisdom and insight.

Self-evaluation may occur in at least two forms. One is through oral conferences. The teacher confers with the student and raises questions about his or her behavior and performance on sciencing tasks. During the raising of such questions, the teacher remains neutral and nonjudgmental; the student is encouraged to arrive at an assessment without subtle leading by the teacher. In other words, it doesn't work if the teacher has his or her own agenda and manipulates the student's responses toward that agenda.

A list of questions that might be raised during such conferences includes the following. Of course, they are used selectively.

- What science centers did you participate in today?
- Tell me about the way you worked.
- Tell me about some discoveries you made.
- Tell me about some of the things that didn't go too well for you.
- Tell me about some of the things that gave you trouble.
- What comments would you like to make about your behavior in the group?
- What were some of the things that you could do for yourself?
- What were some of the things you needed help with?
- How do you feel about your work in the cleanup of the centers?
- How do you feel you got along with the other members of the group?
- Tell me about any new inventions that you created.
- Where do you think you need help from me?
- What did you discover about the materials you worked with? And how might you account for what happened?
- Tell me how you classified those objects.
- What were some of the decisions you made and how did they work out for you?
- Tell me about some of the experiments you conducted and what you found out.
- What questions do you have about what happened?
- Tell me how you think the work in science is going for you?

A second form of self-evaluation is through students' written reports. Students are asked to make careful and thoughtful appraisals of what they have done with respect to the quality of their science work.

Two examples of self-reports are offered here. Teachers may, of course, use these as a basis from which to develop their own forms, singularly appropriate to their own classes. Also, as students' work in science becomes more sophisticated, the report forms should be modified to reflect that growth.

Self-evaluation Report, Type 1

Name   **Date**

1. In my work with my group I am (check one)
    Usually very responsible
    Mostly responsible and cooperative
    Sometimes responsible and cooperative
2. In my work with my groups, I (check one)
    Usually get right down to work on the science tasks
    Need a little time to get down to work
    Have a hard time getting down to work
3. In my work in the science centers, I (check one)
    Usually help with the cleanup and do my jobs
    Sometimes help with the cleanup and do my jobs
    Have a hard time getting down to helping with the cleanup jobs
4. This is what I want to say about my behavior in the group:

5. In my work on science tasks I think I am (check one)
    A good problem solver
    Learning to be a good problem solver
    Having a hard time as a problem solver
6. In my work on science tasks, I (check one)
    Have a lot of confidence in myself
    Have some confidence in myself
    Am not sure about my confidence in myself
7. In my work on science tasks, I am able to (check one)
    Work on my own with little help from others
    Work on my own with some help from others
    Work on my own with a lot of help from others
8. This is what I want to add about the way I work on science tasks:

9. In working on thinking tasks, I am able to (check all that I can do)
    Make accurate observations
    Identify assumptions
    Make comparisons
    Classify objects

Gather data
Make decisions
Invent new things
Design projects
Make up experiments
Use my imagination
Ask good questions

10. This is what I want to add about my work on thinking tasks:

11. In my science work I am learning that:

12. When the teacher says, "It's time for science," I feel:

13. This is what I want to add about my work in the science program:

Self-evaluation Report, Type 2: Weekly Summary

Name **Date**

1. After thinking about my work in the science program this week, I think I need to (check all that are relevant)
   Concentrate on working more responsibly in my group
   Get more confidence in myself
   Try to work more on my own
   Concentrate more on the thinking activities with which I have difficulty

2. This is what else I think I can do to improve my work in the science activities:

3. These are the good things I'd like to say about my work in the science centers:

4. This is how I see that my work has improved since the beginning of the school year:

PORTFOLIOS

Portfolios kept by students offer another means of gathering information from students' performance over time. A large folder, or envelope, or other container can be used if hard copy is preferred. Alternatively, students who have their own tablets can create files of their work to be stored digitally.

These documents may include students' written work and other tasks; they may include notes about science center participation. Students may be the sole contributors to the portfolios, or they may be a collaborative record with teachers adding materials they see as relevant. Portfolios provide a longitudinal record of student growth in knowledge, attitude, and skills, revealing both quality and quantity. They provide a documented picture of how the student has been progressing.

In many classrooms where portfolios are used, students have ownership over them and are given choices about what they want to include. This ownership puts students into the role of evaluator; they assess and decide: "This is what I have chosen as representative of my best work."

Teachers may keep their own ongoing records (portfolios) for each student containing those documents that the teacher deems significant. One or both methods of keeping documentation add immeasurably to the wealth of material that profiles a student's work over the school year.

At the end of a designated interval, the student's portfolio is presented in a conference with the teacher, the student, and the parent. The documents are examined, and the quality of the student's work is discussed. Teachers who work collaboratively with students (and parents) in this process will confer together about standards of performance and make explicit plans for next steps in learning.

REPORTING TO PARENTS

When teachers have on hand the learning goals for science, the data from the students' self-evaluation reports, and the portfolios containing work gathered by students over a particular time period, they have, in hand, the necessary materials to give parents the information they are seeking.

Based upon this accumulated data, the teacher is in the best position to provide jargon-free, genuine, and professionally sound judgments about a student's work, making the reporting to parents clear and easily understood.

In many schools, students are welcomed as participants in parent–teacher conferences. The history of this practice has proved not only successful but also additive. Students' inputs into the conference are not only helpful but also allow them a voice in showing their parents their best efforts as learners.

SOME LAST WORDS ON EVALUATION

Evaluation is an onerous job in any field. It may be easier in a context when judgments lie in the calculation of right and wrong answers—although such judgments are hardly illuminating. It is definitely more challenging when judgments come from professional discernment about the nature of "what is good."

To sum up the authors' positions about evaluation practices in sciencing, it may be helpful to recapitulate the beliefs that lie at the heart of the classroom practices that have been documented in the earlier chapters.

1. Evaluation is a highly personal, very subjective process in which teachers assess student performance in terms of their own professional bias. Bias is reduced when teachers' judgments rely more on informed observations rather than on assumptions and attributions of attitude and motive.
2. The primary purpose of evaluation is to provide feedback to students that enables them to take the next steps in growing and learning.
3. A secondary purpose of evaluation is to provide clear and well-informed feedback to parents about student growth, behavior, and classroom performance.
4. Feedback to students that is not useful in promoting learning is not only unhelpful but may be detrimental to their growth and progress.
5. Teachers' observations of student performance in a variety of classroom contexts over a long period of time are likely to be more helpful in assessing student learning than formal, standardized tests. Portfolios provide important records that document an individual's growth and learning over time.
6. Standardized and teacher-made tests often supply spurious data about student performance. These are rarely helpful in diagnosing weaknesses and areas where remediation is needed.
7. Some types of evaluation may be harmful to students' concepts of self. Those that diminish students' ability to grow and learn should be banished from the classroom.
8. Excessive use of teachers' judgmental responses serves to promote student dependence on the teacher. Such procedures militate against the development of student independence and growth toward personal autonomy.
9. Maturity brings with it the ability to maintain the locus of evaluation inside oneself. Teachers may work toward this goal by increasingly emphasizing self-evaluation procedures.
10. Evaluation practices that emphasize single "correct" answers lead to a false picture of science as a concern for finding "truths." True science, what has been labeled "sciencing" in this text, is more concerned with processes of discovery, experimentation, testing hypotheses, taking risks, and searching—learning to err and to bounce back to try again.
11. Evaluation in sciencing must lead to information about student progress toward the stated learning goals. Practices that do not provide such information may be costly in time, and energy, and may lack real value.

Chapter 17

Journey into the Unknown

> Science is a journey into the unknown with all the uncertainties that new ventures entail.—Mary Budd Rowe, Science as Continuing Inquiry

A journey into the unknown is not just any trip into a tunnel of darkness. The trip may have a clear destination, in spite of the fact that one has never actually been there. What makes such a trip successful and enjoyable is likely dependent on a few factors. For example, it begins with some idea of the goal of the journey—that is, will the trip end up with some benefits for me and for whomever else is traveling along with me? It is also aided and abetted by a few advance organizers: "Do I have the right clothing?" "Do I need to make any arrangements at the destination?" "Do I have a clear appreciation of what it might be like to visit a foreign country?" "Is my passport current?"

And, of course, "What will I do if I run into trouble on the way?"

The journey into sciencing may be full of unknowns, but it is supported by the advance organizers that have been spelled out in great detail in this book. Yes, there may be a few impediments along the way. There may be risky grades and curves. Every journey has its rough edges, but we take them nevertheless because they are full of such wonders as to make the few rough moments more than endurable.

Teachers who boldly venture into sciencing will find such wonders. And these will surely compensate for whatever impediments might be encountered.

To give shape to what some of those impediments might be, the next few paragraphs will attempt to address what might be some lingering concerns about implementation. It is hoped that such discussion will diminish the perceived risks and provide teachers with the additional support needed to get the program under way.

TALKS TO TEACHERS ABOUT THEIR CONCERNS

"I don't know enough science. Can I still make it work?"

It's true that if you have been blessed with the background in biology and zoology of Gerald Durrell, the expertise in chemistry of Linus Pauling, and the wisdom in physics of Sir Isaac Newton himself, these would be valuable assets in carrying out any science program. Not possessing such a fount of knowledge, however, does not automatically disqualify you for the job.

If you perceive teaching science as dispensing information about scientific "facts," then yes, it would be imperative that you not only be able to dispense such information accurately and coherently but that you are able to answer questions intelligently as well. Such an approach to science teaching is largely dependent on the teacher's background and knowledge base.

Of course, even with an expert, using such a didactic approach to teaching science is hardly a guarantee that students comprehend the important concepts of what is being taught. Remember Curtis, who was trying to describe what he was taught about evolution? "The fish's feet turned into fins and it took about 100 years."

The approach to science teaching that is being advocated in this text is that of a laboratory. In a laboratory, inquiries are under way for which many responses are as yet unknown. In such an approach, unknowns are allowable, both for you and for the students. When questions are raised for which you do not have answers, neither sciencing nor the walls of the school will come crashing to the ground. In a laboratory, we may admit that we do not know, and we may then open the search for more information. Students and teacher become partners on the road to discovery.

While it may seem more convenient to "know the answers" than to have to search for them, the searching is much more in the spirit of science than is the knowing, and it is such openness to searching that the sciencing program seeks to cultivate.

"Am I covering the curriculum?"

There are several questions implicit in this concern:

"Will such an approach allow me to cover adequately the body of knowledge assigned to my grade level?" "What if all the science content does not get covered?" "Will my students be in deficit with respect to their scientific 'know how' on year-end assessments?"

In these questions lie, perhaps, the greatest perceived obstacles to sciencing. We authors want to make our strongest arguments here to provide such reassurance as you may still need.

First, the fifty-eight activities contained in the earlier chapters have been included because most scientific concepts for elementary school programs are embedded in these activities.

Second, the activities provide you with a wide variety of choices and, more important, they illustrate the type of treatment that all science topics for your grade might undergo.

Myths die hard in educational practice, and we tend to hold onto them long after research data has taught us otherwise. The press to "cover the curriculum," despite its documented shortcomings, continues to be embraced by educators as the way to develop students' scientific literacy. In fact, such "covering" generally leads to overwhelming emphasis on didactic presentation of information, leaving students substantially shortchanged in concept development and higher-order thinking skills, not to mention the short "mind-life" of the acquired information (AAAS, 1990).

Sciencing will most assuredly address grade-level curriculum concepts more richly and intelligently than the "fact shoveling" that passes for science teaching in other programs.

"The students may get the wrong answers. Shouldn't I correct their mistakes?"

The world of science is indeed a journey into the unknown and that notion is, for many of us, scary. We like certainty. We are more comfortable with answers than we are with questions. We feel more secure with facts than we do with hypotheses. When we have arrived at a "truth," we relax, physiologically and psychologically. Whew! Now we KNOW! To be searching, questioning, and putting out tentative answers are often fraught with dissonance. And dissonance, like atonal music, can be disquieting.

There are prices to pay as well as benefits for both closure and for living with uncertainty. For the price of uncertainty, of journeying into the unknown, we benefit from the thrill of the search and the cognitive stimulation. For the benefit of closure, we pay the price of putting cognitive functioning to rest. We cannot have higher-order thinking without dissonance. We cannot have a becalmed physiological state and still have the thrill of inquiry. They are mutually incompatible states.

Unhappily, in many classrooms, the path of calm has been the primary mode of teaching and learning. Finding the "right answers" in almost every curriculum area is the modus operandi, rather than the exception. They are prized out of all proportion to their real value, and schooling has become a means of acquiring as many "right answers" in as many subjects as is humanly possible. Such orientation is not only destructive of higher-order thinking, but it also fosters the dangerous impression that "right answers" are the keys to a life worth living. In worst-case scenarios, preposterous "answers" are proposed as solutions to the most complex and far-reaching problems.

A "right answer" orientation in the teaching of science presents other problems as well. It gives a false view of what science actually is. Students learning with sciencing inquiries are learning to respect and value the tentative answer, the hypothesis, the toleration of uncertainty, the role that testing plays in the determination of validity.

All of this is not to say that a teacher *never* "corrects" a student within the context of sciencing. A student may be attempting procedures that are potentially harmful and that need "correction." There are times when the teacher must be very certain and directive. There are times when a student will ask for information and the best response is to give it.

Yet, when students are engaged in sciencing—conducting investigations and thinking—and they are asking about strategies, designs, or solutions, about what's right or wrong, good or bad, it is much more fruitful to use questioning strategies that put the ball back in the students' court, encouraging them to seek the ways for themselves.

Allowing students the time and the space to find their own ways, to find their own answers, and to correct their own mistakes is not an easily acquired teaching behavior. Yet, developing such teaching strategies is much more likely to result in a more intellectually healthful classroom climate, not to mention the harvests reaped from sciencing than could ever be gained from the narrow parameters of a right-wrong approach.

"It will be too noisy (messy, dangerous)."

Teachers who have read this far in this book will not be surprised to read here that the ideal classroom for the authors is not one in which students are always seated quietly, listening to the teacher talking, and carrying out written and oral directives on command. Sciencing, as we have advocated, will be more noisy and messy than what occurs in the classroom down the hall. What's more, we believe that sciencing, like life, should be noisy and messy, and with more ventures into the unknown. It's the extent to which each of these factors operates that a teacher would wish to control, not the factor itself.

Investigative play, at the very heart of sciencing, means students working and inquiring together. There will, inevitably, be some noise and mess—but you, the teacher, have the opportunity to decide how much of this is acceptable. Noise and mess do not mean that students are unruly, allowed to become chaotic and out of control. Keeping students' investigations within purposeful and productive boundaries is always the job of the good "classroom manager," and specific suggestions to the students for what is acceptable behavior is part of the job.

When you are able to see that your sciencing program is exuberant and purposeful, you may find yourself more comfortable with the by-products of noise and mess. Noise, after all, comes from students learning together. Mess, after all, can and should be cleaned up in the aftermath.

With respect to "danger," we believe that in no circumstance should any teacher allow activities that put a student's life in danger. Here again, it is up to you, the teacher, to make certain choices, for only you can know the maturity and capability of students involved and weigh the risks against the potential advantages. Should students be allowed to light matches? Should they handle hot liquids? Age and grade are not the best determinants to answer these questions. A teacher's judgment is the best guide.

"Where will I get the science materials and equipment to do the job?"

In chapter 7 you will find an extensive list of materials that may be acquired for a sciencing program. Most of the materials are normally found in school storage rooms housing science equipment. Some materials may be found in one's own kitchen. Some need to be acquired through more imaginative searching—parents, garage sales, flea markets, and the butcher shop.

In no way have we suggested you try to find materials that are hard to come by (dinosaur bones), exotic (unicorn horns), expensive (Rolls Royce engines), or idiosyncratic to a particular geographic area (Sasquatch footprints). All the materials listed are accessible to most teachers in one way or another. It is true, however, that you will have to get them. We cannot offer you any help other than to commiserate that the teacher's life is a demanding one, full of extra duties. Only you can decide if yet another task is worth your effort.

A materials list is also included for each of the fifty-eight sciencing activities. A cursory glance at the materials section of each activity will quickly reveal not only what is needed but also where you are likely to find it and how much effort it will take. Perhaps on your most burdensome days, it might be wiser to choose sciencing activities for which materials are easier to come by, saving those that require more extensive searching for lighter days.

If you begin gathering materials early in the school year and can liberate a small corner of a storage closet for those materials, you can eventually accumulate and maintain a sufficient supply of materials to last throughout the year.

"What will the principal say?"

For many teachers, the specter of the principal as an uninvited guest—shocked speechless by students moving about the room and . . . *talking!* (gasp!) . . . to each other—is unnerving enough to put them off trying anything new for a lifetime. Though we hate to admit it, we know there are such folk out there, occupying administrative positions and collecting large "educational leadership" salaries, who actually impede educational progress. There are, lamentably, principals whose primary concerns are quiet, clean, orderly classrooms where no one talks except the teacher, and who still cling to archaic notions that such classroom environments foster healthful learning.

If your principal is one of these, there is very little anyone can offer you in terms of advice, for the sciencing program is entirely antithetical to such beliefs. We can only offer condolences, for in such a school climate, with such obstacles to face, professional growth and curriculum development are the enemy. All forces operate to maintain the status quo, and sciencing is not a program that would either be acceptable or valued.

On the other hand, there is a large group of school administrators whose very raison d'etre is to promote professional growth and curriculum development; administrators who are dedicated to students' learning and who wish to be part of the growing movement to foster and nurture students' thinking skills. If your principal belongs to this group, he or she wants to know certain things: For example: Are your students learning science in this program? Are they working purposefully and productively together? Are they learning to be responsible? Are they loving science? Are they learning problem-solving skills? Are their thinking skills improving?

We believe that teachers should be able to demonstrate, successfully, to their school administrators that these learning goals are indeed occurring and, in doing so, potential questions about methodology would be adequately addressed.

It is more than likely that to show such learning gains in science may result not only in a principal's tacit approval but his or her explicit regard as well.

"What will the parents say?"

Most parents, like most good school administrators, want the very best for their children. Most parents want to know: Is my child learning? Is he or she happy at school? When parents see that their children are happy and learning, they are usually content. Where the evidence is abundant, parents are usually delighted.

The Play-Debrief-Replay model of sciencing ought to satisfy and delight parents in several ways. It should clearly demonstrate their child's increasing familiarity with science, with respect to knowledge and conceptual understanding. It should clearly reveal their child's enthusiasm for the subject. It should clearly demonstrate their child's increased capability as a thinker and as a responsible, cooperative learner. When such learning goals can be adequately demonstrated to parents, it seems reasonable that these very same parents will be among your strongest allies.

Some teachers who are getting ready to launch a new program believe it's a good idea to invite parents for an after-school "tea." During this session the new program is described in a clearly articulated statement. Perhaps charts or even a YouTube presentation of students working at sciencing are made to give some visual "punch" to the oral presentation. Students may also be included in talking to parents about what they have been doing.

Learning goals are also spelled out:

"This program will help your child become a better thinker, problem solver, cooperative learner, inquirer. It will increase your child's understanding of scientific principles; enable your child to become more responsible, more self-initiating, more independent."

Faced with such important learning goals, parents may understand how Play-Debrief-Replay may more successfully bring such goals into realization. When parents understand, truly understand, the learning goals and how the means being used are consistent with those goals, they are more likely to be supportive than critics.

"What about the student who . . . ?"

In almost every in-service session we give to teachers, there is a question raised about "that certain student who . . ." Variations on the theme include the student who behaves badly, who takes a much longer time to learn, who cannot concentrate, who is aggressive, who hurts other students and destroys property, who is disrespectful, who doesn't listen—the list goes on and on. There are many such students in many classrooms, and their needs are great. These are the students who are always a source of much pain to teachers and over whom teachers anguish and spend sleepless nights. In virtually every classroom there is at least "one student who . . ."

The Play-Debrief-Replay model of sciencing offers no panacea for all those "students who . . ." The model promises no magic cures, no tricks to bring socially unacceptable behavior into line. We can't even say to teachers that this model offers a quick route to success. Actually, the contrary is more likely to be the case, that is, it is not an effortless route to success. But the success, when it comes, is sweet.

In any program that respects the dignity of each student, in any program in which students are listened to and cared about, in any program that attends to and respects students' ideas, we can expect positive changes in students' behavior. The data for such claims exist in abundance in the literature on child growth and development, and these data are incontrovertible. No one claims that such changes come about overnight or that they are easily won. Behavioral change, especially in students operating out of grave social-emotional deficits, comes about only after much long-term, consistent application of the right conditions. But it does come, and when changes occur, they are likely to endure. Such claims cannot be made by others who would seek to circumvent the long-term process by short term "cures."

What do teachers do in the interim? How do they keep from going under, maintain balance, and keep the program alive in the face of students who manifest such behavioral symptoms? How do teachers cope until the signs of change can be seen?

Here's where we fail you. We do not know how. We only know that if you are able to "stick it out" and apply the strategies advocated with consistency, changes will occur. This is an incomplete answer, and we wish we could offer more. As former classroom teachers ourselves, we are well aware of the toll such students take on the minds and hearts of teachers. Yet if we will not be there to help them, who will?

"Does sciencing always have to involve experiences with manipulative materials? Are there times when other types of experiences may be appropriate?"

No teacher is unaware of the role that experience plays in learning. We can have experiences of many kinds, and each one will contribute to learning in its own way. However, as most teachers realize, the quality of an experience is fundamentally connected to the quality of learning.

For example, one is not very likely to learn much about mollusks from experiencing Fred Cipher's delivery of the world's most boring lecture on the subject. Yet, a lecture delivered by that charismatic zoologist Stephen Jay Gould would almost certainly result in a "better" experience and consequently a different kind of learning.

It has been said that experience is the best teacher and we may learn from the experience of books, newspapers, television, theater, film, and the Internet, as well as from the experience of lectures, group discussions, and debate. Experiences from reading, viewing, and listening may all be valuable, but it is the extent to which the learner actively engages in the experience that contributes substantively to a higher quality result. That is why a boring lecture fails us while an exciting one "turns us on."

The same is true for experiences with other media—books, plays, films, discussions, social media; they may contribute substantively to our overall learning, only to the extent that we engage. Adrenaline must pump in order for the learning "juices" to flow.

That is why experience's reputation as the best teacher almost always refers to the experiences of life. To spend two weeks in Venice is a far more engaging experience than hearing a lecture about Venice. An experience that generates less personal/cognitive engagement is therefore less substantive and offers less in terms of learning opportunity. If all the options were open, how would we choose to learn about Venice?

In this text, the advantages of experiences with manipulative materials as a way of promoting conceptual understanding and enthusiasm for science have been stressed. Playing with the materials is much like going to Venice. You are there, right in the thick of it. You are not learning second hand or third hand, from someone else's experience. If hands-on primary experiences with manipulative materials produce such good results, we believe they should be used whenever possible.

But it is not always possible to go to Venice. Sometimes we must settle for a different quality experience acknowledging that it is second best. We may look at beautiful photographs, a film, and a travel book. Such experiences may also engage us and offer us a different potential for learning and knowing.

In providing sciencing opportunities, we may not be lucky enough to get to see whales from the deck of a boat, to experience their beauty, their grace, their intelligence, their size, from real-life experience. But that does not mean we should not turn to second-best experiences—photographs, films, and books—in our studies. We may not have a Museum of Natural History a subway ride away to experience the real-life adventure of gazing on the skeletal structure of a dinosaur. But we may study these incredible animals through secondary experiences. Being able to visit the seashore is a much more valuable experience than reading about it, but if books and films and photographs are all we can gather about the seashore in a classroom in Colorado or Manitoba, we must make as much of these second-best experiences as we can.

Second best need not mean second rate, so how the experience is offered becomes an equally crucial factor in generating the kind of learning opportunity that will engage students.

Studying about whales, for example, can occur from "playing with ideas" substituting for actual real-life experience. Playing with ideas rather than with manipulatives also calls for students' active engagement in the learning experience. In organizing playing with ideas, the same model is followed. The students play and are cognitive engaged, but they do so with pictures, diagrams, articles, and a variety of other audio-visual media. Instead of manipulating manually they manipulate ideas. But in these "minds-on" tasks, they must be actively engaged with the ideas in order for the results to be effective.

In playing with ideas, the teacher might ask that observations be made from photos of whales. Comparisons of whales and other mammals might be asked for. Students might imagine what a whale's life is like. They could be asked to generate hypotheses about the intelligence of whales. They might be asked to reflect on whether we should bother to "save the whales" and why this species has value. Many thinking operations might be used to promote students' inquiries about whales, and it is understood that in such play, students are sharing ideas and thoughts and recording their ideas from their examination of the materials. Thus, play with manipulatives is translated into play with ideas and becomes a substitute, an alternative; second best, but not second rate.

"Many of my students are computer literate. Can technology be used to support the Play-Debrief-Replay model of teaching science?"

While the authors remain unapologetically committed to real-world, hands-on experience as fundamental to learning in the elementary grades in science, technology can play an important role in furthering certain kinds of scientific inquiries, even within the Play-Debrief-Replay curriculum framework. There is no question that computer programs have played essential roles in teaching and learning during the long COVID-19 closure of schools.

Even with schools open, with more access to tablets and desktops and laptops, there are opportunities for students to engage in science experiences that can be enriching and productive. For example, in an online notebook that can be accessed from one's tablet, students can make comments, record observations, ask questions, and carry out other ways of gathering scientific data. Other members of the learning network, other students, teachers, or experts can insert their own comments to create an ongoing dialogue. Inquiries on a topic or in a learning center such as "Pond Life" can include field trips that are debriefed on the Internet. Virtual experiences with "Pond Life" (or other natural habitats) can be added when access to ponds is inaccessible.

Multimedia systems also provide ways of enhancing work in science that are compatible with the instructional framework. The Internet is a treasury of YouTube videos that offer realistic views of geography, biology, chemistry, and zoology that are only a touch away. These can offer the kind of introduction to scientific adventures out of the reach of real experiences of many students.

With students' increased and more sophisticated use of computers and tablets, they are also able to create their own web designs, and illustrations to demonstrate their growing awareness of science concepts.

CONCLUSION

This book has been full of promises for teachers who choose to embark on a sciencing program for their elementary-grade students. Those promises come from the authors' extended experiences with Project Science-Thinking, in which twenty elementary teachers volunteered to participate in a two-year guided experiential approach to teaching science that emphasized the development of students' higher-order thinking skills integrated with the teaching and learning of important science concepts.

In this program, students were engaged in learning concepts and skills that led to the improvement of their scientific literacy—a process that enabled them to have wide-ranging learning experiences. They had many opportunities for engaging in hands-on and "minds-on" activities and for the promotion of their intelligent habits of mind, making meaning of their experiences, as well as connecting science with mathematics, the arts, and humanities, and, of course, technology.

The benefits reaped in these classes were manifold; students gained skills in their ability to describe scientific phenomena and did so with intelligence and understanding. They advanced in their ability to solve problems, to make thoughtful and intelligent decisions, and to widen their knowledge base. They grew in their independence as learners and as cooperative members of their working groups. What's more, they grew to love science.

Teachers who are embarking on sciencing programs have before them a many-splendored adventure. To all, we wish the success and the satisfaction that such a program is likely to offer.

For when the teacher announces that there will be sciencing that afternoon and the students cheer—how can that not be sweet?

Appendix
Selected Readings in Science for Primary and Middle Graders

CHILDREN'S SCIENCE BOOKS BY MELVIN AND GILDA BERGER

101 Animal Babies.
Do Bears Sleep All Winter?
Planets
101 Animal Secrets
Baby Animals
Hurricanes Have Eyes But Can't See
Storms
101 Animal Superpowers
Dangerous Animals
What Do Animals Do in Winter: How Animals Survive the Cold
Reptiles
Your Brain
Bees
Why Don't Haircuts Hurt?
Can It Rain Cats and Dogs? Questions and Answers About Weather
Did it Take Creativity to Find Relativity, Albert Einstein?
Do Tarantulas Have Teeth? Questions and Answers about Poisonous Creatures
Mammals
Chomp: A Book About Sharks
Your Heart
The Byte Sized World of Technology
Fish Sleep but Don't Shut Their Eyes: And Other Amazing Facts about Ocean Creatures
Rocks and Minerals
Think Factory: Solar System
What do Sharks Eat for Dinner?
Amphibians
Visit to an Apple Orchard
Life on a Coral Reef
Farm Animals
From Chick to Robin
Brrr! A Book About Polar Animals
Why do Volcanoes Blow their Tops?
Howl: A Book About Wolves
Your Muscles
Penguins Swim But Don't Get Wet
Pumpkins
Pets
Dogs Bring Newspapers but Cats Bring Mice
Your Bones
Can Snakes Crawl Backward?

Where Have All the Pandas Gone?
Grub to Ladybug
Can You Hear a Shout in Space?
Screech! A Book About Bats
Sting! A Book About Dangerous Animals
How's the Weather?
Snap! A Book About Alligators and Crocodiles
You Touch with Your Fingers
Whales
Why Did the Dinosaurs Disappear? The Great Dinosaur Mystery

CHILDREN'S SCIENCE BOOKS BY SEYMOUR SIMON

Big Cats
Oceans
Earthquakes
The Brain
Wolves
Sharks
Storms
Tornadoes
Animals Nobody Loves
Rocks and Minerals
Wildfires
The Universe
Hurricanes
Spiders
Our Solar System
Weather
Eyes and Ears
Horses
Sea Creatures
Lungs
Snakes
Bones

Climate Action
Insects
Cats
Dogs
Lightening
Trucks
Muscles
F is for Fart: A Book about Farting Animals
Mountains
The Heart
Guts
Tropical Rainforests
Global Warming
Volcanoes
The Sun
Earth
Coral Reefs
Gorillas
Comets, Meteors and Asteroids
The Ultimate Book of Space

Others

Jodie Shepherd. *It's a Good thing There Are Earthworms.*
Wynne, Patricia. *My First Human Body Book.*
Wade, Jess and Castrillon, Melissa. *Nano: The Spectacular Science of the Very Small.*
Smith, Robyn. *Horse Life.*

Mooney, Carla and Carlbaugh, Samuel. *Forensics.*
Diehn, Andi and Li, Hui. *Forces: Physical Science for Kids.*
Macaulay, David. *The Way Things Work Now.*
Ignotofsky, Rachel. *What's Inside a Flower?*
Zommer, Yuval. *The Big Book of Blooms.*
Willis, Kathy and Scott Katie. *Botanicum: Welcome to the Museum.*
Lyon, George Ella and Tillestrom, Katherine. *All the Water in the World.*
Mulder, Michelle. *Every Last Drop.*
Green, Jen. *Why Should I Save Water?*

Bibliography

American Association for the Advancement of Science. 1989. *Science for All Americans Summary*. New York: Oxford University Press.
American Association for the Advancement of Science. 1993. *Benchmarks for Science Literacy*. New York: Oxford University Press.
Ashton-Warner, Sylvia. 1985. *Spearpoint*. New York: Knopf.
Beichner, Robert and Dobey, Daniel. 1994. *Essentials of Classroom Teaching: Elementary Science*. New York: HarperCollins.
Bloom, Benjamin. 1956. *Taxonomy of Educational Objectives. Vol. 1: Cognitive Domain*. New York: McKay.
Bronfenbrenner, Urie. 1979. *The Ecology of Human Development*. Cambridge, MA: Harvard University Press.
Brown, Mary and Precious, Norman. 1970. *The Integrated Day in the Primary School*. London: Ward Lock.
Bruner, Jerome, Sylva, Kathy, and Genova, Paul. 1974. "The Role of Play in the Problem Solving of Children Three to Five Years Old," in Bruner, Jolly and Sylvia. 1974. *Play—Its Role in Development and Evolution*. London: Penguin,
Carin, Arthur and Sund, Robert B. 1984. *Teaching Science Through Discovery*. Columbus, Ohio: Charles Merrill.
Clarke-Stewart, Alison, Friedman, Susan and Koch, Joanne. 1985. *Child Development: A Topical Approach*. New York: Wiley.
De Vito, Alfred. 1984. *Creative Wellsprings for Science Teaching*. West Lafayette, IN: Creative Venturing.
Dewey, John. 1964. *On Education*. Chicago: University of Chicago Press.
Duckworth, Eleanor. 1990. *Science Education: A Minds-On Approach for the Elementary Years*. Hillsdale, NJ: Lawrence Erlbaum.
Elkind, David. 1982. *The Hurried Child*. Boston: Allyn & Bacon.
Featherstone, Joseph. 1971. *Schools Where Children Learn*. New York: Liveright.
Fein, G. G., ed. 1986. *The Play of Children: Theory and Research*. Washington, DC: National Association for the Education of Young Children.

Feynman, Richard P. 1985. *Surely You're Joking Mr. Feynman!* New York: Norton.
Fort, Deborah C. 1993. "Science Shy, Science Savvy, Science Smart." *Phi Delta Kappan*, 74, pp. 674–683.
Fraenkel, Jack. 1980. *Helping Students Think and Value.* Englewood Cliffs, NJ: Prentice Hall.
Getzels, Jacob and Jackson, Philip. 1962. *Creativity and Intelligence.* New York: Wiley.
Gillies, Robyn. 2007. *Cooperative Learning: Integrating Theory and Practice.* Newberry Park, CA: Sage.
Goldberg, Lazar. 1970. *Children and Science.* New York: Scribner.
Goodlad, John. 1983. *A Place Called School.* New York: McGraw Hill.
Hazen, Robert M. and Trefil, James. 1990. *Science Matters: Achieving Scientific Literacy.* New York: Macmillan.
Herron, R.E. and Sutton-Smith, Brian, eds. 1971. *Child's Play.* New York: Wiley.
Howes, Virgil. 1972. *Informal Teaching in the Open Classroom.* New York: Macmillan.
Ivany, J. W. George. 1975. *Today's Science.* Chicago: Science Research Associates.
Jackson, Philip. 1990. *Life in Classrooms.* New York: Teachers College Press.
Jacobs, Geroge M., and Powers, Michael. 2016. *The Teacher's Sourcebook for Cooperative Learning.* New York: Skyhorse.
Jacobsen, Willard and Bergman, Abby. 1994. *Science for Children.* New York: HarperCollins.
Johnson, James E., Christie, James F. and Yawkey, Thomas D. 1987. *Play and Early Childhood Development.* New York: Harper Collins.
Johnson, David W., Johnson, Roger T., Holubec, Edythe Johnson, and Roy, Patricia. 1984. *Circles of Learning.* Washington, DC: Association for Supervision and Curriculum Development.
Joliffe, Wendy. 2007. *Cooperative Learning in the Classroom. Putting it into Practice.* Newberry Park, CA: Sage.
Kaplan, Paul S. 1986. *A Child's Odyssey: Child and Adolescent Development.* St. Paul, MN: West.
Karlis, Nicole. 2021. "A Generation of Kids has Used Social Media Their Whole Lives. Here's How it's Changed Them." *Salon.* https://www.salon.com/2021/02/11/a-generation-of-kids-has-used-social-media-their-whole-lives-heres-how-its-changing-them/
Kotlowitz, Alex. 1991. *There Are No Children Here.* New York: Doubleday.
Martin, Ralph, Sexton, Colleen, Wagner, Kay and Gerelovich, Jack. 1994. *Teaching Science for All Children.* New York: HarperCollins.
Meyrowitz, Joshua. 1985. *The Impact of Electronic Media on Social Behavior.* New York: Oxford University Press.
Packard, Vance. 1983. *Our Endangered Children.* Boston, MA: Little Brown.
Pepler, D. J. and Rubin, K. H., eds. 1982. "The Play of Children: Current Theory and Research." *Contributions to Human Development*, 6, pp. 64–78.
Pinker, Steven. 2021. "Modern Miracle: What Accounts for the Doubling of the Human Life Span Since the mid-19th Century?" *New York Times Book Review, June*, 13, p.11.

Postman, Neil. 1982. *The Disappearance of Childhood.* New York: Dell/Delacorte Press.

Raths, Louis E., Simon, Sidney B., and Harmin, M. 1980. *Values and Teaching*, 2nd ed. Columbus, OH: Merrill.

Rowe, Mary Budd. 1973. *Teaching Science as Continuous Inquiry.* New York: McGraw Hill.

School Council Publications. 1973. *Minibeasts: A Unit for Teachers.* New York: Macdonald Educational.

Segal, Julius and Yahraes, Herbert. 1978. *A Child's Journey: Forces that Shape the Lives of Our Young.* New York: McGraw Hill.

Silberman, Charles. 1973. *Crisis in the Classroom.* New York: Random House.

Suchman, J. Richard. 1966. *Developing Inquiry.* Chicago: Science Research Associates.

Suransky, Valerie. 1982. *The Erosion of Childhood.* Chicago: University of Chicago Press.

Sutton-Smith, Brian, ed. 1979. *Play and Learning.* New York: Gardner.

Thomas, Lewis. 1983. *The Youngest Science.* New York: Viking.

Vandenberg, B. 1980. "Play, Problem-Solving and Creativity," in K. H. Rubin, ed., *Children's Play.* San Francisco, CA: Jossey-Bass.

Wassermann, Selma and George Ivany, J.W. 1988. *Project Science Thinking* was a two-year field study carried out by the authors of this text with 20 classroom teachers in 12 elementary schools in British Columbia. The objectives of the study were (a) to develop and implement a training program to retrain practicing teachers in the principles and instructional strategies of science and teaching for thinking and (b) to observe and assess pupil learning outcomes related to the implementation of such practices.

Wassermann, Selma. 2009. *Teaching for Thinking Today: Theory, Strategies and Activities for the K-8 Classroom.* New York: Teachers College Press.

Wassermann, Selma. 2017. *The Art of Interactive Teaching.* New York: Routledge.

Winn, Marie. 1983. *Children Without Childhood.* New York: Pantheon.

Wood, David. 1983. *How Children Think and Learn.* Oxford, UK: Blackwell.

Index

absorbency activity, 116–19
activities: absorbency, 116–19; air and aerodynamics, 143–45, *146*; balances, 146–48; birds, 185–89; bones and shells, 180–83; bouncing balls, 209–11; bubbles, 121–23; categorization of, 94–95; colors, 255–57; earthworms, 249–52; eggs, 252–55; electricity, 139–43; flowers, 171–74; foods, 174–77; friction and inertia, 211–14; garbage (midden heap), 263–66; germs, 221–24; growing plants from seeds, 159–62; hands and feet, 227–50; humans and the environment, 232–35; ice, 123–26; kites, 207–9; levers, 219–21; life in water, 128–31; light and shadow, 153–56; live animals, 246–49; magnets, 214–16; magnifiers, 150–53; measuring, 156–59; metals, 258–60; minibeasts, 243–46; molds (tiny plants), 166–68; parachutes, 192–94; pendulums, 148–50; plastic, 260–63; presentation of, 95–96; pulse and heartbeat, 230–32; rain, 106–9; reflecting surfaces, 134–36; seeds from fruit; fruit from seeds, 163–66; selection of, 96–98; sinking and floating, 109–12; siphoning, 114–16; skeletons, 183–85; skins, 177–80; solutions, 119–21; sound and pitch, 112–14; sounds with strings, 202–4; spiders, 240–43; squids, 237–39; static electricity, 204–7, *206*; suction, 126–28; thermometers, 137–39; time, 224–27; tools and machine, 194–97; water fountains, 103–6, *106*; wheels and axles, 216–19; wind energy, 199–202; wind sounds, 197–99; World Wide Web, 189–92; yeast (tiny plants), 169–77

Activity Card, 84–86, 95
air and aerodynamics activity, 143–45, *146*
American Association for the Advancement of Science (AAAS), 6, 93
anti-vaxxers, 81
appreciations, 270, 273
Ashton-Warner, Sylvia, 11
attitudes, 270, 273

balances activity, 146–48
Benchmarks, 93
big ideas, 5, 22, 95
birds activity, 185–89
bones and shells activity, 180–83
bouncing balls activity, 209–11

British Infant School movement, 16
Bruner, Jerome, 16
bubbles activity, 121–23

children, 14; from classroom, 9–11; developmental history of, 11–12; healthful and intellectual development, play relationship to, 17; implications for teaching, 12–13; learning needs, 12–13; play with science materials, sciencing program, 31
classroom observations, 271–73
classroom practice, teaching for, 20–24
closure, 32, 33, 69–70, 281
cognitive behavior, 272–73
colors activity, 255–57
cooperative learning groups, 65
creativity, 16, 96

Debriefing, 28, 30, 32, 33, 67–68, 95, 99–101; awareness of individual behavior, 76–78; coding sheet, 74–76; interactions that analyze and inform decision-making, 86–88; investigations of locusts, 79–80; learning teaching for thinking interactions, 74
decision-making, 86–88; for "minds-on" play activities, 84–86
Dewey, John, 15
Durrell, Gerald, 280

earthworms activity, 249–52
effective learning, 64
eggs activity, 252–55
Einstein, Albert, 16
electricity activity, 139–43
Elkind, David, 11
experiences, 286–87
experiential teaching-for-thinking program, 89
extending activity, 96

Featherstone, Joseph, 16
Feynman, Richard, 16

floating-sinking tests, 29
flowers activity, 171–74
foods activity, 174–77
foolish choices, 83
friction and inertia activity, 211–14

garbage (midden heap) activity, 263–66
germs activity, 221–24
Goodlad, John, 22
Gould, Stephen Jay, 286
grade-level application, 93
Grade 3 sciencing, 28–31
growing plants from seeds activity, 159–62
guidelines and ground rules, sciencing program, 55–65

hands and feet activity, 227–50
higher-level mental functions, 21
higher-order mental processing, 69
higher-order tasks, 21
higher-order thinking skills, 6, 20, 30, 83
humans and environment activity, 232–35

ice activity, 123–26
Information Age, 11
inquiry-based approaches, 68
inquiry teaching, 67
inquiry-type learning, 16
instructional materials, 21–22
intellectual behavior, 272–73
interactions: call for students to think, 71–74; delimit students' opportunities to think, 70–71; learning to use, 69; that inhibit thinking, 69–70
investigative play, 68, 282
investigative play centers, 28, 52

Karlis, Nicole, 11
kites activity, 207–9
Kotlowitz, Alex, 11

learning: inquiry-type, 16; by interacting with students, 23; role of experience

in, 286; role of play in, 15–17; to use interactions, 69
learning centers approach, 51
learning sciencing, 4–5
learning teaching, 74
levers activity, 219–21
life in water activity, 128–31
light and shadow activity, 153–56
live animals activity, 246–49
live-animal study, ethical considerations for, 97
lower-level mental functions, 20
lower-level tasks, 21

magnets activity, 214–16
magnifiers activity, 150–53
materials, for sciencing program, 41–50, 95, 283
measuring activity, 156–59
metals activity, 258–60
Meyrowitz, Joshua, 11
middle-grade students, 10–12
middle-grade teacher, 10
minds-on play activities, 84–86, 287
minibeasts activity, 243–46
molds activity, 166–68
multimedia systems, 288

Newton, Sir Isaac, 280
"No Fuss, No Muss, No Sticky Stuff" (Category B): air and aerodynamics, 143–46; balances, 146–48; birds, 185–89; bones and shells, 180–83; bouncing balls, 209–11; electricity, 139–43; flowers, 171–74; foods, 174–77; friction and inertia, 211–14; germs, 221–24; growing plants from seeds, 159–62; hands and feet, 227–50; humans and the environment, 232–35; kites, 207–9; levers, 219–21; light and shadow, 153–56; magnets, 214–16; magnifiers, 150–53; measuring, 156–59; molds (tiny plants), 166–68; parachutes, 192–94; pendulums, 148–50; pulse and heartbeat, 230–32; reflecting surfaces, 134–36; seeds from fruit; fruit from seeds, 163–66; skeletons, 183–85; skins, 177–80; sounds with strings, 202–4; static electricity, 204–7, *206*; thermometers, 137–39; time, 224–27; tools and machine, 194–97; wheels and axles, 216–19; wind energy, 199–202; wind sounds, 197–99; World Wide Web, 189–92; yeast (tiny plants), 169–77
no pencil-and-paper classroom test, 271
notes to the teacher. *See* teacher, notes to

orientation, 39–40

Packard, Vance, 11
parachutes activity, 192–94
Pauling, Linus, 280
pendulums activity, 148–50
personal behavior, 272
plastic activity, 260–63
play, 15–17; opportunities for middle graders, 84; relationship to children's healthful and intellectual development, 17
Play-Debrief-Replay instructional model, 31–33, 284, 285, 287–88
portfolios, 276–77
Postman, Neil, 11
problem-solving, 20
pulse and heartbeat activity, 230–32

rain activity, 106–9
reflecting surfaces activity, 134–36
reflective responses, 57, 59, 71, 72, 86, 88
responsible group behavior, 64
"right answer" orientation, 281–82

science: readings for primary and middle graders, 291–93; *vs.* sciencing, 5–7; teaching, 3–4; thinking and decision-making in, 81–89

Index

science education, 6, 82
sciencing, 281; investigative play in, 30; journey into, 279; learning, 4–5; preparing students for, 37–40; science vs., 5–7; student work in, 270–71
sciencing program, 38–39; children's play with science materials, 31; gathering materials for, 41–50; goals for, 269–70; guidelines and ground rules, 55–65; making room for, 51–53; organizing space and storing materials, 52–53
scientific inquiry, 94
scientific literacy, 82
seeds from fruit; fruit from seeds activity, 163–66
self-directed investigations, 32
self-evaluation, 273–76
sinking and floating activity, 109–12
siphoning activity, 114–16
skeletons activity, 183–85
skins activity, 177–80
social group behavior, 272
social media, 11
solutions activity, 119–21
sound and pitch activity, 112–14
sounds with strings activity, 202–4
spiders activity, 240–43
Sputnik, 15
squids activity, 237–39
static electricity activity, 204–7, 206
student, evaluation of growth, 269, 277–78; classroom observations, 271–73; goals for sciencing program, 269–70; portfolios, 276–77; reporting to parents, 277; self-evaluation, 273–76; work in sciencing, 270–71
Suchman, J. Richard, 67
suction activity, 126–28
Suransky, Valerie, 11
systematic focused observations, 271–72

teacher: implications for, 83–84; tools for, 74; work-play context, 16
teacher–student interactions, 22–23, 68
teaching: implications for, 12–13; thinking and classroom practice, 20–24
teaching-for-thinking approach, 67, 89
teaching-for-thinking interactions, 87
teaching science, 3–4, 280; as inquiry, 67; principles of, 24
thermometers activity, 137–39
thinking interactions, 20; learning teaching for, 74; teaching for, 20–24
thinking skills, 95; higher-order, 6, 20, 30, 83; that inhibit, 69–70
Thomas, Lewis: *The Youngest Science*, 5–6
time activity, 224–27
tools and machine activity, 194–97

value-laden issues, 82
values-related issues, 87

water fountains activity, 103–6, *106*
"Wet, Wetter, Wettest" (Category A): absorbency, 116–19; bubbles, 121–23; ice, 123–26; rain, 106–9; sinking and floating, 109–12; siphoning, 114–16; solutions, 119–21; sound and pitch, 112–14; suction, 126–28; water fountains, 103–6, *106*
wheels and axles activity, 216–19
"Who's Afraid of Spiders?" (Category C): colors, 255–57; earthworms, 249–52; eggs, 252–55; garbage (midden heap), 263–66; live animals, 246–49; metals, 258–60; minibeasts, 243–46; plastic, 260–63; spiders, 240–43; squids, 237–39
wind energy activity, 199–202
wind sounds activity, 197–99
Winn, Marie, 11
"work-play" environment, 16
World Wide Web activity, 189–92

yeast activity, 169–77
The Youngest Science (Thomas), 5–6

About the Authors

Selma Wassermann is professor emerita in the Faculty of Education at Simon Fraser University. She is the author of more than twenty books and the recipient of the University Excellence in Teaching Award.

J. W. George Ivany is president emeritus of the University of Saskatchewan and an author of texts and research papers on science teaching.

www.ingramcontent.com/pod-product-compliance
Lightning Source LLC
Chambersburg PA
CBHW021847300426
44115CB00005B/42